D1580328

TITIAN

PHAIDON

THE MAN WITH THE GLOVE. About 1520. Paris, Louvre.

TITIAN

THE PAINTINGS AND DRAWINGS

WITH THREE HUNDRED ILLUSTRATIONS

BY HANS TIETZE

LONDON · MCML · THE PHAIDON PRESS LTD

SECOND EDITION REVISED: 1950

MADE IN GREAT BRITAIN 1950
TEXT AND MONOCHROME PLATES PRINTED BY WAGNER'SCHE UNIV.-BUCHDRUCKEREI
GES. M. B. H. · INNSBRUCK
COLOUR PLATES PRINTED BY HENRY STONE & SON (PRINTERS) LTD · BANBURY
BOUND BY KEY AND WHITING · LONDON

CONTENTS

FOREWORD

THE first edition of this book—with a more detailed text than that now offered—appeared in 1936 and reflected the impressions received a year earlier from the Titian Exhibition in Venice. There the figure of the great artist, presented against the most dignified background, triumphed by its individual perfection. It seemed that the essential task of the biographer was to isolate his figures as much as possible, in order to give the clearest outlines to Titian's personal achievement.

When, in starting to revise the introductory text for this long overdue new edition, I consider in what respects my ideas have been most perceptibly modified during this interval of thirteen years, I find that the answers is an enhanced appreciation of Titian's close connection with his environment. Thirteen years' concentration on the material offered by American collections and by the international art market—in place of that choice selection of works which spread a glorious halo around the Master—could but dim his outlines, in the sense that he now derives more distinctly from the art of his predecessors, and his own achievement is now fused more closely with that of his school and his time. His isolation seems less striking and his œuvre has to a greater extent become a component, though certainly an essential and decisive one, of sixteenth-century Venetian art.

This modified conception, however, must not be allowed to interfere with the supreme obligation of the biographer of a great artist, or of any other great personality, to endeavour to penetrate and to capture his very essence. The wider the margin which frames the personal art of Titian in his early and his late years, the greater the preponderance of his individual characteristics over those which he shares with others. It remains the biographer's principal task to defend the integrity of Titian's artistic personality against unjustified expansion and excessive tolerance.

A critic of the first edition of this book took exception to my habit of quoting divergent judgements on certain controversial attributions without offering a pontifical decision. The inclusion of a painting in my selected list, and my comment on it in the Catalogue, give a sufficient indication of my own opinion in each case. But experience has taught me that such an opinion must necessarily

remain subjective—a reflection of the idea of Titian's art which a long and inces-
sant study of the subject has implanted in my mind. The opinions of other critics,
though differing from mine, may be equally well founded, and I shall therefore
continue to include them in my notes, which after all are intended, in part, for
expert readers. This tolerance has seemed the more desirable as I have myself
made use in numerous cases of the privilege which is accorded to every critic—
for a critic is at one and the same time pupil and teacher—to change a previously
held opinion, yielding at times to criticism by others of my former statements,
at times to my own conviction of the need to modify my point of view. These
corrections have for the most art been relegated to the Catalogue, while the
essential structure of the book remains unchanged. I still feel, as I did thirteen
years ago, indebted to many colleagues, above all to the late Theodor Hetzer,
whose analysis of Titian's colour still seems to me to be one of the greatest
achievements of modern art criticism.

New York, 1949   H. T.

I

The sources

W HAT we know about Titian, the artist, comes from our knowledge of his work. What we know about Titian, the man, is mainly derived from three contemporary writers, whose evidence is supplemented by numerous documents. Of the three, the earliest to write about Titian was Lodovico Dolce, a literary hack, who was certainly very devoted to Titian, but was hardly capable of formulating an independent opinion of his work. The second, Pietro Aretino, was for many years Titian's most intimate friend and the framer of his official letters ; he was also a gifted writer in many fields, with a keen appreciation of art, but too much filled with a sense of his own importance to be a reliable reporter. Lastly there is Giorgio Vasari, whose series of biographies is our most important source of knowledge regarding the conditions under which the artists of the Italian Renaissance lived. In the second edition (1567) of his famous work, he strove to eliminate the mistakes contained in the first edition published seventeen years earlier and to be fairer in his judgement of Venetian artists. Vasari's information on Titian was derived mainly from a meeting with the great artist in 1566, but as a stranger to Venice Vasari was naturally unfamiliar with conditions in the city and had, moreover, to rely on the statements of a old man, whose memory, especially as regards remote events, was no longer trustworthy.

The next biographers of Titian wrote long after his death, at a time when direct knowledge was no longer available. One of them, the so-called Tizianello, a distant relative of the master, recorded in 1622 the Titian tradition as it had been preserved in the family, while the other, the dry and pedantic Carlo Ridolfi, elaborated Vasari's statements and added everything that was known in Venice about Titian in the middle of the seventeenth century.

All these sources must be read and evaluated with a critical mind. They hardly suffice to give us the most important data of Titian's life, more especially concerning his youthful period.

Date of Titian's birth

We cannot even answer with certainty one of the fundamental questions of all biography—we do not know when Titian was born. According to a tradition dating back to Titian's lifetime he lived to be ninety-nine years old ; as he is known to have died on 27 August 1576, this would mean that he was born in 1477. Since Sir Herbert Cook, writing in 1900, first cast doubts on this tradition, there has been an increasing tendency to doubt whether Titian really attained this partriarchal age. Titian's own statements, other indications and certain well-documented events in his life, all point to his having been born about ten years later, closer to the date given by Vasary, ' about 1490 '.

If that is so, Titian's early career would have been approximately as follows: He was born about 1487-1490 at Pieve di Cadore, in the northernmost extremity of Venetian mainland territory. At the age of nine he left his mountain valley and went to Venice to be trained as a painter, being apprenticed to some painter of the city, perhaps to Sebastiano Zuccato. He soon left this painter's atelier and went to that of Gentile, and then to that of Giovanni Bellini. The first reliable information we have about him concerns his share in the frescoes which Giorgione was commissioned to paint on the walls of the Fondaco de' Tedeschi, the warehouse of the German merchants in Venice. In 1511 we find him in Padua; two years later he was back in Venice, where he applied for an official post, making no mention in his application of any earlier works, but merely giving promises for the future. In the following years he widened the circle of his connections and activities and in 1516 he was commissioned to paint the ' Assunta ', which laid the foundations of his fame. All these facts are in harmony with his having been born about 1487-1490, rather than ten years earlier. His share in Giorgione's frescoes on the Fondaco is that of a youth just ending his apprenticeship, not that of a man of thirty-two, and the rapid progress which he made from 1513 to 1518 points to his having been at that time on the threshold of maturity rather than a man in his late thirties.

In the first edition of this book I dealt at greater length with the question of Titian's birth, which is important when we try to judge his early development. If he had been born in 1477, an artist of such exuberant creative power would certainly have produced some notable works before 1508, the first year in which we have news of him as an artist. Efforts have been made to fill this gap by attributing to him a number of undated works, some of them very doubtful, thus creating a vague and misleading youthful œuvre, but subsequently many of these supposed early pictures, if they really are Titian's, have been given later dates, while others have been assigned to other artists. The more recent theory as to the date of his birth enables us to obtain a better picture of Titian's entry into art.

Arrival in Venice The boy Titian must have come to Venice about the beginning of the new century. If he was, in fact, only nine years old at the time, he can hardly have received any artistic instruction in his home. We must assume, however, that in some way he had shown a talent and inclination for painting. We can follow the history of his family a long way back, and most of its male members seem to have adopted a military or a judicial career, some of them a combination of the two. No artists can be traced among his ancestors, but that does not exclude the existence of a talent for art, or even of amateur indulgence in it, for this is common among the wood-felling and wood-carving population of the Alps. In any case we cannot assert that Titian brought anything from his home except the robust physical constitution and lively imagination typical of those who come from the mountains and the dogged perseverance of a community toiling under adverse conditions. The transplantation of the country boy to the great city must have affected him profoundly.

To Sebastiano Zuccato, who is mentioned as his first teacher, Titian can hardly have owed anything but training in the first elements of his craft.

Titian does not seem to have stayed very long with Zuccato; according to Dolce he soon went on to the workshop of Gentile Bellini and then to that of the latter's brother Giovanni, while his first real teacher was Giorgione. Either under Giorgione's supervision or in collaboration with him, Titian, when he was only just twenty, painted the wall on the street side of the Fondaco, whereas Giorgione himself painted the frescoes on the canal side. Dolce's statements show how these early years appeared to Titian when he thought of them in his old age. Titian did not like to think of himself as having been subordinate or indebted to any older painter, but denied any such close collaboration, just as Michelangelo in his old age would not admit that he owed anything essential to any of his supposed teachers. Later biographers, especially Crowe and Cavalcaselle, whose authority still carries weight, had a feeling that those tentative suggestions—Zuccato, Gentile and Giovanni Bellini—were an inadequate reconstruction of the process of Titian's education, and we too must ask ourselves whether the results of more recent investigation do not justify our amending those sketchy lines.

His first teachers

Dolce's assertion that it was the dry and tiresome manner of the Bellinis which drove Titian to Giorgione, is an obvious reflection of values as seen by the mature Cinquecento. In the first decade of the sixteenth century the Bellinis were by no means a declining force—in 1506 Dürer wrote of Giovanni that, although he was very old, he was still the greatest painter in Venice. In fact it was precisely at that time that Giovanni, on the death of his brother, was officially recognized as the leading painter of the city; through the granting of a broker's patent he became painter to the Republic. If Titian, who according to our reckoning would then have been seventeen or eighteen years old, came to Giovanni or worked with him about that time, their relationship must be considered as having been other than the academic relationship between teacher and pupil. It was a case of a young painter coming to an old master, as an assistant rather than as an apprentice; not merely to learn, but to help—and by helping he naturally learned a great deal.

The Bellinis

In this respect the workshop of Giovanni Bellini in his later days offered incomparable opportunities. In addition to the important state commissions, some of which Giovanni had inherited from his brother, there were also the late altar-pieces, the portraits, which thanks to Giovanni became the fashion in Venice, and even a few mythological subjects, which the ageing master undertook although he had previously not executed such paintings. In the last ten years of Giovanni Bellini's life his workshop was extremely busy, despite the great age of its owner. The earliest results of Titian's artistic activity might well be hidden in this abundant production.

Bellini's late works are, in fact, so lacking in uniformity, in some cases so different from his earlier works and in others so full of new conceits, that they cannot possibly have all been executed by the old master alone. The most striking novelty was the 'Feast of the Gods', which Bellini delivered to Alfonso

The 'Feast of the Gods'

of Ferrara in 1514, but on which he may have started working as far back as 1506. We know from Vasari and from the testimony of our own eyes that it was later revised and modernized by Titian. This revision, during which the picture was enriched with a fine and typically Titianesque landscape, must have been executed during the late 1520's, at the time when Titian was carrying out many other commissions for the same court and even for the very room which housed Bellini's painting. We shall return to this subject later. The natural manner in which the later additions fuse with the original composition to form a harmonious whole, and a closer analysis of Vasari's statement, as given by John Walker in his monograph on the 'Feast of the Gods', make it appear highly probable that Titian had a share in the original version produced in Bellini's workshop. The very presence of such a young artist in his workshop may have induced the master to accept and execute this unusually large mythological painting, whereas only a few years before he had refused to carry out a similar commission for Alfonso's sister, Isabella d'Este.

It is, of course, impossible to establish with absolute certainty such a participation of a young assistant, for it was a characteristic feature of Renaissance workshops that the individual shares of the various collaborators should be merged in the art of the leading and responsible master. But if it is correct that the 'Feast of the Gods', is one of the works in which Titian anonymously prepared himself to become an independent painter, then other works of Bellini from the same period might also furnish examples of Titian's early manner. Very tempting in this connection is the Allendale 'Adoration of the Magi' in Washington, which, since it left the Allendale Collection, has been ascribed by most critics to Giorgione, though that keen-eyed scholar Berenson maintains emphatically that it is a very early, perhaps the earliest work of Titian. In an article written by E. Tietze-Conrat and myself, we attempted to prove that this is the "Adoration' which Giovanni Bellini painted in 1504 for Isabella d'Este, or at least that it is connected with it, and that some slight participation of the young Titian in the painting of it, though not probable, cannot be altogether excluded. Our analysis, which inevitably had to remain a hypothesis, sought to bring out those points where Titian's style, in general, grows out of that of Bellini.

Votive picture of Jacopo Pesaro

1

At a similar point of transition stands the votive picture of Bishop Jacopo Pesaro in the museum at Antwerp, which was formerly, for external reasons, assigned to a date before 1503, but which is now considered to have been executed later—according to some scholars, much later. It is difficult to assign a date to this picture because it is not all cast in the same mould. The left half, with the awkward figure of St. Peter enthroned, produces an archaic effect in comparison with the right half, in which the kneeling donor and the accompanying Pope are fused into an animated group. There is a similar contrast in the colouring of the two halves. These differences have been explained in different ways, either by assuming that Titian completed a panel begun by an artist of the older generation by adding the group on the right, or else that he himself began the picture in his early years and completed it after a long interval. As Titian signed the painting and thus claimed the whole of it for himself, the second theory appears more likely. Titian might have painted the St. Peter while he was still a pupil of Bellini, and I myself once tried to explain the sudden transition to the much freer group on the other side as due to Dürer's stay in Venice from 1505 to 1507, for Dürer could have taught Titian, as he did many other painters, something about monumental painting. To-day, however, it seems to me that this does not suffice to explain the marked difference in style, and I would prefer to date the picture from the second decade of the century, when Titian, through his contact with Giorgione, was beginning to feel his way towards the achievement of a monumental style.

The frescoes on the Fondaco de' Tedeschi remain the point at which Titian's *The Fondaco de' Tedeschi* art emerges from the impenetrable mists of his early schooling into the light of day, though even so the light is still obscured, for these paintings, which figure *286—291* in all old descriptions of the city down to the Baroque period as one of its artistic treasures, have been almost completely ruined by the action of air and water and have to be reconstructed fragment by fragment from much later engravings, which give a false impression of the originals. The Fondaco de' Tedeschi, which was the hub of Venetian trade with the North, was restored in 1505—1507 after a destructive fire. Since it was a Venetian custom that marble ornamentation was reserved for the Ducal Palace, the exterior of the Fondaco was to be decorated with frescoes. The commission was given to Giorgione and had been completed by November 1508; on 8 December Giorgione received a payment of 130 ducats. Giorgione's is the only name mentioned in the documents, but contemporary writers—Dolce and Vasari—agree in stating that only the façade towards the canal was painted by him and that the side of the building facing the street was entrusted to Titian. Thus Giorgione was the chief artist and the agreement was made with him alone, and Titian was merely an assistant, though one who was allowed a considerable degree of independence. According to an old anecdote, Giorgione felt that his assistant had outshone *Giorgione and Titian* him, but it must be remembered that the source of this anecdote would appear to have been Titian himself. If Titian was about ten years younger than Giorgione, who was born in 1477, the relationship between them would be a normal one. In an age of rapid development they were representatives of two different generations, linked by dependence and contrast. Giorgione was the pioneer of the transformation of Venetian painting which Titian effected. Giorgione's new conception of nature, his treatment of spatial depth, his contrasting colours, were all departures from Venetian tradition, which he was unable, in the short span of life he was granted, completely to transform. Paradoxical though it may sound, although Giorgione exercised a decisive influence on every artist of his own time, instilling a drop of Giorgionism into each of his contemporaries, he did not alter the course of Venetian art. Artistically and sociologically he was an alien. Ludwig Justi has shown how this young provincial failed to enter the closed circle of the official painters of Venice and had to seek other fields of activity such as the painting of frescoes and the production of cabinet pieces for dilettanti, to which Ansaldo Ferriguto added that Giorgione's clients

were drawn from a small circle of literary-minded sons of patrician families.
He was the idolized painter of a young generation conscious of its modernity,
which imposed upon him its choice of subject and its language of form, and
with his rendering of human life in its subjection to nature he gave unsurpassed
expression to its specific ideal of humanism.

*The Fondaco
frescoes
286—291*

In the frescoes on the Fondaco, where the mature master was competing
with the fledgling pupil, it was Titian who asserted the survivor's right to the
future. Unfortunately a comparison of the shares of the two artists has become
a philological and archaeological question; philological because Miturbi has
recently interpreted Vasari's statement, to my mind wrongly, in such a way that
our ideas of the distribution of the work between the two painters would have
to be changed; archaeological because we have to rely almost entirely on reproductions made at a time when the frescoes were half destroyed, though less completely than to-day. Our chief source is a series of etchings made and published by
an enthusiastic dilettante of the eighteenth century, Antonio Zanetti. A hundred
years earlier, in 1658, Piccino had engraved two of Titian's compositions, and a
comparison of the two versions, one baroque and the other rococo, provides a

290

check, especially as regards the so-called Judith, reproduced by both Piccino
and Zanetti. This figure seems to have been one of the most important in this
scheme of decoration, the scope and meaning of which were obscure even to
the old writers. Vasari, who was unable to find out from anybody what exactly
the frescoes were supposed to represent, describes them as a free play of artistic
fancy, and however unwilling we may be to believe that, we are not in a position
to disprove it. It is impossible to deduce any definite story or deeper meaning
from any of the figures, and even in the case of the twice reproduced Judith,
it has been suggested that the figure might be intended to represent Justitia.

*Titian and
Giorgione*

The formal language of the two artists can, however, be distinguished
despite the dimness of the mirror. The most instructive contrast is to be found
in two pairs of standing and sitting nudes. If we compare Giorgione's seated

286, 287

woman in Zanetti's etching with Titian's as engraved by Piccino, we note Giorgione's slender, delicate type, with its frontal stance, its motionless tranquillity
and silhouette effect, as against Titian's massive, compact and pathetic figure.
The manner in which the head rests on the neck and the arms emerge from the
shoulders, reveals a fundamentally different feeling for corporeal values. The

289

seated pair as seen in Zanetti's reproduction confirms the impression received
from the standing pair. We find the same contrast in the type of body: while
Giorgione's figure—which has been aptly compared with that of the woman
in his 'Tempest'—with its complicated pose and intersections, is clearly striving
towards plastic opulence and spatial depth, Titian's more solid female figure
is bound more strictly to the surface of the pictorial plane. To judge from
the sharp differentiation which Zanetti gives to it, the colouring must also have
served the same contrasting aims. Giorgione set glowing reddish light against
deep shadows, thus strengthening the impression that the figures were merged
in the surrounding space, but Titian used a brighter fundamental tone and

subdued shadows, which accentuated the surface modelling. Even in this youthful work Titian has unhesitatingly taken up his position.

He took up a position in Giorgione's milieu, not in his school. Titian can hardly be said to have been Giorgione's pupil in the sense that he grew up in his workshop, according to mediaeval and Renaissance custom. He must have achieved a high standard of training elsewhere before Giorgione engaged him to execute part of the Fondaco frescoes in the role of an independent assistant. We have the unanimous testimony of the literary sources and his works themselves to prove that the starting-point was the art of Bellini, and that is why I consider it wrong to attribute to Titian works which conform to an earlier stage in Giorgione's development, e. g. the 'Circumcision' at Yale, which Berenson and Suida both assign to Titian. When Titian came into contact with Giorgione at the Fondaco, he had already been working with Bellini. Only after Giorgione's death did he come more deeply under his spell.

Before that happened, Titian may from time to time, either consciously or unconsciously, have vied with Giorgione, whose artistic example, aided by the unusual attraction of his personality, exercised a profound influence on all the artists of his generation. Certain pictures seem from the very beginning to have been wrapped in obscurity, which modern investigators have not been able to dispel, the problem being rendered more difficult in several cases by their derivation from older types and their bad state of preservation. The 'Dead Christ' in the Scuola di San Rocco follows the type of the Gregorian 'Man of Sorrows' which is also frequently found in the Bellini circle, and the 'Bearing *284* of the Cross' in the church of the same confraternity is another type from the Bellini school. In both pictures a coating of dirt and overpainting has made it impossible to discern the original features; it is more a question of guesswork than of judgement if we assign them to one artist or the other. In the 'Dead Christ' neither tradition nor style supports the attribution to Titian. There are stronger reasons for assigning the 'Bearing of the Cross' to him—the testimony of most of the literary sources, the fact that the lunette of the altar-piece contains a painting by Titian's brother Francesco, and lastly the style of the figures, which reveal more of his conception of the human body than they do of Giorgione's. Nevertheless, in view of the condition of the picture, which makes it impossible to see more than a little of the original painting, these suppositions have more value from the archaeological than from the artistic point of view.

Greater artistic interest is attached to certain portraits, in which Titian *The early* may have consciously followed Giorgione. Even Vasari realized that Titian *portraits* sometimes came so close to Giorgione that there was risk of confusion, and he mentions in this connection a portrait of a member of the Barbarigo family, painted so carefully that it might well have been taken for a work of Giorgione's if Titian had not written his name on it in an inconspicuous place. This passage has been thought by many scholars to refer to the half-length portrait *4* now in the National Gallery in London, which in the seventeenth century was believed to be a portrait of Ariosto, but most certainly is not. Its soft chiaroscuro and the masterly way in which blooming manhood is attuned to a lyrical mood, have led many critics to doubt the authorship of Titian, despite the presence of his signature, and to attribute it to Giorgione.

That Titian's style in this picture should resemble Giorgione's would be only natural if it were really the picture which Vasari praised on account of that very similarity. But what distinguishes it is the difference in the character of the two artists, which emerged when they were working together on the Fondaco and which is rendered even clearer if we compare the 'Ariosto' with the likewise disputed 'Maltese Knight' in the Uffizi. In the latter picture, the attribution to Titian is supported by the heroic and dominating attitude, which, however, might also be due to the sitter and the nature of the commission.

19 Titian's 'Flora' which hangs in the Uffizi close to the 'Maltese Knight', makes the latter look bloodless, despite his tense, almost swaggering posture. What distinguishes Titian's human beings is the organic wholeness of their physical and spiritual appearance and their fusion with the pictorial plane, whereas Giorgione's figures are still children of the Quattrocento and need outside help to make them look impressive. In the 'Maltese Knight', in the 'Schiavona',

3 formerly in Sir Herbert Cook's collection at Richmond and now in the National

2 Gallery, London, and in the 'Portrait of a Gentleman' in the National Gallery, Washington (formerly H. Goldman collection), Titian speaks his own language in a Giorgionesque tone. Before he could come closer to Giorgione, he had first to consolidate his own position in art.

Titian's prospects   What professional prospects existed at that time for an ambitious young painter like Titian? The Bellinis had a firm grip on the big official commissions; even Giorgione found it difficult to compete with them. In fresco-painting, Titian in his début had shown that he was Giorgione's equal, but could he hope to rival him in his own speciality, in intimate figure-painting? In this field Giorgione had inimitable gifts—a power of invention hovering between lucidity and vagueness which appealed to the initiated, an inner feeling for nature which endowed his figure-compositions with cosmic infinity, a sense of proportion, charm and modernity which flattered the new type of connoisseur. Here there seemed to be little prospect for Titian, whose gifts were of a different kind; he was not an inventor, he was not a humanist, and he did not know how to exploit charm and modernity. To all these inner reasons were added external difficulties—the disruption caused by the war which Venice was waging against the powerful League of Cambrai, the consequences of which, as Crowe and Cavalcaselle have pointed out, were as catastrophic for Venetian artists as was the sack of Rome a few years later for the artists of the Eternal City. 'Sebastiano Luciani moved to Rome, Lotto went to Romagna, and Titian eventually to Padua and Vicenza.'

Titian in Padua   Since the middle of the fifteenth century, when Donatello and Mantegna were working in the city and the Bellinis were producing their first works, Padua had declined in importance as an art centre. The masters from other cities had left and the indigenous artists were of merely local importance. But in the first decade of the new century, artistic talent was attracted to the city from all sides. Among those who went there was Titian, though we do not know when or under what circumstances. Only three frescoes in the Scuola del Santo can be attributed to him with certainty on the basis of documents and certain stylistic features. We have Titian's receipt, dated 2 December 1511, for his fees for the painting of three murals in the Scuola, and three compartments of this extensive *The three* cycle of pictures are outstanding for their masterly execution. Paduan artists of *murals* *8, 11, 12* unequal talent contributed to this series of episodes from the life and deeds of St. Anthony, and to Titian was given the execution of three simple legends—episodes, one might almost say, of everyday life—showing St. Anthony giving a suckling the power of speech so that it may testify to its mother's innocence ; St. Anthony bringing to life a woman murdered by her jealous husband ; and St. Anthony restoring the leg of a youth who kicked his mother and then cut off his leg in remorse. These scenes of truly Franciscan naïveté were raised by Titian to a higher level and bathed by him in a glow of colour, which still makes an irresistible appeal, despite all the neglect and restoration, deplored as long ago as the eighteenth century. We realize with sorrow how much of the effect of the originals must be lacking in the colourless etchings made from the frescoes on the Fondaco.

The frescoes in the Scuola del Santo show clearly that they are by the same hand as those on the Fondaco, but they also reveal the young master's striving for independence. On the Fondaco he was restrained by the authority of Giorgione and the exigencies of a planned scheme of decoration, but now the young artist, still barely twenty, had to paint compositions for which no models existed.

He seems to feel most restraint in the ' Testimony of the Newborn Infant '. *8* In the general arrangement of the figures with the heads all on the same level one is tempted to see the influence of Donatello's reliefs, and in the division of the background into two halves, one architectural and the other landscape, both without any spatial relationship to the scene in the foreground, an echo of the Mantegna school. The influence of Giorgione is shown by the affinity of this scene to Giorgione's late painting in Glasgow. The robust vitality of the figures is Titian's. Taken separately, they are typically Titianesque figures, but they still lack Titian's cohesion of movement.

The 'Healing of the Youth's Leg' shows further progress. The group of *12* onlookers is more closely connected with the landscape by the big tree behind them, and the protagonists of the episode are more effectively contrasted with the crowd of onlookers. This heightens the pathos of the action ; the tender solicitude of the offended mother, the humble plea of the young woman and the gesture of the Saint are new dramatic touches.

The third painting stands alone, not only in its location, but also in its *11* format and character. The story of the jealous husband is represented on a stage, preserving many of the traditional elements. But in the disposition of the figures Titian shows his independence by relegating the culminating episode of the legend—the remorse and redemption of the sinner—to the background, and making the dramatic episode of the murder of the wife the main theme of the picture. At the same time he abandons the archaic arrangement of the figures in rows, as seen in the other compositions, in favour of a steep pyramid of figures, which raises a commonplace murder to the heights of symbolism. Mad with rage, the murderer towers above his victim, who wards off the thrust of the dagger with a gesture which even in death reveals a tender and erotic yielding—all this is genuine Titianesque comprehension, springing not from deliberation and analysis, but from the instinctive feeling of an exceptional genius for all the facets of human life.

These three frescoes denote a decisive step forward, expressed in an irregular way, but with striking freshness. In the colouring Giorgione's favourite juxtaposition of red and green—later to be replaced by red and blue—still predominates, but the meaning of the colours is no longer limited to flowery brilliance; they are used to stress vertical and horizontal lines and become an integral part of the picture.

Titian's new style exercised a profound influence on the motley crowd of artists who flocked to Padua during these years. Echoes of it can be detected in many of the other frescoes in the Scuola del Santo and the Scuola del Carmine; a whole school of painters found stimulus in these works, and one of them, Domenico Campagnola, who later became the leading local painter of Padua, imitated Titian so closely that his works are sometimes mistaken for those of the master.

The 'Triumph of Faith' Folding plate

Titian proved his superiority over all the other artists whose works some critics attempt to group with his, in a by-product of his stay in Padua, the mighty series of woodcuts of the 'Triumph of Faith', to which Vasari, our only more or less contemporary source, assigns the date 1508, but which must be dated not earlier than 1511 by reason of certain borrowings from Raphael. They represent a revolution in the history of woodcuts. Among the graphic arts, the engraving of woodcuts had achieved special popularity in Venice and a new style of illustration had developed, which with its daintiness, attention to minute details and charm is reminiscent of the childlike attractiveness of the Venetian dialect. Titian abandoned all this. He saw possibilities in the woodcut which nobody before him, even in Northern Europe, had recognized. He wanted his woodcuts to vie not with miniature-painting, but with frescoes.

The idea of a procession, showing Christ enthroned on the triumphal car of the Church and accompanied by the hierarchy of the faithful, is Italian. Jacob Burckhardt has pointed out that many details of Titian's composition correspond with a description of the 'Triumph of the Cross' by Savonarola and believes that these and similar representations of Christ's triumphal processions in art and literature are derived from actual processions which took place on the occasion of religious festivals. In any case the transposition of a spiritual conception into the vivacious dynamism of such a procession was in accord with the spirit of the Italian Renaissance. The timelessness and grandeur of the Church unroll before our eyes like the pomp and circumstance of the Roman

YOUNG WOMAN AT HER TOILET. About 1512-15. Paris, Louvre.

Empire in Mantegna's 'Triumph of Caesar', which had appeared a few years before in woodcut form after drawings by Benedetto Bordone.

The essence of Titian's 'Triumph' is Mantegnesque. In relief-like arrangement and slow-moving rhythm heroic figures pass before our eyes, beginning with Adam and Eve and the patriarchs, continuing with Moses und the Prophets, down to the Good Thief and the Innocent Children, the last witnesses of the Old Testament. Behind the triumphal car drawn by Fathers of the Church come the Apostles, Martyrs and Saints, and lastly the founders of the religious orders, who at that time were considered almost as contemporaries. Here all Giorgionesque modernity has been abandoned in favour of Mantegnesque solemnity. The general idea and the execution of the details are archaic, except for a few figures which are echoes of Michelangelo and Raphael.

While Titian was busy in Padua, an event took place in Venice which altered *The death of Giorgione* his prospects considerably. At the end of October 1510, there occurred the sudden and premature death of Giorgione, leaving a void which Titian was determined to fill. The share which, as a semi-independent assistant, he had had in the Fondaco frescoes, may even have given him a kind of right to this succession. But he may also have had to compete in this respect with Sebastiano Luciano, whose relationship to Giorgione and talents made him Titian's most redoubtable rival, but who preferred to go to Rome and leave the field to his competitor. Be that as it may, Titian was allotted part of the task of completing the works which Giorgione had left unfinished. That there was a considerable number of these we learn from that very reliable source of information on private collections in Northern Italy at that time, Marcantonio Michiel, who mentions several works begun by Giorgione and finished by Titian or Sebastiano, and later research has made one or two tentative additions to these.

The most celebrated of these paintings is the 'Venus' which Michiel saw *Giorgione's* in 1525 in the house of Jeronimo Marcello in Venice and which, since its redis- *paintings finished by Titian* covery in 1890 by Senator Morelli, has been identified by most scholars as the *294* 'Venus' now in Dresden. That it is Giorgione's 'Venus' for which Titian painted the landscape and the Cupid, as mentioned by Michiel, has more recently been doubted by several scholars, who hold that it is entirely by Titian's hand. These doubts seem to me unjustified, though the picture lacks indeed that unity between figure and nature which was the aim, and at the same time the charm, of all Giorgione's principal pictures. The landscape which Titian is supposed to have contributed is an addition, taken from the formal stock-in-trade of Giorgione, but not breathing his spirit. His, on the other hand, is the recumbent Venus, differing from Titian's mythological beauties in those very qualities which examination of the Fondaco frescoes shows to have been the keynote of Giorgione's work—minuteness, fine articulation and spatial depth; renunciation of organic unity and cohesion with the surface. What sensitive writers so often described as the chasteness of Giorgione compared with the sensuality of Titian's Venuses is precisely this lack of compelling organic power, which makes Titian's female figures appreciable in another sense.

292

The 'Noli me tangere' in the National Gallery, London, has the same lack of unity in the composition as the Dresden 'Venus' and also the same landscape motive in the right background. The attribution of this picture to Titian goes back as far as the eighteenth century, but even those older writers who support it, have emphasized the general affinity to Giorgione and the abundance of Giorgionesque details. The figures and landscape do not constitute an indivisible whole; the figures, with brilliant lightness of touch, are placed upon an already existing landscape ground, as Crowe and Cavalcaselle have stressed in their analysis of this picture. G. M. Richter, who has made the closest study of it, proposes a solution which to me appears to be the best—that we should consider this composition as one which was begun by Giorgione and finished by Titian.

A third painting belonging to this group is the 'Christ supported by an Angel', which Michiel saw in 1530 in the house of Gabriel Vendramin. This picture, for which various unsatisfactory identifications have been suggested, may perhaps more rightly be identified with a painting now in a private collection in Italy, which corresponds exactly with Michiel's description and analysis and which would appear to be a composition designed by Giorgione, but modernized by Titian. This picture, of which no reproduction is at present available, leads us to another painting similar in style, as regards which I must now change the

13

negative opinion I formerly expressed—the 'Tobit and the Archangel' from Santa Caterina, now in the Accademia in Venice. Vasari maintains that he learned from a reliable source that Titian painted a version of this subject in his early years and assumes that this must be the other 'Tobit' in San Marcuola, which however originates from a later period and is only a work of the Titian school. The fact, first noticed by A. L. Mayer in 1936, that the coat of arms on the Santa Caterina 'Tobit' is that of the Bembo family, lends considerable support to the theory that it is a painting of Titian's early period. Pietro Bembo was one of Titian's earliest patrons and probably arranged that invitation to Rome which Titian mentions in his application of 1513. The 'Tobit' must have been painted slightly before that date. It shows Titian still in the orbit of Giorgione, and certain clumsy details, such as the seated dog, also point to its being an early work.

The 'Concerts'
20, 29

To the group of works which have alternately been attributed to Titian and Giorgione, belong two paintings traditionally known by similar names— the 'Concert' in the Pitti Gallery at Florence and the 'Concert Champêtre' in the Louvre. The reproduction of the two paintings facing each other in Suida's book on Titian—together with the claim that they were both painted by Titian about the same time—seems to me to be the most conclusive evidence that they have nothing in common but their similarity of name and their Venetian origin. The elimination of the Louvre 'Concert' from Titian's œuvre, despite Hourticq's brilliant defence of its attribution to him, is a simpler matter than proving that the attribution to Titian of the Pitti 'Concert' is correct, especially as I here come up against opposition in my own household. E. Tietze-Conrat recently expressed herself very definitely as favouring the attribution to Sebastiano del Piombo; she is not the first to advance this theory, but she draws attention to certain important links, hitherto unnoticed, between him and Titian. This new phase of an old controversy bases its chief arguments on the middle figure of the three, the musician with his head turned, and, since the other figures are still further from Sebastiano than this one, would lead us to ask whether Sebastiano, like Titian, may not have departed from his normal manner during this period of transition.

Titian, too, had to struggle against the influence of Giorgione in order to regain his own complete independence. We can follow his progress through a series of female half-lengths, some secular, some religious. At the beginning of this series stands the 'Gipsy Madonna' in Vienna, whose gentle shyness has always been recognized as a characteristic surviving from the Quattrocento. Within Titian's œuvre this picture marks the beginning of a Giorgionesque transitional phase. The general conception still reminds us of Giovanni Bellini's devotional pictures, but the change from a high, narrow format to a wider format already denotes a tendency towards increased worldliness. The greater energy and the compactness of the bodies carry us to a stage beyond Giorgione, though the expression of Mother and Child is akin to him. The 'Gipsy Madonna' is the spiritual sister of the worldly heroines whom Titian depicted in half-length. Closest to her is the 'Salome with the head of the Baptist' in the Galleria Doria in Rome. A second version of this picture has recently been claimed for Giorgione, without any attempt to explain its close affinity with the other half-lengths of this group, the attribution of which to Titian has never been disputed. In this picture, too, we are struck by the worldly element, as compared with the older versions of the subject so popular among the artists of the school of Leonardo. The real subject of Titian's picture is the representation of female beauty. If the external attributes were to be omitted, it would be difficult to give these young women names. Many of them have, in fact, been given improvised names or a subjective explanation of their allegorical meaning, e. g. the 'Vanity' in Munich, the 'Flora' in Florence, the 'Young Woman at her toilet' in Paris. The interpretation of the last-named picture gave rise to the most daring guesses; it was supposed to represent various pairs of lovers of high rank famous at that time. The inventory of Van Dyck's estate, made in 1644, was probably nearer the truth when it bluntly described a picture of this sort as *una corteggiana con un specchio et un uomo*. In Titian's hands Giorgione's world of mythological allegory was transformed, scenes and figures over whose significance secret cults seemed to cast a mysterious twilight, are now seen as discreet forms of homage to female beauty.

The most beautiful of these Venetian 'ladies of the town' is generally acknowledged to be the 'Flora' in the Uffizi, equally perfect in the harmonious proportions of the human figure in relation to the pictorial plane and in the robust, yet gentle colouring, which has passed beyond the Giorgionesque play of broken tones. In pure harmony the auburn hair, dissolving into gold at the edges, the white of the chemise tinged with bluish-grey and the strawberry red of the dress stand out against the olive-green of the background.

Giorgione's influence on Titian

9

15

17—19

19

II*

30

The most important and the last in this series of pictures from Titian's preparatory period is the celebrated painting of two women in the Galleria Borghese in Rome. It is only since 1700 that it has been known by the high-sounding name of 'Sacred and Profane Love'. An older description of the Villa Borghese, in which the picture is mentioned for the first time, gives it a simpler designation—'Beauty Adorned and Unadorned'—and is probably closer to the original meaning. For among the numerous attempts to interpret the picture, as anything from an illustration for some classical or contemporary work of literature down to a pictorial representation of a supposed love-affair between Titian and Palma's alleged daughter Violante, the suggestions most likely to have good foundations are those which find in this picture a parallel to the Platonic dialogues on love so popular during the Renaissance period—a contrast between two principles, such as the Middle Ages were wont to depict by means of similar associations—Chastity and Lewdness, Saintliness and Worldliness—and such as we find in a celebrated Venetian romance of more recent date, Colonna's 'Hypnerotomachia Polifili'. Numerous details in our picture may well have been derived from this curious book, as W. Friedländer and R. Wischnitzer have recently shown. At the time when the picture was painted, the contents of the book were a concrete reality, whereas for us they have faded to the point of being incomprehensible.

The picture was commissioned by the Grand Chancellor of Venice, Niccolò Aurecchio, and it thus originated in the same social atmosphere as Giorgione's cabinet pictures, though the difference between it and them is very noticeable. A new style is here ushered in, which passes over the Giorgionesque interlude and links this composition with the frescoes which Titian executed in Padua. The way in which the figures are fitted into the picture and form one surface with the landscape is nothing new, because that is part of the essence of Titian. But the solution is a richer one. The long horizontal lines of the rim of the basin give a greater impressiveness to the two seated women and bind them more closely together despite the distance which separates them; any thrust into depth is eliminated by the concealment of the narrow ends of the basin; the way in which the colours are interwoven gives us a foretaste of Titian's subsequent mastery of colour, although in other respects the picture suffers from the unavoidable weaknesses of youthful exuberance, overcrowding and lack of proportion.

27

24

Looking back into the past and forward into the future, the Borghese painting closes a period of transition in Titian's life. To the same period belong a couple of pictures which, though well authenticated by literary sources, have given rise to many doubts. One of these is the 'Three Ages of Man', assuming that the best of several extant versions, that in Bridgewater House, London, is the original which Titian, according to Vasari, painted in 1515 for Giovanni di Castel Bolognese of Faenza, or, if we take into account a certain hardness of execution, an old copy of it. Another bone of contention is the 'Baptism of Christ' in the Capitoline Gallery in Rome, which, despite the fact that it is well authenticated—Michiel saw it in 1531 as a work of Titian's in the house of Giovanni Ram—

THE TRIBUTE MONEY About 1518. Dresden, Gallery.

has had doubts as to its authorship cast upon it by Hetzer. The most disturbing feature is the almost obtrusive prominence given to the figure of the donor in the foreground, though it is true that analogies to this can be found in other works of that time. Even if we admit this and other weaknesses, the intensity of the reproduction of nature in this picture is a decisive argument in favour of its attribution to Titian. About this time (1515-1516) Titian's feeling for nature received a powerful stimulus from his impressions of Dürer's woodcuts, especially those of the 'Life of the Virgin', and it was no mere coincidence that a writer who has made a special study of Titian's attitude to landscape, should detect for the first time in this despised 'Baptism of Christ' the 'rustling of the mountains forests'. In other works of the same period, e. g. the magnificent study of a tree in the Metropolitan Museum, New York, and the large woodcut 47 320 of 'Abraham's Sacrifice', we have further proofs of this important event in Titian's artistic life. A recent discovery has added an important link to this chain. The 'Flight into Egypt' in the Hermitage at Leningrad has been identified as the picture which Vasari—and after him, much more accurately, Ridolfi—describes as a youthful work of Titian's, immediately after he has dealt with the frescoes in the Scuola del Santo. The resemblance of the figures to some of those in the great woodcuts of the 'Triumph of Faith' and 'Abraham's Sacrifice' confirms the dating and indicates the source from which Titian drew the inspiration for his new interpretation of nature. The inner relationship to Dürer's woodcuts goes so far that one might almost assume the collaboration of German assistants in Titian's large woodcuts, who might also have helped to execute some of the landscapes of his paintings. Vasari mentions that in Titian's early days he had Germans in his workshop, whom he employed on his landscapes. The 'Flight into Egypt', in which for the first time we find Titian rendering landscape with deep feeling, is his earliest claim to be considered the founder of Italian landscape painting. He has a right to this title and it has long been accorded to him. For although Titian never painted landscapes in the narrower sense of the term, under the influence of Dürer he opened the eyes of his fellow-country-men to this new artistic world.

Return to Venice AFTER TITIAN returned to Venice from Padua, his position underwent a considerable change. He quickly filled the void which had been left by Giorgione's death and his achievements as the dead master's executor and successor were such that in 1513 he aspired to become the official painter to the Republic and thus the successor of the eighty-year-old Giovanni Bellini. In a petition to the Council of Ten, dated 31 March 1513, Titian formally applied to be granted the next broker's patent at the Fondaco de' Tedeschi, on the same conditions as had been granted to Giovanni Bellini. In his application he mentioned receiving attractive offers from the Pope and other high personages, but stated that he would prefer to serve his native city and pledged himself to paint the battle picture in the Hall of the Grand Council, which no other artist had ventured to undertake. There was some opposition to Titian's application. It is true that his offer was at first accepted and that he was installed in the Council Hall with two assistants in June 1513, but a few months later this decision was reversed, perhaps at the instigation of a coterie which did not favour Titian, and it was not until 1516, the year of Bellini's death, that he finally obtained the coveted post, with all the advantages pertaining to it.

Official painter to the Republic His first task as official painter to the Serenissima should have been the painting of the battle picture in the Doges' Palace, but once he had reached his goal, he seems to have been in no hurry to fulfil his obligations. In the same year, 1516, he began working for Duke Alfonso of Ferrara, for whom he executed all kinds of artistic commissions during the following years and through whom he came into contact with other princely courts related to that of Ferrara by blood or marriage—the Gonzagas in Mantua in 1523 and the Rovere family in Urbino in 1532.

The large number of orders which Titian received did not dismay, but stimulated him, and his faculties seem to have been braced to the utmost. Nor did he limit himself to his work for the Venetian Republic and the court of Ferrara. Ecclesiastical patrons commissioned him to paint the 'Assunta' for the *35, 65* *49, 54* *69* Frari, the 'Annunciation' for Treviso, the altar-piece of the Virgin Mary for San Domenico at Ancona and the polyptych for Santi Nazaro e Celso in Brescia, while his old patron Jacopo Pesaro ordered the great family altar-piece for the Frari. Within fifteen years Titian had completely transformed the current conceptions of the altar-piece, the private devotional painting, the mythological picture and the formal portrait. His capacity for work seemed to grow and to be insatiable. This astounding development was helped by the mighty strides made by painting in Northern Italy. Even that representative of the older generation, the aged Giovanni Bellini, was involved in this movement and none of the younger artists could remain untouched by it. In such stirring times the bold and enthusiastic generally take the lead, and thus in Venice the movement was headed by the impetuous and gifted Antonio de Sachis, known from his birth-place as Pordenone, who influenced all his own contemporaries and also the slightly younger Titian. Pordenone's frescoes in Corbolone anticipated the 'grand manner' of Titian's 'Assunta', a fact to which Fiocco was the first to draw attention.

Pordenone owed his lead not only to his impetuous temperament, but also to his direct acquaintance with Central Italian art, which he had acquired during his journey to Rome in 1515. To his fellow-countrymen he brought back a knowledge of the aims and achievements in the heart of the artistic world at a time when Venice was ready and eager to absorb these Central Italian and classical influences.

Even in works of his preceding period, such as the 'Allegory of Love' in the Galleria Borghese, Titian had demonstrated his new understanding of the antique. On the threshold of manhood, this tendency becomes more marked. The ideal female type of the 'Assunta' is permeated with the vigorous form language of classical art, just as the putti in the same painting are akin to the cupids round the throne of Saturn. The mythological paintings are full of borrowings from antique art, of a kind differing from those found in Titian's frescoes in the Scuola del Santo and from the classical fragments which Floren-tine artists inserted in their compositions as ornaments. There is one figure, in particular, in which the new conception is clearly seen—the St. Sebastian in the altar-piece of the Resurrection at Brescia. The special care which Titian devoted to this youthful nude is confirmed by literary sources and emphasized by the conspicuous signature beneath this very figure. The foot resting on the broken shaft of the column, formerly a purely decorative motive in Venetian painting, is here used as a means of heightening expression and intensifying the pathos of the fettered arms and the bowed head.

Freiherr von Liphart believed that this St. Sebastian was inspired by one of Michelangelo's slaves in the Louvre. There is a parallel to this in Titian's borrowing of a figure from the battle cartoon for his 'Andrians' in Madrid— the youth resting on his arm, next to the young woman raising the saucer, is the recumbent man on the extreme right of the grisaille at Holkham Hall. A fragment of the cartoon, which was broken up in 1515—1516, was in a private collection in Mantua in the sixteenth century. Was it already there when Titian came to Mantua with Dosso in 1519, at the very time when he was painting the 'Andrians', and inspected Isabella d'Este's art treasures? It is intriguing to think that it may have been an original fragment of Michelangelo's lost work which led Titian to make an exact replica of this figure and to borrow others.

At the same time as he gained an insight into Michelangelo's rendering of form, Titian also learned to understand Raphael's method of composition. His altar-piece of the Virgin in Ancona (1520) is often cited as the Venetian counter-

Titian and the antique

35

52

51, 53

43

49

part of Raphael's Madonna in Foligno. The most fruitful result of this contact with this artistic tendency was the 'Assunta', in which the influence of Raphael's last manner is apparent. The sonorous pathos, the skilful disposition of the figures, the classically exalted type of the Madonna and the Apostles filled with deep emotion, all that is Titian's interpretation of Raphael's language—*lingua toscana in bocca veneziana*. To appreciate the new scale of values, one must think of renderings of the same theme by leading masters of the earlier generation, for example Giovanni Bellini's late work in San Pietro Martire at Murano.

We have already mentioned that Dürer was also one of the artists from whom Titian drew inspiration in these years when he was thirsting to absorb new ideas. Other artists, too, enriched Titian's art, but it would be fruitless to try to establish which of these influences led him to his great style. In its essence it was a natural phase in accord with Titian's development. It was not Pordenone or any other forerunner of Venetian art, it was not antique art or Michelangelo or Raphael or Dürer who made Titian great; it was his desire for greatness which enabled him to absorb all they had to offer. They came to him at a favourable time together with favourable opportunities. Great orders resulted in a great style, and that great style enabled him to execute these orders in a great manner. Influences and opportunities do not create geniuses, but are exploited by them. Titian's contact with the art of others and the works he produced during these years are the result of the same enhanced vitality.

The point to be remembered is that the essential element in Titian's art did not come to him from outside, but was already present within him. For this reason it is advisable to begin our study of his masterpieces by considering that which is considered to be the earliest of this category—the altar-piece of St. Mark

in the sacristy of Santa Maria della Salute. It was painted at the time when he was closest to Giorgione, and it may be that the outbreak of plague in 1510, to which Giorgione fell a victim, prompted the donation of this altar-piece. Crowe and Cavalcaselle assume that this was the first work produced by Titian in Venice after his return from Padua. The pattern of the 'Santa Conversazione', developed by Giovanni Bellini and still visible in Giorgione's Madonna in Castelfranco, is here abandoned. The elegant architecture in which such compositions were enframed is reduced to a pillar motive on one side, such as is found for the first time in the Fondaco frescoes. Instead of the simple juxtaposition of figures, there is a definite subordination to the central figure of St. Mark, who is sitting enthroned like a Roman emperor above the others. The elaboration of the construction and the new dignity seen in the play of the draperies have been ascribed to the influence of Fra Bartolomeo, who came from Florence to Venice in 1508. It does not, however, seem necessary to assume Florentine influence, for Giorgione's late style, as seen in the 'Judgement of Solomon' at Kingston Lacy, provided a model nearer home. In other respects, too, the relationship to Giorgione is evident. The Salute altar-piece shows the same predilection for small figures as the Castelfranco Madonna, the same striving to achieve spatial depth by means of the geometrical pattern of the pavement, the same types of ardent youths, steeped in light and shadow.

Far more important than all this is a new pictorial homogeneity. The central figure is not isolated from the others as it is in Castelfranco, but is in close relationship to them; the secondary figures are not arranged in a row, but in two pairs, harmonizing both bodily and spiritually and culminating in the principal figure; the architecture ceases to be a framework, and has the function of heightening the impression of grandeur and monumentality; there is no distant view of a landscape, only a patch of cloudy sky links the group with infinity. Everything has become simpler, heavier—one might almost say more unwieldy— and bigger. The colouring has undergone a corresponding change. The clash of colours is more violent and in the robe of St. Mark we find for the first time that harmony of ultramarine and carmine, that note of blue and red, which was to become Titian's keynote. The picture is not only rooted in the past, but points to the future.

With its heightened feeling for life the St. Mark altar-piece is a prelude to Titian's heroic period, which lasted for about fifteen years until 1530. During this period all categories of pictures attained that form which was to remain predominant for the next three centuries. This new form is the expression of a fundamentally new conception of art, for it is the starting-point of the idea of the enrichment of life by art which is so characteristic of modern times. To reality, whose elements art grasps, concentrates and intensifies, art opposes its own effect, different in substance and ruled by other laws. The era of the Fine Arts is beginning.

On its threshold stands like a sonorous overture, anticipating all its essential *The 'Assunta'* elements, the first great masterpiece of the new style—Titian's 'Assunta'. He *35* painted this picture in an unusually short time. It was ordered in 1516 and unveiled on 20 March 1518. The State chronicler Martin Sanudo considered the event of sufficient importance to merit being recorded in his diaries, which were normally reserved for matters of State.

With one bound Titian leaves all his contemporaries behind him. There were, of course, harbingers of the 'Assunta' in Venetian art and outside it. The reliefs on the Barbarigo tomb, completed in 1515, show a similar grouping of Apostles in one row beneath the ascending Madonna, and slightly older compositions by Fra Bartolomeo and his school are filled with the same pathos. But such facts merely tend to show that Titian's development was in harmony with that of the whole Cinquecento and they provide a yardstick by which we can measure the distance between his achievement and other, sometimes even earlier solutions.

The miraculous event of the Assumption is clearly divided into its two essential episodes—the departure of the Virgin from this earth and her reception in Heaven. This clear division into three tiers holds the composition in one plane and the 'Assunta' has, in fact, been described as the flattest of all pictures, comparable in its two-dimensionality only to the works of Byzantine art, to which other critics add that the marked effect of depth in the main tiers of the construction counterbalance this unilateral element, that the Apostles with the vivacity of their gestures and their daring intersections give the impression of lively bustle and that the semicircle of angels encloses the Virgin as in a niche. The darkness at the bottom of the picture, in which the Apostles stand out like silhouettes, serves not only to mark the contrast with the centre of the picture, where the Virgin, dark against light, achieves concentrated vitality, and to stress the difference between the three zones, but also to give the impression of upward movement, which becomes a physical uplift and a dissolution of all that is earthly in the heavenly sphere. The yearningly raised arms of the Apostles, the sweep of the garland of angels around the Virgin, the foreshortening of the upper part of her body, all contribute to create an impression of energetic movement upwards, impetuous and stormy, but at the same time irresistible and tranquil. The simplification of the colouring enhances the impression of certainty, inevitability and sanctity. The picture is tuned to a full harmony of red and blue, which in the altar-piece of St. Mark had appeared only as an isolated note.

We are told that the Franciscan monks at first refused to accept his painting. The novelty which offended their aesthetic, and of course even more, their religious ideas, was the heightening of the sensual effect. All the human forms are idealized, but they remain the enhanced expression of a subjective sensual experience, and this imparts to the picture a pathos, an exuberant vitality and a self-sufficiency which was bound to seem frightening, and even offensive, to the champions of an older conception. We have only to think of the altar-pieces of Giovanni Bellini and his contemporaries, or even of Giorgione's Madonna in Castelfranco. They, too, strive to be true to life and to achieve solemnity, but they were filled with a naive religiosity and an ingenuous realism which made them seem simpler, more mysterious and more godly. It was by means of their childlike simplicity that they gained entry to the holy of holies. Titian's 'Assunta', which transforms a significant subject, presented in a significant form, into a sensual experience, produces a very different impression; it *represents* what its predecessors merely *were*. This aesthetic motive endows the picture with a worldly and theatrical element which confused and frightened the worthy friars and has made subsequent art critics with Romantic leanings distrustful of Titian.

The 'Pesaro Madonna'
69—73

A few years later Titian was given the opportunity of installing in the same church of the Frari a new version of the 'Santa Conversazione', but this he owed, not to the friars, but to the Pesaro family, to whom he had been known since his early years. The payments for the altar-piece of the Pesaro family run from April 1519 to May 1526 and the painting was unveiled in the latter year on 8 December. It represents a more radical departure from the normal scheme of votive pictures than the 'Assunta'. The traditional elements—the group of saints round the enthroned Madonna, the relationship between them and the donors, the architectural framework—have all acquired a new significance. The most important novelties are the shifting of the whole construction from the normal frontal to an oblique position and the elimination of the landscape view, the function of which has been taken over by the architecture. The two huge columns, which were inserted while the picture was being painted, heighten the impression of spaciousness and give firmness and proportion to the figures. These form a pyramid, to the apex of which—the Madonna—two arms, a long and a short one, lead up. The shifting of the vanishing point to the extreme left gives the spectator a constant impulse to follow the stately avenue which the chain of figures draws through the picture. Many details in the style of the individual figures are reminiscent of the 'Assunta', but the effect is different. The fact that members of the Pesaro family are intermingled with the saints deprives the picture of that ecstatic agitation which gave the 'Assunta' spiritual unity. In the Pesaro altar-piece the divine and the human are more intimately fused and the atmosphere is one of peace and bliss. Pure and unbroken colours predominate, not with the robust impetuosity of the 'Assunta', but more softly, more soothingly and more lustrously.

The third of the great altar-pieces with which Titian directed religious The lost 'St. Peter Martyr' monumental painting into new channels, has not been preserved. The 'Murder of St. Peter Martyr', which Titian painted between 1525 and 1530 for Santi Giovanni e Paolo, was destroyed in 1867 when the chapel of the Rosary in this church was burned. To the fact that this painting, more than any other, was studied and imitated by artists of Venice and other cities, we owe the existence of some good old copies, which, together with the preliminary drawings in Lille 297—299 300 and a number of engravings, help us to reconstruct the original. The subject is an assassination; rigid tension on the part of the dastardly assailant, helpless prostration on the part of his victim. The escorting monk recoils from the triangular main group—as if jerked away by the inclined tree-trunk in the background—and his horrified gesture epitomizes the craven human reaction to the onslaught, just as the gestures of St. Peter Martyr — his attempt to write 'Credo' on the ground, his arm raised, not in self-defence, but in a gesture of appeal to Heaven—typify the religious reaction. The greatness of the figure composition is heightened by the grandeur of surrounding nature; the mighty tree-trunks with their storm-lashed foliage, the sinister clouds in the sky, the panorama of mountains in the far background—all reflect the spiritual mood of the human beings in the foreground.

These three great classics, with their power of creating types, had a Other altar-pieces momentous influence on the subsequent evolution of European painting. They were followed by others moving in the same direction, though at a certain distance—the signed altar-piece donated by Aloysius Gotius to San Francesco in Ancona (now in the Museum of that city); the altar-piece in six compartments 49 for Santi Nazaro e Celso in Brescia, the donor of which, the Papal Legate 54 Altobello Averoldo, perhaps insisted on the archaic form of an altar-piece in several panels, but which, by way of compensation for this retrogression, contains one of the most beautiful of Titian's single figures, the St. Sebastian; and lastly 52 the 'Annunciation' in Treviso, which has perhaps not come down to us in its 65 original form. The magnificent figure of the kneeling Madonna is certainly Titian at his best and may have been painted about 1516—1520, but the ambitious spatial construction and the unfortunate placing of the miserable little donor between the Madonna and the disproportionately small angel, that is to say in the very holy of holies, are a contradiction of Titian's principles and skill. Among the various explanations of this lack of uniformity, the best appears to be that of Oettinger, who suggests that a composition by Titian was adapted by Paris Bordone to make it fit into this altar-piece, which was completed in 1523. It is also noteworthy that the Treviso 'Annunciation', unlike other works by Titian, had no influence on other artists and was never imitated. Even Titian himself, in his later versions of the 'Annunciation', never returned to this arrangement.

The 'Madonna with the cherries'
34
*9*The three pictures mentioned above, despite their somewhat inferior character and their lack of uniformity, nevertheless played a part in the great task of this period of Titian's life—the transformation of traditional old types into new ones. Titian also developed the private devotional picture along the same lines as the altar-piece. His 'Madonna with the Cherries' is a reformed version of the 'Gipsy Madonna', which was rooted in the old Venetian tradition. A new element in this picture is the firm way in which the central group is built into the plane by the stress laid on the horizontal parapet in the foreground and by the arrangement of the broad triangle of figures within the rectangular format. The two saints on either side of the lighter-coloured figure of the Madonna were added only during the execution. The maturity of the composition makes it probable that it was painted about 1515, not in the early years of the century, as was previously assumed; the resemblance to Dürer's 'Madonna of the Goldfinch' of 1506, which does not necessarily imply a direct derivation, supports this dating, as does also the affinity of the picture to the 'Tribute Money'.

The 'Tribute Money'
*25*The 'Tribute Money', painted for Duke Alfonso d'Este, is an illustration of his motto: 'Render therefore unto Caesar the things which are Caesar's, and unto God the things that are God's.' This fact alone makes it unlikely that the picture was painted before 1516, the year in which Titian's connection with this prince began. The artistic theme of the picture is based on the contrast between the light-coloured, mild oval features of Christ and the dark, pointed profile of the Pharisee. This is an echo of Leonardo da Vinci's 'Last Supper' and a forerunner in the œuvre of Titian, or Giorgione, is the 'Bearing of the *284*Cross' in San Rocco. The hands repeat the dramatic contrast—the pale, flesh-coloured hand of the Saviour and the dark-brown hand of the Pharisee. These contrasts serve to fuse composition and colouring into an ornamental pictorial whole, closely akin in this respect to the 'Assunta'; as in the 'Assunta' deep red and blue are juxtaposed and opposed, luminous and transparent as in a painting on glass and, as they would be in such a painting, joined together in a firmly defined plane.

Mythological works

*41, 43?*For the same patron Titian executed the three mythological pictures which may be described as analogies to the three great religious paintings of this period, in the sense that they show the same advance of style in the field of mythological painting. They were destined for the study of the prince, who wanted to compete with the famous study of his sister Isabella d'Este in Mantua. The 'Feast of Venus' and the 'Andrians' are both based on descriptions of imaginary

BACCHUS AND ARIADNE. 1523. London, National Gallery.

pictures by the late classical writer Philostratus, whose text the compositions follow with astonishing fidelity, without thereby losing their artistic independence. Literary invention is transposed into the language of art and a classical quotation is given an independent interpretation. There is no whiff of the midnight oil in these pictures, such as we occasionally discern in those executed for Isabella; they are redolent of forests, wine and humanity. Inner comprehension has re-created the subject-matter.

The starting-point for these new compositions was Giovanni Bellini's 'Feast of the Gods', which since 1514 had been in the room for which they were intended, though it is hard to imagine a greater contrast than that which exists between them and it, despite the affinity of subject. Bellini endowed his theme, a somewhat coarse episode from Ovid's *Fasti*, with the solemnity of his religious paintings; Titian's pictures, on the other hand, are filled with music and fragrance, with love-making, dancing and exuberant joy. They breathe a cosmic consciousness which might be called pagan, but which is even more a reflection of that self-identification with the universe which filled the 'Assunta' with such deep religious serenity. Figures and colouring are attuned to this change of sentiment. The putti of the 'Feast of Venus' are the brothers and sisters of the angels in the 'Assunta' and their blue wings and yellowish-red apples spread a gay network over the picture. The 'Andrians' is dominated by the striking contrast of blue and red in the dancing pair on the right and between the bluish-white of the sky and the healthy flesh-colour of the Bacchantes.

The first two paintings may have been executed in 1517 and 1518; the third, 'Bacchus and Ariadne', was not completed until 1523, after many impatient reminders from the Duke. It is based, not, as was hitherto supposed, on a passage from Catullus, but, as E. Wind has convincingly proved, mainly on Ovid's description of the departure of Bacchus and the metamorphosis of Ariadne. This mature, thoughtful conception is Titian's most perfect embodiment of his new ideas concerning mythological pictures.

I am inclined to date Titian's revision of Bellini's 'Feast of the Gods' from about the time when he finished the 'Bacchus and Ariadne'. It is possible that the uniform style of his three pictures rendered a modernization of the older one in the same room necessary. The grandiose forest and mountain landscape, which is painted over the previously existing curtain of parallel tree-trunks and occupies the upper left quarter of the picture, belongs to the late 1520's. On this occasion, Titian naturally went carefully over the whole of the rest of the picture and X-ray photographs reveal how radically he altered many details. Nevertheless, the 'Feast of the Gods' retains its harmonious tranquillity, which is an argument in favour of the previously mentioned theory that Titian may have collaborated in the original version of this picture.

Portraits

During these fruitful years portrait-painting moved in the same direction as the other branches of painting, but did not assume the importance within Titian's œuvre which it afterwards achieved. He cultivated it occasionally rather than systematically. Here too, he strove to create an independent prototype transcending Giorgione's conception. The series of early portraits begins with

58
23
62, 59

those of two functionaries at the court of Ferrara—Tommaso Mosti, Alfonso d'Este's secretary (now in Palazzo Pitti), and Lodovico Ariosto, the court poet (now in Indianapolis). More mature and probably painted a little later are the 'Man with a glove' and a bearded young man in the Louvre, whom Hourticq, for interesting but not quite convincing reasons, attempts to identify as Girolamo Adorno and Pietro Aretino. This would bring us at least to about 1527, which hardly agrees with the style of the portraits; they are close to the portraits of donors in the great altar-pieces and have that solemn rigidity which is reminiscent of Byzantine art. Above all, they have no trace of that lassitude, relaxation and softening which become characteristic of Titian's style about 1530.

The new spirit which speaks from Titian's creations during the preceding fifteen years might be defined as the proclamation of the aesthetic motive in the artistic consciousness of the period. Mediaeval art had subjected itself to the service of the religious idea; in the fifteenth century art strove to achieve knowledge of the universe. The aim of Titian's pictures is to enhance the pleasure of living by offering assurance and happiness. Art begins to be a means of raising life to a higher level; the encouragement of art becomes a duty of the State and a badge of social distinction. Ecclesiastical patrons are replaced more and more by lay patronage and, especially in Venice, where the pattern of politics and civilization tended to suppress the individual, by the State.

Official commissions

We have already seen how Titian, while still comparatively young, applied for and obtained the post of official painter to the Republic. To him with his peasant cunning a fixed salary seemed the most desirable form of remuneration. His broker's patent at the Fondaco, which he finally obtained in 1516, placed him under an obligation to execute certain works, among which a battle picture in the Sala del Gran Consiglio is specifically mentioned. Nevertheless, it was a quarter of a century before Titian fulfilled this obligation, and even then it needed a threat that he would be replaced by his competitor Pordenone and would have to refund all the payments received during all these years, to induce him to complete and deliver the battle picture.

This excessive delay may not have been entirely Titian's fault; other commissions for the State may sometimes have appeared to him to be more urgent. In 1517, the government of Venice, always compelled to hold the balance between the German Emperor and the King of France, was anxious to gain the favour of the latter's representative in Italy, Marshall Lautrec, by bribing him. Among the numerous costly gifts which it was intended to present to him, a painting by Titian of St. George, St. Michael and St. Theodore occupied a prominent place. The Venetian chargé d'affaires in Milan repeatedly urged upon Titian the need for haste and the picture was, in fact, ready for presentation only at the last moment. Modern research has overlooked this work of Titian's, mentioned a dozen times in Sanudo's chronicle, despite the fact that at least part of it has been preserved. I, at all events, am firmly convinced that the St. George from the Audley Neeld collection, now on the art market in England, is a fragment, or, to be more exact, a third of the lost work. It has been attributed to Giorgione and to other artists, but years ago Longhi, though he

50

did not know how strong was the documentary evidence, recognized in it Titian's early style. That it is not a complete picture in itself is obvious, for there would have been no point in producing a large figure, full of animation and seen from one side, unless it had been intended to form part of a larger picture—the three-panel painting for Lautrec. The haste with which Titian was compelled to work is still discernible in this magnificent improvisation, in which Titian develops reminiscences of Giorgione in the same way as he does in the Apostles of the 'Assunta' or the Saints in the altar-pieces at Ancona and Rimini.

In addition to this urgent order, the second commission for the Sala del Gran Consiglio may have diverted Titian from completing the battle picture. Since the beginning of the fourteenth century well-known artists had been commissioned by the State to execute mural paintings in this hall depicting episodes from the semi-legendary early history of Venice, but in the course of time most of these deteriorated owing to the humid climate and had to be renewed, the new pictures being as far as possible replicas of the old composition. The painting representing the Emperor Frederick Barbarossa doing homage to Pope Alexander III, actually a second edition of a fourteenth-century painting, had been left unfinished by the Bellinis and to Titian was given the task of completing it. His version was destroyed by fire in 1577 together with the rest of the decoration of the hall, so that we have to try to reconstruct it from the version executed by Federigo Zuccaro to replace it. But Titian's great achievement in this hall was not the completion of the Bellini picture, but the 'Battle' which he had been commissioned to paint as long ago as 1513. This, too, has been lost, but we possess designs for it, engravings and one painted copy of it. Tradition is not clear as to what battle is represented, and it would almost seem as if this vagueness were deliberate. In any case, the original theme was the battle of Spoleto, an episode from the legend of Barbarossa; this designation, however, was abandoned in the seventeenth century in favour of a more recent feat of arms, the victory which the Venetians won in 1508 in Cadore against the imperial troops.

The lost 'Battle of Cadore'

78, 105, 302

The lucky discovery of a complete design for the whole work, which is worthy to rank with the two other Renaissance masterpieces of battle-painting, Leonardo's 'Battle of Anghiari' and Raphael's 'Victory of Constantine', enables us to follow in part Titian's procedure during the long years devoted to the completion of this picture. At the outset the arrangement was more Leonardesque and more genre-like, a scene of combat rather than an episode of military history. It was not until later that the picture was adapted to the rectangular wall-space and the commander, whose place was originally occupied by a humble artilleryman, was made to dominate the battle, while the tumult of battle and the grandiose mountain landscape, full of memories of Titian's native Cadore, were integrated into one plane.

Most of the other works which Titian executed in his capacity as official State painter have likewise been lost. The chapel of St. Nicholas, which Doge Andrea Gritti commissioned him to adorn with paintings, no longer exists. His portraits of the Doges, the execution of which formed part of his official duties,

Other lost works

were destroyed in the fire of 1577; his votive pictures of these dignitaries, another branch of his official duties, were all lost in another fire three years earlier, except one, the 'Fede' with the Doge Grimani, which was saved by chance. Everywhere we have to rely on fragments, reproductions and reconstructions. The only official painting by Titian still in its original location is the St. Christopher in the Ducal Palace.

271
67, 68

Titian's official portraits of the Doges have been destroyed, but it is legitimate to assume that he executed replicas of these for the families concerned or for other purposes, and that, in order to do this, he kept preparatory sketches or models of them in his workshop, as well as of other works suitable for duplication. Several such hastily executed portraits, to which Titian contributed only the essentials, while the accessories were left to the discretion of whoever executed the replica, have been preserved, not always in their original form, as additions were often made, in order to improve the prospects of selling them. To this category we must assign the portraits of Gritti in the Metropolitan Museum, New York, and of Francesco Donato in San Diego (California), whereas the portrait of Gritti in the Czernin collection in Vienna might well be a variant executed by Titian himself. The latter portrait is more pompous than is usual for a Titian portrait, but this may have been a concession to the character of the sitter. In the votive picture of the same Doge, the composition of which is somewhat freely repeated in an almost contemporary woodcut and which was still further transformed by Tintoretto in the replacement painted after the fire, Titian adhered more closely than usual to the traditional type.

168, 169

303

*The fate of
Titian's works*

This survey of Titian's production for the State during the most fruitful years of his life gives rise to a feeling of surprise. Some writers, in order to justify the increasing avalanche of attributions to Titian, stress the quantitative disproportion between the authenticated works and the master's potentiality of production during so many years. Our survey of the official part of his artistic activity proves, as does a survey of his work for the court in Madrid, the weakness of such an argument. Of these well-authenticated works in well guarded locations, the greater part has perished. What destruction must the centuries have wrought upon works of less importance, such as portraits, which were of a more personal nature and were kept in private houses ! 'What rich man would not have liked to have his portrait painted by Titian ?' exclaims Sansovino in 1581 in his description of the wonders of Venice. And we might add, what grandson or great-grandson would not have lost interest in a portrait, to him anonymous, of an ancestor whom he no longer remembered ?

More favourable conditions for the safe preservation of works were offered by the smaller courts, where a keener personal interest in the artist combined with the conservatism typical of such princely establishments to ensure their preservation. The works executed for such courts therefore form a fairly numerous group, but they are no longer in their original locations. The works executed for Mantua are now for the most part in the Louvre, while those originally in Urbino have passed to the Florentine collections. What Titian painted for Alfonso d'Este, the first of his princely patrons, has been completely

*Works for
Ferrara*

LANDSCAPE WITH FLOCKS.

Detail from the 'Madonna and Child with Saint Catherine and Saint John.'   About 1530.   London, National Gallery.

scattered. We have already discussed the choicest fruits of this association—the three Bacchanals for the alabaster room and the 'Tribute Money'. From 1525 to 1528 there appears to have been a pause in Titian's activity for the Duke, but the association was then resumed and lasted until Alfonso's death in 1534. During these years the Duke received an unusual confirmation of the quality of Titian's works. First Francesco Covos, secretary and favourite of Charles V, and then the Emperor himself fell in love with them. By sacrificing part of his picture-gallery Alfonso was able to purchase the goodwill of the new rulers of Italy. It was at this time that his portrait by Titian, painted about 1523, went to Spain, where it disappeared. The version in the Metropolitan Museum, New 75 York, is probably a replica, and the substitute, which Titian painted after the loss of the original and shortly before Alfonso's death, seems to have survived only in copies. The other portraits which he painted for this court have had no better fortune. A copy of his portrait of the hereditary prince Ercole d'Este recently came to light; of the portrait of Lucrezia Borgia nothing is known; of that of Laura Dianti, the mistress and perhaps the secret morganatic wife of the widower Duke, there are two versions, one in Modena and the other in 309 the collection of Sir Herbert Cook, both of which are perhaps only copies of a lost original.

Through the court at Ferrara Titian came into contact with Mantua, where Works for Mantua Alfonso d'Este's sister, Isabella Gonzaga, had her court. When Titian came to Mantua, the palmy days of this court were over. He painted two portraits of Isabella—one of them, now in Vienna, from an existing portrait by Francia, 95, 310 while the other, perhaps not painted from life either, exists in the form of a replica in Paris. Isabella seems to have taken no particular interest in the artist, his real sponsor in Mantua being her son Federigo. In his portrait by Titian in Madrid he appears as an elegant dandy, with veiled glance, stroking a lapdog, 76 the representative of a different generation in comparison with his old warhorse of an uncle, who rests his hand tenderly on the barrel of a cannon. When Italy became the political battlefield between Spain and France, the power of these petty princes was reduced to a mere semblance, but the importance of art patronage, which added lustre to this semblance, became all the greater. The painter who was best equipped to satisfy Federigo's demands was Giulio Romano, who had settled in Mantua after the sack of Rome; two qualities, which qualified Giulio to be a court painter during the late years of the High Renaissance—an unfailing power of invention and decorative facility—were lacking in Titian. This explains why the latter made only one contribution to the embellishment of the Mantuan palaces, so overrated by his contemporaries—the twelve figures of Roman 304—307 emperors which were carried off by the imperial troops during the sack of Mantua in 1630 and now survive only in copies and engravings. In these portraits, highly esteemed by his humanistic contemporaries, Titian strove to enhance the lifelikeness of these historical personages, for he was convinced that he could paint portraits of people he had never seen in a more vital, and consequently more lifelike way than the average artist. We shall find an avowal of Titian's to this effect when we come to discuss his activity as a portrait-painter.

Hourticq has endeavoured to trace among the treasure of the Louvre the other works which Titian executed for the court of Mantua and to date them

84, 89
83, 157

with the aid of documents—the 'Virgin with the Rabbit', the 'St. Jerome', the 'Christ at Emmaus' and the 'Entombment'. In view of the reminiscences of Giorgione in the figures and the chiaroscuro of the last-mentioned painting, it is possible that it was designed at an earlier date—about 1516—and completed for the court of Mantua later.

Works for
Urbino

It was thanks to his stay in Mantua that Titian came into contact with the third of his princely patrons, Federigo's brother-in-law Francesco Maria della Rovere, Duke of Urbino, whose predilection for Titian was inherited by his son and successor, Guidobaldo II. The ducal palace was full of pictures by

107
94, 130

Titian when Vasari visited it. He mentions the 'Venus of Urbino', a Magdalen and portraits of Charles V, Francis I, Guidobaldo II, Popes Sixtus IV, Julius II and Paul III, the Cardinal of Lorraine, the Sultan Mahomet and Hannibal. Gronau's thorough investigation enables us to add to these a 'Nativity', a 'Resurrection', a 'Lady in Blue'—perhaps the famous 'Bella' now in the

92
101—103

Palazzo Pitti—and last but not least, the portraits of Francesco Maria and his wife Eleonora, the culminating point of Titian's activity for this court.

These 1530's mark a caesura in Titian's life. During the preceding fifteen years he had won for himself his place in the artistic and social world. He had established his household, for he was married in 1525 and in 1531 moved to the house he had purchased in the district known as the Birri Grande, where he lived until the end of his days. In 1527 began his close association with Jacopo Sansovino and Pietro Aretino, which lasted until the deaths of these two friends. This association made him a power in Venetian art politics and his meeting with the Emperor in 1532 brought him to the threshold of his international fame.

Change of
style

Titian had reason to look back with satisfaction on his years of struggle, but he must also have felt the need for relaxation after all this effort. As he grew older, he felt a desire for refinement of form. Looking back on the works of his period of storm and stress, he must have seen in them not only power and grandeur, but also a certain coarseness and over-simplification. The change in Titian's style about 1530 is a typical reflection of the stage of life he had reached. His virtues and defects before 1530 are those of youth; the change is the crisis of manhood. The fervent devotion which had felt earth and heaven as a harmonious unity gives way to cooler reflection, a greater absorption in the concrete, a more manly approach, for which the names of scepticism or refinement are equally appropriate.

This refinement, which first becomes perceptible in his colouring, may be interpreted either as lassitude and pettiness after the tension and grandeur of the preceding works, or else as a finer comprehension of what he had achieved by great bounds. It determines the character of a phase in the master's development, the boundaries of which are sharply defined in either direction. It is epilogue and prologue, relaxation and a gathering of strength, a connecting link between two periods the aims of which were different. Like every period in the life of a man, it is the crest and trough of a wave in the eternal movement of the waters.

From the standpoint of the heroic period which preceded them, the 1530's represent an attenuation and a softening, a quieter and more homely tendency. It is obviously no coincidence that at this time the monumental altar-pieces, previously his chief preoccupation, become less numerous in Titian's work, and the few pictures of this category which he did paint in the ten years after 1530, vary considerably from their predecessors in quality. This contrast becomes particularly clear if we compare the 'Assumption' in the cathedral of Verona *82* with the 'Assunta' in the Frari. Instead of the sonorous pathos of the latter *35* picture, we find the miracle taking place amidst a solemn silence; there is hardly any connecting link between the Apostles standing in amazement round the empty tomb and the 'gloria' above. The Virgin is aloof from the worldly scene; deep blue and mauve against whitish-grey clouds, she hovers above those she has left behind, who follow her only with longing looks. This altar-piece was painted at the beginning of the 1530's, about the same time as the 'St. John Elemosynarius' in the Venetian church of the same name. Figures and colouring are the same. Instead of the chromatic idealism which gave such timeless solemnity to the 'Assunta', we find a more intimate, individual solution.

In his need for quiet in which to reflect, Titian withdrew to the half- *The 'Presentation'* religious, half-secular atmosphere of the brotherhood which had offered a spiritual refuge to Venetian painters of the fifteenth century. His principal work of the 1530's is the 'Presentation of the Virgin in the Temple', which was painted between 1534 and 1538 and still adorns a wall of the Scuola della *108* Carità, its original location. This return to the old-fashioned surroundings of the Scuola finds an echo in the old-fashioned style of the composition. The action unrolls itself tranquilly in the pictorial plane; there are architectural motives on either side and a mountain landscape in the background, perhaps the Marmarole as seen from San Rocolo di Sant'Alipio; the heads of the onlookers, each one of whom is a portrait, are on the same level—for all this there are many precedents in older Venetian painting. But the old motives are filled with a new expression and the general effect is far from being old-fashioned. The decisive importance of this picture is due to the systematic way in which the perspectival construction is developed into a motive of expression and to the fact that here for the first time we find a colour-scheme based, not on the individual component parts of the picture, but on the pictorial plane as a whole. One continuous movement pervades the whole picture with its many figures, and similarly, an abundance of broken and graded colours without dominants is woven into the painting. The colour-scheme is not a product of the various objects depicted; it is an independent, self-contained factor.

The pleasing atmosphere and the marked interest in an abundance of details *Other religious paintings* which we find in the 'Presentation', are also visible in other religious paintings created at this time. The gem of this category is considered to be the 'Virgin with the Rabbit' in the Louvre, generally held to be the 'Virgin with *84*

St. Catherine' mentioned in 1530 in letters from Mantua. At first glance it looks like a small-scale repetition of a painting designed by Titian, but this is a characteristic feature of Titian's style about 1530. The pleasure which the artist takes in details is striking. The rabbit in the Virgin's hand, the fruit-basket near it, the flowers in front and the farmhouses in the background are all pictures within a picture. The colours have lost all relationship to the objects to which they belong and strive to achieve a harmony of their own. Although this idyllic scene in format, composition and spiritual content is a little Titian, its colour-scheme makes it worthy to rank among his great masterpieces.

86

Nearest in quality and style to this picture is the 'Virgin with the Child, St. Catherine and St. John' in the National Gallery, London, which might equally well be the painting referred to in the above-mentioned letter of 1530. Though it cannot compare with the Paris picture in its colouring, it surpasses it in the statuesque compactness of the central group and in the grandeur of the landscape. In the preceding period Titian had been striving to penetrate the beauties of nature, and now he has mastered them.

Treatment of nature

This new conception is characteristic of his work during the 1530's. Whereas in the earlier great pictures in which landscapes figure—the 'St. Peter Martyr' and the mythological pieces for Ferrara—the landscape was strictly subordinated to the human figure, we now find it being given equal importance. Previously Titian had experienced nature as an astounding phenomenon, but now he enjoys it to the full; so strongly does he now feel its mood that the human element is in danger of becoming a mere accessory. The 'St. Jerome', seen in the midst of a vast landscape, in the Louvre, generally identified as the picture of this subject the receipt of which Federigo Gonzaga acknowledged to Titian with words of delight on 5 March 1531, is one of the pictures in which nature is treated with such respect that the solitary penitent seems to be lost in the midst of it. Of another great composition of Titian's, the 'Adoration of the Shepherds', painted in 1532 for the Duke of Urbino, at about the same time as the 'St. Jerome', two versions exist—in Palazzo Pitti and at Christ Church College, Oxford—both of which are perhaps only school copies of a larger composition which found many imitators both inside and outside Titian's entourage. Many decades later, Titian caused a fresco after this picture to be painted by his pupils at Pieve di Cadore.

89

323

The 'Pardo Venus' 116

A similar case of a composition to which Titian returned later in life is the 'Pardo Venus' in the Louvre. About 1567 it came into the hands of King Philip of Spain and in his list of the '*fantasie*' which he dispatched, Titian describes it as 'the nude woman with the landscape and satyr', just as if the old painter had forgotten what specific mythological episode he had depicted. It has long been recognized, but not sufficiently stressed, that the design of this picture cannot date from the 1560's. Important elements in the composition point to the 1540's, and among them there are even some which are reminiscent of Titian's Giorgionesque period. The Antiope, or whoever the fair sleeper may be, is a relative of the Dresden Venus. The satyr at her feet has the sentimental amorousness of the faun in Lille, which we have restored to Titian, and the

40

seated satyr crowned with a garland on the other side is directly derived from *7*
the drawing formerly in the Oppenheimer Collection, which belongs to the same
early period. The mood appears to be related to that of the 1530's. The design
of the 'Pardo Venus' must therefore date in the main from these years. The
compactness of the group of figures on the left reminds us of the 'Virgin with   *86*
St. Catherine' in London, while the stress on horizontal lines on the other side
is found again in the 'Venus of Urbino'. Other characteristic features are the   *107*
relationship of figures to landscape and the respect for detail, which makes it
possible to divide the painting up into a number of charming scenes. In Titian's
late period this luscious green meadow would have been an anachronism, but
it is perfectly in keeping with the middle distance and the backgrounds of the
Madonnas in Paris and London.

The Christian counterpart to the 'Pardo Venus' is the 'Rest on the Flight *The 'Rest on*
into Egypt', which is severely criticized by most modern writers, although in the *the Flight'*
old days it was considered one of Titian's principal works. The original is   *90*
generally supposed to have been lost in transit while on its way to Spain, but
the version in the Prado, which can be proved to have been in the possession of
the Spanish royal family since 1644, is of such high quality that it may very
well be this allegedly lost original. Unfortunately, as with the 'Pardo Venus',
subsequent overpainting, or perhaps the completion of the picture many years
later, has left a thick veil over the original painting.

The mythological pieces painted about this time likewise express Titian's
changed attitude towards the world. Just as he renders his religious subjects
more human, so does he bring down the mythological themes from their solemn
pedestals. The distance between the 'Venus of Urbino' and Giorgione's   *107*
Dresden Venus is the clearest proof of this transformation, because the coherence
of motive and the derivation of the later picture from the earlier are so obvious.
In the correspondence between Titian and the court of Urbino, the picture is
always referred to as the '*donna ignuda*', the nude woman. That does not imply
that it is a study from the nude and nothing more; the grandeur of the recumbent
pose is still full of memories of the antique. But this addition does not suffice
to re-evoke the mood of the Dresden Venus; the indoor setting, the genre-like
scene in the background, with maidservants lifting toilet articles out of a chest,
help to heighten the intimacy of the scene and to deprive the goddess of some
of her divinity. She is awake and returns the spectator's gaze with very
conscious eyes. Individualization has made undeniable progress and it is no
coincidence that some have tried to maintain that the 'Venus of Urbino' is an
individual portrait! The same difference exists between the 'Flora' and the   *19*
'Bella'. The former, despite her glowing vitality, remains timeless and   *92*
impersonal; when we look at the 'Bella', we are tempted to ask what is
her name.

It is obvious that the wishes of Titian's patrons, who were becoming more *Wishes of*
and more important, must have contributed to this change of conception. We   *Titian's*
have ample evidence of their erotic interest in nudes. It is as if the worldly   *patrons*
aspect of the Renaissance spirit, which was being gradually repressed by the

rising current of religious feeling, were seeking a last refuge here. The moral laxity in this field was the farewell gesture of an intellectual movement which had begun on a much higher plane. Of course, Titian would not have acceded to such wishes on the part of his patrons, if this development had not been in accord with his own artistic needs; this derogation of divinity was not only a cultural, but also an artistic process, the basic outlines of which are visible in pictures of religious subjects as well. As in the latter pictures, we find in the 'Urbino Venus' a stressing of the lines leading into depth and an attention to detail so uniform that here too, as in the 'Presentation in the Temple', it would be possible to cut out a number of charming details.

The Louvre
'Allegory'

91

Similar merits of colouring distinguish the pleasing picture in the Louvre, which, in default of a better interpretation, we must continue to call by its makeshift name, the 'Allegory of Alfonso d'Avalos'. It represents an allegory of marriage, and the fact that it seems to demand a more personal explanation is an additional reason for assigning it to the same period as the 'Venus of Urbino'. The 'Allegory of Alfonso d'Avalos' has the same compact grouping of the figures and the same glowing colouring as we find in the 'Venus' and other paintings of the same period.

Portraits

As Titian during this period was showing more and more interest in the things of this earth, it is only natural to expect that portraiture would attain more importance in his work. And in fact, he did during these years become a specialist in this field, which formerly had attracted him only from time to time. In a letter dated 9 November 1537, Aretino mentions that the world at that time looked upon Titian primarily as a great portrait-painter.

62

What distinguishes the portraits created after about 1530 from Titian's earlier portraits, such as the 'Man with the Glove', is the attempt to grasp the whole appearance of the sitter as an organic whole. This is not yet the psychological penetration and creative evocation which he achieved ten or twenty years later, but rather a form of artistic interpretation which is in accord with the general refinement of his colouring during these years. Titian's portraits do not start from his impression of the external appearance of his sitter. That he was capable of grasping it with the utmost penetration is shown by the undermost layer of his painting, as revealed by X-ray photographs. The so-called

163—165

Varchi portrait in Vienna is a good example of this. He seizes the essential features of his sitter with surprising vehemence, but after this first reaction, Titian develops the model's appearance by artistic means in so logical a manner, that he appears to live not with his own, but with Titian's vitality.

This growth of the portrait independently of the sitter is partly due to the special requirements of Titian's clientele. He began his career as a portrait-painter in the service of high-ranking personages, some of them living outside Venice, who could not grant him many sittings, but who attached more importance to the formal character of a portrait than to psychological penetration. In such a milieu an art of portraiture was bound to mature which aimed at reproducing the typical.

*Portraits of
Charles V*
94

The classic example of Titian's portraiture at this time is the full-length
of the Emperor Charles V with his dog in the Prado, which Titian copied in
1533 feature by feature, dog and all, from a portrait of the emperor by the
Styrian court painter, Jakob Seisenegger. It is highly instructive to note how
the copy surpasses the original in every detail, how a living entity is created
out of a pedantic inventory of all the characteristics of the Emperor's coun-
tenance and costume, how even a chromatic harmony results, in which the pale
complexion of the Emperor, his greyish-white hose and the grey dog are brought
into accord. That was what his sitters expected; and it was this paraphrase
of Seisenegger's portrait which induced the Emperor to appoint Titian his por-
traitist-in-ordinary on 3 May 1533. From then on, to him alone would be
reserved the privilege of painting the monarch in that enhanced aloofness which
is the ideal of formal portraiture.

The difference between this and the ordinary portrayal of a human being
was recognized in the sixteenth century. When a worthy burgher like Hans
Fugger wanted portraits made of the members of his family, he ordered his
agent in Italy to find 'a good counterfeiter, no matter whether he be otherwise
skilled in painting, provided only that he be a master of counterfeiting', but
in 1543 the Emperor sent Titian a portrait '*molto simile al vero, benchè di
trivial pennello*' —'very lifelike, though by a mediocre hand'—of the dead
Empress, whom Titian had never seen, in order that he might make a proper
portrait of her. So well did Titian understand what kind of portrait of his
wife the Emperor wanted, that it was his imaginary portrait which Charles V   *185*
took with him when he withdrew to the solitude of the monastery of Yuste.

Similar achievements were Titian's portraits of the Sultan (1538), which
in the opinion of those who had been in Constantinople was a most striking
likeness, and of King Francis I of France, which may have been done from a   *123*
medal. It was in this portrait, and not in the products of the French court
painters, that the features of the King acquired their definitive and convincing
stamp, for it brings out all his merits and weaknesses, his chivalrous gaiety, his
sex-appeal and his exuberant vitality. Every inch a king and in every fibre of
his body the opposite and enemy of Charles V! Titian painted a whole series
of such portraits of people he had never seen. Whether he was painting Hannibal or the Roman Emperors, dead Doges—Niccolò Marcello in the Vatican—   *131*
or Popes—Sixtus IV and Julius II in Florence—Titian always aimed at achieving   *130*
the same directness as when he was portraying from the living model. What
the intermediate model offered him, even if, as in the case of the portrait of
Julius II, it were by Raphael's hand, was for Titian merely raw material. Even
the living sitter was little more than that. On the occasion of one rather delicate
commission in 1532, Titian gave a particularly striking example of this point
of view. Francesco Covos, the Emperor's minister, had fallen in love with Cornelia, one of the Countess Pepoli's ladies-in-waiting, and the Margrave of
Mantua wanted to present this important personage with a portrait of the lady
by Titian's hand. When Titian arrived in Bologna to execute the commission,
the girl was not there. But he at once offered to paint her portrait on the basis

of descriptions of Cornelia and a painting by another artist. He was quite confident that his version would not need any corrections when compared with the living model.

This assertion epitomizes Titian's programme during the first phase of his activity as a portrait-painter. His task was, not to represent the individual as such, but to extract the typical elements from the individual. The new rulers of a radically changed epoch were his models; he accepted them as representatives of a species, but he grasped every one of them with such penetration that the portrait becomes the definitive image of the person portrayed.

Titian's sitters

What a gallery of international society in the Cinquecento is spread before our eyes in these pictures! The Emperor and Empress, the King of France, the Duke and Duchess of Urbino, the princely military leaders of the great powers, *93, 99, 122,* Alfonso d'Este and Alfonso d'Avalos, the smooth Duke Federigo of Mantua *123, 124,* and the light-hearted Ippolito de' Medici, Giacomo Doria, Antonio Porcia and *128* Admiral Giovanni Moro! Even the anonymous sitters are filled with the unassuming noblesse which the period prescribed—the 'Man with the Falcon', the young man with his hand in his belt and the old warrior in Milan, who is more likely to be Titian's father than, as was formerly supposed, the Condottiere Gian Giovanni de' Medici.

A new phase

About 1540 we come to the end of that pause in Titian's creative develop-ment during which his powerful nature was constrained to devote itself to the careful penetration of more delicate problems and during which he became absolute master of all the means at his disposal. He now returns to problems and conceptions which remind us of his heroic period between 1515 and 1530. In the case of a great artist like Titian, in whom productivity and receptivity were equally above the average, it is difficult to determine to what extent he was thereby obeying the inner laws of his life and to what extent outside influences contributed to this evolution.

During the preceding decades Central Italian art had made several incursions into the realm of Venetian art. Giulio Romano deployed in Mantua a much-admired activity, which was also esteemed by Titian, and other artists had also become known in Venice. Vasari and the two Salviatis, Francesco and Giuseppe, produced works in the city which conflicted with the style current there. With one of these works Titian had a direct connection. Vasari relates that when he *Ceiling pain-* was in Venice in 1541, he was commissioned to execute ceiling paintings in the *tings in Venice* church of the Santo Spirito and that, as his departure made it impossible for him to carry out this work, it was taken over by Titian. The three ceiling paintings now in the sacristy of Santa Maria della Salute differ so noticeably from Titian's previous productions that we are bound to ask ourselves whether Titian did not derive much of them from Vasari's designs—for one of the compositions, 'Abraham's Sacrifice', we possess a remarkably similar preliminary sketch—or whether he was not deliberately trying to compete with Florentine-Roman art in the very field in which its pre-eminence was most unconditionally acknow-ledged—in the correctness of draughtsmanship, in the plastic value of the human form and in the boldness of the foreshortening.

Three deeds of violence are represented—the 'Slaying of Abel', 'Abraham's *149—151*
Sacrifice' and 'David's Victory over Goliath'—all three pronouncedly fore-
shortened, which was necessary in the case of ceiling paintings seen from below,
a type of painting which for Venice was a novelty. The powerful figures seem
to burst forth from the pictorial plane with the might of their bodies and the
expressive violence of their movements. A weird gloom, in which harsh light
effectively sets off the forms, serves to heighten the tragic mood. Three other
pictures of similar subjects, but unfortunately preserved in an unsatisfactory
state, form stylistic appendices to the paintings in Santa Maria della Salute. One
of them is the 'Vision of St. John the Evangelist' painted by Titian at an
unknown date for the Scuola of that name; for a long time it could not be
traced and was known only through an engraving, but recently it has come to *318*
light, though, so far as one can judge from a photograph, it has been heavily
overpainted. The others are the 'Sisyphus' and the 'Tityus' in the Prado, *201, 202*
which Queen Maria sent in 1549 to her castle of Binche in Flanders; they are
in such a condition of deterioration that it is impossible to say with certainty
whether they are originals or not, and many critics hold that they are copies
by the Spanish painter, Alonso Sanchez. The relationship of these compositions
to the Salute pictures is evident. Here, too, the mighty, agitated figures fill the
whole pictorial plane and are fused with the gloomy, rocky surroundings by
means of a web of brownish and greenish-grey tones. The warning of torments
in Hell and eternal punishment is in accord with the reawakening of religious
feeling at the time. The tragic mood of Michelangelo's 'Last Judgement' casts *Titian's
impressions
in Rome*
a shadow over the art of Titian. The paintings in Santa Maria della Salute
were executed before Titian's journey to Rome and those of the condemned
sinners after it. It was therefore not the direct impression received from the
Sistine Chapel which influenced Titian to transform his style, nor was it, in
general, his visit to Rome or his newly-acquired knowledge of the works of
antique and modern art. On the contrary, Titian had reached a point in his
evolution at which the influences of Central Italian art, accessible in various
ways, could be more effective, thus rendering the journey to Rome, which he had
failed to make in earlier years, more fruitful. To see with mature eyes the
celebrated works of antique art and those of his great contemporaries, must have
seemed all the more desirable to Titian at this time of changing conceptions. And
in fact, he looked eagerly around him in this world of strange art during his
stay in Rome, which lasted from autumn 1545 to the spring of 1546. Humanists
and academicians welcomed his visit as a kind of artistic repetition of Henry IV's
visit to Canossa and Vasari kindly let it be known that Titian might have become
a really great artist if, like Sebastiano del Piombo, he had come under Michelangelo's influence at the proper time; but that as it was, since he had not
sufficient mastery of draughtsmanship and had not made a thorough study of
the antique, he could only hope to achieve a lesser degree of beauty. Titian's
reaction to such observations was probably rather ironical. The works which
he was shown in Rome gave him no reason to regret the path which he had
followed as an artist, far from this dangerous milieu. His instinct must have

told him that he understood far more about the spirit and form of antique art than the imitators of dead models.

The 'Danaë'
173

His own interpretation of its ideals is the 'Danaë' now in Naples, which he painted, according to Vasari, in the Belvedere in the Vatican, that is to say in the stronghold of the worshippers of the antique. It is a Venetian plea against Rome, and all the more effective because it takes its stand on the ground of the opposing party. In both figures we see the influence of sculptural models—in the Cupid, a well-known Praxitelean type; in the recumbent Danaë, perhaps one of Michelangelo's river-gods—but these reminiscences are heightened by Titian's increased interest in values of this kind. The human form dominates the picture completely. The magnificent female body, closely confined within the frame, and the passionate eyes combine with the Cupid turning away in frightened astonishment to express the significance of the divine event. All the accessories—column, cushion, curtain—are merely indicated, in order to avoid any impression of sensual intimacy and to leave the composition undisturbed. Unlike everything else which Titian created before and after, it tempts us to evoke the impression of a work of sculpture.

174

The extent to which the 'Danaë' must be considered as Titian's homage to Rome becomes clear if we compare it with another mythological painting which he must have executed about the same time, but away from the Roman sphere of influence. The 'Venus and Cupid' in the Uffizi forms part of that series of Titian's paintings of Venus which later became part of the stock-in-trade of his atelier. The whole picture is attuned to a gamut of reds and browns, thus forming a sharp contrast to the flowery motley of the 'Venus of Urbino', and this, like the grandiose, serious composition, is in accord with the spirit of the 1540's.

I have discussed elsewhere the autumnal melancholy of this painting and the prevalence of the same mood in Titian's general attitude during this decade. The enthusiasm of youth and the joie-de-vivre of manhood were followed by a deeper insight into the grandeur and might, and also the grimness and inexorableness of human life. This induces a mood of revolt which is not yet tempered by resignation, a scepticism which is still far from the charitableness of old age. This attitude towards the world gave Central Italian art its power over Titian. Heightened forms are now better suited to his intentions ; even colour, his own element, loses something of its charm. The paintings he produced at this time, stirring though some of them may be, have not the magic colouring which distinguishes those of other periods in his life.

136

139

A transformation of this kind does not occur all at once. The 'Address of the Marchese del Vasto to his Troops' in the Prado, ordered in 1540 and delivered in 1541, illustrates the transition from the style of the 1530's. There is a jingle of arms and a confusion of military signals in this picture, which contains numerous echoes of the antique, both thematic and formal. Delight in colour is still predominant, but in the principal picture of this group, the 'Ecce Homo' in Vienna, this is abandoned altogether. The latter picture was painted in 1543 for the Flemish merchant Giovanni d'Anna (van Haanen), a personal

friend of Titian, and its subject and composition make it suitable for comparison
with the chief work of the preceding decade, the 'Presentation of the Virgin in *108*
the Temple'. In both, the action unrolls parallel to the pictorial plane; in both,
perspective expedients have been turned into a medium of expression. But the
movement pervading the composition is, in the 'Ecce Homo', no longer a gentle
flow, but a violent heaving to and fro. In comparison the 'Presentation' seems
primitive, almost Quattrocentistic, whereas the 'Ecce Homo' might be described
as a harbinger of the Baroque period, an impression which is augmented by the
increased individualization of the heads, in which many have claimed to discover
the likenesses of famous personages.

Despite all this, the combination of unusually glittering splendour and *New religious works*
almost painfully stressed cruelty reveals an uncertainty which is at variance
with the proud self-assurance normally found in Titian's works. This may be
due to the religious crisis at that time, which shattered the ground beneath the
feet of the creator of religious paintings. Nothing has been handed down to us
which shows that Titian was as irresistibly caught up in this movement as that
old pagan Michelangelo, but somehow he must have been affected by the transformation which the spirit of the times demanded. He created new religious *206*
types to comply with the wishes of his patrons. His 'Ecce Homo' and his *191, 207*
'Mater Dolorosa', which exist in several versions, were so dear to Charles V that
he took them with him to Yuste.

At the same time he produced many indifferent works. Pictures like the
'Last Supper' and the 'Resurrection' in Urbino (1542—1544), the altar-pieces *154—156*
in Castel Roganzuolo (1544) and in the cathedral at Serravalle (1547), although
they are better authenticated than some of his principal works, are nevertheless
only occasional pieces of secondary value, for which his workshop is in the
main responsible. Other pictures from the same period show us Titian at his
best. The 'Crowning with Thorns' in the Louvre, originally in Santa Maria delle *143*
Grazie at Milan, must belong to the middle 1540's on account of the vigour of
the action, the plasticity of the bodies and the passion revealed in the gestures.
The colouring is tuned to a nocturnal gloom, to which the carmine of the
Saviour's draperies and the ultramarine of the raised cloak of one of the
executioners add a solemn and soothing note.

Closely related to the last-mentioned picture is the 'John the Baptist' in
the Accademia at Venice. The essential elements are the same—stress on plastic
exactitude in the figures together with simplification of the colouring, pathos of
the gestures, passionate excitement combined with rigid constraint. Noteworthy
is the contrast between the grandiose freedom of the landscape and the primitive
character of the figures, for which Titian may have gone back to an older design,
as he did with increasing frequency during his later years.

To this Indian summer belong also two pictures frequently assigned to much *'St. Jerome' 'St. Lawrence'*
later dates, the execution of which might actually be as late as the following
decade, though the conception must be older. These are the 'St. Jerome' in Milan *211*
and the 'Martyrdom of St. Lawrence' in the Gesuiti at Venice. It is instructive *209*
to compare this 'Jerome' with the earlier version of the theme in the Louvre. *89*

In the latter, the important element is the subordination of the figure to the landscape, but in the Brera painting it is the figure which dominates the scene.

201, 202

This active and muscular saint is akin to the 'Sisyphus' and the 'Tityus' in the Prado and, like them, has antecedents going back to classical antiquity. Recent documentary research has proved that the 'Martyrdom of St. Lawrence' also dates from the end of the 1540's, despite the fact that it did not appear in its present location until 1559. There is hardly any other picture by Titian so full of reminiscences of his journey to Rome as this. Not only are the general conception and many details taken from Michelangelo's 'Sacrifice of Noah' on the ceiling of the Sistine Chapel, while there are also other echoes of this ceiling and of Raphael, but the scene of the martyrdom ist transferred to an architectural setting of truly Roman grandeur. Efforts to pay homage to Michelangelo and to vie with Central Italian art are clearly visible in this picture; the fact that there

208

exists in the Uffizi a magnificent study for the turbaned executioner on the right, may be evidence of the particular care which Titian devoted to the draughts-manship of this work. The attempt to rival Central Italian art may be responsible for the presence of an unusual atmosphere in this picture—as it was in the case of the 'Ecce Homo' and the 'Crown of Thorns'—something elaborate and forced, which is eloquent of influences not fully absorbed. So long as it was assigned to a later date, critics claimed to see in it the influence of the youthful Tintoretto, but in actual fact the reverse is the case. The common feature is a manneristic element which Titian saw in being in Rome. The rationalization of the lighting effects—in the varying effect of the torches, the fire beneath the grill

258

and the 'gloria' in the sky—can likewise be ascribed to the same external influence. In the much later version of this picture in the Escorial, Titian introduced many corrections, both in the treatment of light and in the composition as a whole. He purged the picture of foreign elements and returned to his own artistic essence.

Titian had not yet reached that stage of wisdom which is called resignation. Direct contact with antique art and Michelangelo on the one hand, and his role as the Emperor's confidential adviser on art matters on the other, combined in these years to strengthen Titian's self-assurance, to enlarge his scope and to kindle his energy. Again, as at the end of the second decade, painting alone was not a sufficient outlet for his exuberant vitality. He began to take an interest in mosaics, which had a natural attraction for the leading painter of Venice, and in woodcuts, for which, as he had done before, he chose a gigantic format in keeping with his whole manner of thinking. In 1549 Domenico delle

321

Grecche cut the 'Destruction of Pharaoh's Host' on twelve blocks after drawings by Titian. For the numerous figures all sorts of odds-and-ends from earlier works were used, but their fusion into one composition by means of the agitated seascape is a creative achievement in keeping with the spirit of the 1540's.

Titian and Charles V   Even more than in other fields, these years saw Titian reach the zenith of his art as a portrait-painter. Many shoots which had been budding in the 1530's now began to bear fruit. This applies also to his position as portrait-painter to Charles V, the new Apelles of the new Alexander. His appointment as court painter in 1533 had at the time been a promise rather than a fulfilment. During the next fifteen years the Emperor was so occupied with campaigns and matters of State that he did not claim from Titian what he expected of him and what was indeed the new social task of court painting. Among the services which the absolute ruler demands from his entire entourage, art also has its place ; it has to serve his glory, and so far as portraits are concerned, to enhance the glory of his personal appearance. The greatness of the painter signifies increased importance for the man he portrays. A man who employs an Apelles, is bound to feel like an Alexander. The Renaissance doctrine that it is the function of art to dispense fame, became in the sixteenth century a recognized part of the general conception of culture.

Titian had gradually acquired the style which this task demanded, and the *The Farnese portraits* first proofs of his new style in portraiture are the Farnese portraits. What his meeting with the Emperor had initiated, was notably furthered by his meeting with the Pope. The first member of the family whom Titian portrayed was the eleven-year-old Ranuccio Farnese, grandson of Paul III, who in 1542, *144* already a prior, came to Venice in order to study at the University of Padua. Several versions of this portrait exist, of which that in Richmond has the best claim to be considered the original. Similar difficulties as regards distinguishing versions by Titian's own hand from replicas are encountered in connection with the other Farnese portraits, and above all the character of the most famous of them all, the portrait of Paul III without his biretta, is not easy to determine, *Pope Paul III* as the investigations of E. Tietze-Conrat have shown. This interpretation of the *160* distinguished sitter not only differs from Titian's other portraits of him, but is also so unlike the portraits of the old Pope by other contemporary artists, that one is tempted to conclude that in 1543 Titian did not paint this portrait from nature, but on the basis of some other portrait, the author of which is most likely to have been Sebastiano del Piombo. The latter, with his heroic style, might well have painted the Pope without revealing that frailty which Paul III already manifested at the time of his election and which Titian made no attempt to conceal in the portrait of him with his two nephews. If this theory is correct— and it is far more acceptable than the other theory, that the portrait is not by Titian at all, but by Sebastiano—it means that Titian repeated his achievement with the portrait of Charles V after Seisenegger, and in fact surpassed it. For here he has, one might say, undisturbed by the presence of the individual sitter, created a formal portrait of the highest quality. It shows a man, great and small at the same time, dignified by his human superiority and his high office and yet helpless by reason of advancing years and the stress of stormy times.

The whole moving comedy of human and political activity is revealed in the family group in Naples. The fact that it was not completed and that it was *170* Titian's habit to cover up natural truth in the course of the work, gives this picture even more the character of a *document humain*, of a sensational revelation. Gronau opined that the picture was left unfinished because the Farnese family did not wish to see dragged into the light of day the truth about themselves and the profound dissensions among them, and that competent judge, the historian Leopold von Ranke, confirms the intuitive grasp of the characters and of the whole situation. This abundance of psychological penetration is, however, but the overflow of the resources of a painter, for whom the composition was primarily a fascinating symphony in red.

Visit to Augsburg

The broadening of Titian's outlook on the world was completed by his stay at the imperial court of Augsburg in 1548—1549 and 1550—1551. Charles V's position had been strengthened by his victory at Mühlberg in 1547 over the Protestant League under the Elector Johann Friedrich of Saxony. He could now take a rest and indulge in his long frustrated delight in art. The invitation reached Titian towards the end of 1547 and at the beginning of the following year he went to Augsburg with several of his assistants. There he found assembled around the Emperor all the members of the Habsburg family, the military leaders and diplomats, all the leading figures in international politics. One might have said that Titian immortalized this European congress, were it not for the fact that most of the pictures he painted there have been lost or exist only in the form of copies or doubtful replicas. Nowhere did Titian

Portraits of Charles V

display his style of portraiture to better effect than in his two portraits of the Emperor, which penetrate to the core of this dual personality and epitomize a

187

whole period of history. The portrait of the Emperor in his arm-chair in the Ältere Pinakothek at Munich shows him plagued by gout and sunk in deep

183

melancholy, which was his prevalent mood, whereas the equestrian portrait in the Prado shows the great military commander to whom the extraordinary occasion of a fateful day has restored his strength and his youth. The first is one of the most intimate, the second one of the most formal portraits Titian ever painted.

We have said before that the Emperor's personality is, so to speak, split in these two portraits, and we might add that each of them nevertheless contains the whole of it. In the sick man in Munich we find the indomitable energy, in the victor in the Prado the sorrowful knowledge of things. On seeing the latter painting, an Italian critic was reminded of Dürer's engraving, 'The Knight, Death and the Devil', and though hardly a single detail supports this analogy, it nevertheless represents a correct description of the mood of fatalism and symbolism in the picture.

Other portraits in Augsburg

To a certain degree the other portraits painted during the Augsburg period have the same monumental conception as those of the Emperor. Titian saw even the Crown Prince Philip, who was later to become his master and patron,

199, 200

as a reflection of his father. Two studies from life, perhaps made in Augsburg, were used afterwards for full- and half-length portraits. The other Augsburg portraits, too—and those artistically related to them—form a chorus round the

190

towering figure of the Emperor—the younger Granvella, General Giovanni di

181, 194

Castaldo, the Elector Johann Friedrich of Saxony, the so-called Don Diego

188, 197

Mendoza in Palazzo Pitti, the 'Man with the Maltese Cross' in the Prado. Even the humbler sitters were raised to a higher social level by Titian's art. One of the most pompous of these character portraits is that of Titian's old

166, 167

friend, Pietro Aretino, in which the freshness and directness of conception are heightened even more by the improvised character of the execution. To a painter like Charles Ricketts, the intellectual lightness of psychological and material characterization in this portrait seemend so outstanding that he did not hesitate to call Titian the greatest portrait-painter of all time, superior to Rembrandt, Velazquez and Van Dyck.

We mentioned before, when speaking of the X-ray photograph of the *Other portraits* so-called Varchi portrait in Vienna, that the lively directness which makes the Aretino so sparkling, was Titian's first, not his last word as a portrayer of men. Other portraits, too, may have originated from a similar impressionistic early stage, but in the course of the painting were given that mask of reserve and impersonality which to Titian seemed to be the ideal likeness. In the same way, the charming portrait of Clarissa Strozzi as a child, in Berlin, for which Aretino *159* claimed the first place among all pictures ever painted or to be painted, is a prelude to Van Dyck's portraits of princely children. All of Titian's sitters in this middle period became equally distinguished in his hands—Pietro Bembo's secretary and administrator, Antonio Anselmi, the Venetian patrician Daniele Barbaro, *192, 162* and an unknown man (now in the possession of Frank Sabin) whom a slip of paper he is holding describes as a friend of Titian's. Still more characteristic *196* is the tension, mixed with a touch of over-tension, in the portrait of the jurist Ippolito Riminaldi. In the eyes of this sitter, formerly, for no reason whatsoever, *134* known as 'the young Englishman' or the 'Duke of Norfolk', Burckhardt claimed to see 'something which may be not very far removed from madness'. This interpretation implies that the enhancement of nature during these years at some point reached its limit. The historic pose, which Charles V and some of his supporters and enemies carry so easily and naturally, is an embarrassment to more homely natures. They act, while the others merely exist; they have to play a part, whereas the others have only to live it. And this note, too, belongs to the underlying tone of a century which was prone to exaggeration.

III

THE LAST twenty-five years of Titian's life, after his return from the imperial court to Venice, marked the climax and the anticlimax of his existence. His international reputation had now been consolidated and was further strengthened by his regular activity for the court of Spain. At home he was a great man, one of the sights of the city. But the shadows of old age and loneliness were beginning to darken his life. His family life was devoid of joy. It is true that his painter son, Orazio, now began to relieve him more and more of the burden of mass production, but the other son, Pomponio, whose ecclesiastical career Titian had endeavoured to further by intervening on his behalf with all his eminent patrons, was proving more and more to be a ne'er-do-well. Lavinia, his favourite daughter, whose features are familiar to us through many genre-like half-lengths, left home to marry in 1555. The old friends were gradually disappearing; Pietro Aretino died in 1557, and Jacopo Sansovino, for several decades the third member of the trio, followed him in 1570. As a human being, Titian began to feel alone, and even as an artist he must have felt isolated. His position as the leading artist of Venice was hardly disputed. In 1557 there appeared Lodovico Dolce's treatise, which was a panegyric of Titian and a polemic against Michelangelo. Tributes of this kind usually mark the end or a turning point and it is in fact about this time that we begin to hear something of artistic opposition. Michele Parrasio, who was very devoted to Titian, informed him while he was in Augsburg that certain people—obviously a reference to Tintoretto and perhaps also to Schiavone—were trying to profit by his absence in order to corrupt art. It may quite well be true that the master's absence helped the representatives of a younger generation to win the favour of the public. A certain coolness in official circles became noticeable about the same time. Doges began to forgo his services, his offer to the Brotherhood of San Rocco to paint a large picture for their Scuola came to nothing, and Titian, with one ceiling panel, was merely one of several contributors to the decoration of Sansovino's Library of St. Mark.

Some weary pictures produced by Titian after his return were mere random commissions, such as the portrait of the Papal Legate Lodovico Beccadelli in the Uffizi (1552), or the altar-piece of Christ appearing to his mother, in the parish church at Medolle, which Titian hoped would procure a benefice for Pomponio. Nor is the 'Pentecost', painted for the church of the Santo Spirito and now in Santa Maria della Salute, one of his best works. In 1541 Titian had painted a version of this picture which for reasons unknown to us did not satisfy his

DETAIL FROM THE PARDO VENUS. About 1535-40. Paris, Louvre.

clients. In the revised version, which must belong to the early 1550's, the discordant mixture of archaic and manneristic elements strikes the eye. Was it his return to humdrum existence from the exceptional splendour of Augsburg that oppressed the artist? For the Emperor he executed at the same time a large work of his customary high quality—the 'Gloria', in which he depicts in *The 'Gloria'* *230* monumental style the Emperor's withdrawal from earthly to heavenly matters. The painting was completed in 1554, just in time to follow the Emperor to his lonely retreat at Yuste, for which it may have been intended from the beginning.

The 'Gloria' reflects the lofty ambition of earlier masterpieces and preludes that of those to come. Dürer's altar-piece of the 'Adoration of the Trinity' provided the inspiration for the general arrangement of this vision floating far above the earth, and Michelangelo's 'Last Judgement' the mood transcending all earthly things. Later, in his 'Last Things', Rubens developed Titian's conception still further. A hieratic scale, which at the same time is a chain of tightly-packed human bodies, leads from the mortal patriarchs and prophets of the Old Testament to the figures of the Holy Trinity. The figures are graduated accordingly, from the herculean proportions of the lower rows, nearest to the spectator, to the highest sphere of all, in which all corporeality is dissolved. Members of the imperial family, taken from earlier portraits by Titian, are shown, praying humbly, amidst the heavenly host, and a modest place among them is even reserved for the 'humilis pictor'.

This vision offers not only a harmonious garland of human figures, but also a pure symphony of colour. The widely graded flesh tones are blended effortlessly with the blue, red, golden yellow and white of the draperies and the sky streaked with clouds. New colours appear—moss-green and brown— and their blissful strength and beauty are transformed into a feeling of solace, of trust and promise. Like the great altar-pieces of the 1520's, the 'Gloria' is filled with deep religious feeling. Once again Titian succeeded in evoking for his imperial master, for whom this was his last work, the mood which he required.

Titian was a tired man when he came back from Augsburg. As in 1530, after such a period of concentration a reaction was bound to set in, a mood of relaxation, refinement and repose. But what for a man of forty had been a mere pause in his creative development, for a man of sixty might well mark the beginning of the end. In the works created in Venice after his return the negative aspects of this transformation are visible; the positive aspects can be discerned in those works in which Titian turns, or returns, to other fields in order to achieve new fertility. Instead of portraits and religious themes, mythological subjects now become the most important in his work. The most noteworthy of these *poesie*, as Titian called them, were painted for King Philip II, *Works for* *Philip II* an amateur with a good understanding of art, who seems to have taken little interest in Titian's religious pictures and to have enjoyed him more as a painter of pagan mythologies, or even of outspokenly erotic nudes.

That the protector of the Church and the restorer of the Catholic faith throughout his wide domains should have had a predilection for such subjects is a symptom of the transformation which took place in every field of

European civilization about the middle of the century. The aims of the great movement, which had aspired to be a spiritual rebirth, were now disavowed and everything deprecated from the standpoint of the new religious feeling was aesthetically sublimated. This attitude on the part of his new patron was of great assistance to Titian's art at this stage. The sensual enjoyment of the world which determind his style in the 1530's, now finds its expression in a more passive and contemplative attitude which corresponds to Titian's advanced age. Things in themselves no longer attract him, but their reflected splendour does.

Erotic subjects His homage to beauty, which at this period of his life does not even recoil before the sweetish and delicious in form and colour, is imbued with the immaterial tenderness of senile eroticism. It may have been this veiled eroticism which rendered the enjoyment of these *poesie* permissible and even attractive to the pious king. The letter which Titian wrote in 1554 to introduce his new series leaves no room for doubt as to the deliberately erotic character of the pictures. With reference to the 'Venus and Adonis', he writes: '... Since the "Danaë", which I sent to Your Majesty, is seen from the front, I wanted in this second *poesia*, for the sake of change, to show the woman from the opposite side, that the room for which these pictures are destined may appear even more delectable. Soon I shall send the " Perseus and Andromeda ", which will offer yet another aspect than the two earlier pictures, and the same is true of the " Medea and Jason ".'

174 Though the general mood of the mythological pictures of the 1550's is new, the subjects themselves hark back to earlier paintings. The ' Venus with Cupid ' was, as we have already mentioned, the ancestress of a whole series of similar divinities. Titian offered one version to the Emperor in 1545 and took it with him to Augsburg in 1548. Whether this is identical with either of the two pictures of Venus in Madrid is questionable; even if that is so, it does not imply that it is by Titian's own hand, for this subject was naturally one of the most popular and a Venus by Titian is found in the inventory of every princely collection at the time of the Late Renaissance. Titian's workshop and imitators had a large share in this mass production.

220 Of the 'Danaë', too, numerous variants were produced to meet the wishes of patrons. A comparison of the Madrid version, mentioned as the earliest of the *poesie* in the letter of 1554 which we quoted above, and the Naples
173 version of 1545, shows the radical change of conception. The coarser atmosphere is not due merely to the replacement of the Cupid, who emphasized the mythological symbolism of the scene, by an old hag, who is trying to gather as much of the gold as possible in her apron. In addition to that, the majestic corporeality of the Naples 'Danaë' has become soft delicacy, her vigour has become unresisting surrender and her radiant glance sensual desire. The composition, which in the Naples picture was subordinate to the body, now absorbs it in the pictorial whole. We said that the Naples 'Danaë' could be conceived as a work of sculpture; that would be impossible with the Prado version, for in it everything is fused in a chromatic system, in which all the component parts are of equal value.

The third 'best-seller' among Titian's mythological pictures was his 'Venus and Adonis', of which a dozen versions still exist to-day. They may be divided into two classes, differing in format and in many details of composition, both classes having probably been produced in Titian's workshop down to the date of his death. The version in the National Gallery, London, would appear to be Titian's original of the older and larger type. To the later, smaller class, perhaps painted by Orazio Vecelli, belong the versions in the National Gallery, Washington, and the Metropolitan Museum, New York. The 'Perseus and Andromeda', now in the Wallace Collection, London, seems to have been less popular, and of the last picture mentioned by Titian in 1554, the 'Medea and Jason', nothing at all is known. Perhaps when he wrote the letter he was thinking of the composition which he later had engraved by Cornelis Cort and which is commonly known as 'Roger and Angelica'. This fantastic scene, in which the protagonists are a sorceress lying on the ground and a knight riding through the air on a griffin, might equally well be interpreted as the legend of Jason and Medea.

A second group of mythological compositions is mentioned in a letter of Titian's to King Philip, dated 19 June 1559, in which he says that he has already completed the 'Diana bathing' and the 'Diana and Callisto' and begun the 'Rape of Europa' and the 'Punishment of Actaeon'. The two Diana pictures, after many peregrinations, eventually passed to Lord Ellesmere's collection at Bridgewater House; they have always been regarded as pendants to each other and are of the same format, but are not counterparts as regards conception and are composed according to different principles. In the 'Diana and Callisto' two compact groups are dramatically contrasted and the emphasis is on the human figures, which, even considered singly, are more vigorous and more sculptural. The 'Punishment of Actaeon' is more loosely but more uniformly constructed; the figures are more slender and active, and more closely connected with the landscape. This picture is more manneristic than the other and is close to the two *poesie* of 1559 from the stylistic point of view, whereas the 'Diana and Callisto' is based on a conception which is twenty years older. It may be that Titian modernized a bathing scene left over from his productions for one of the minor princely courts. That the older composition no longer appealed to him can be seen from the replica in Vienna, in which the hands of pupils played a large part. The preliminary drawing of the composition on the canvas agrees completely with that of the Bridgewater House painting, but in the course of execution it was altered to bring it into line with modern requirements. The Vienna picture, though inferior in the quality of the painting to the London version, is nevertheless superior to it as an expression of Titian's attitude to life about 1560. Its colouring and spiritual conception are closer to the two other mythological paintings of this period.

Of the two paintings mentioned as having been begun in the letter of 1559, the 'Rape of Europa' was completed in 1562 and sent to Madrid, but whether the 'Punishment of Actaeon' ever arrived there is doubtful, for it is not mentioned in Titian's list of 1574 of the pictures he had delivered to the Spanish court. In both these *poesie* all attempts to follow the pagan legend and to exalt the human figure have been abandoned. The predominating rose-red of the 'Europa' and the gloomy monochrome of the 'Actaeon' express a cosmic feeling, without any intention of provoking an association of ideas. The landscape has ceased to be an echo and an enhancement of lofty sentiments; like the rest of the picture, it is a gleam of light, a strip of colour which passes before our eyes like a dream. Everything has become unreal, a gentle echo of one-time pleasure in life.

Titian's
later style

Whether we can accept Roger Fry's assertion that this mood of the ageing Titian was specifically pagan, is doubtful, and the same applies to the question whether the religious paintings of this last, or last but one, stage in Titian's development can be considered as Christian in the narrower sense of the term. Devotional paintings of this sort were sent to the Spanish court together with the mythological pictures, among them an 'Entombment' of 1556, which has survived only in atelier replicas, and another version of the same subject painted three years later, which modernizes the 'older version' in the same way as the Vienna 'Diana and Callisto' is a modernization of the painting in London. The figures have become more slender and their heads smaller and they lose still more of their supremacy through the looser colouring, which transforms the action from an everyday task into a mystery above all rational comprehension. The aloofness of this late picture becomes still more perceptible if we compare it with the much earlier version of the subject in the Louvre.

249, 250

What affects us most deeply in the later 'Entombment' is perhaps the spectacle of the ageing master's diminishing powers, rather than the pathos of an episode from the Passion of Christ. Religious and mythological connotations are dissolved in a cosmic feeling which embraces all conceptions; classical myths and scenes from the Passion are equally charged with feeling, and so are the portraits. In the tarnished mirror of a soul grown old, the pictures appear blurred. Titian has reached that stage of aloofness from things which makes the style of an artist in his old age so full of foreboding. In the loosening of his forms he takes no heed of the impression the spectator may receive, the subjects represented have for him equal value or lack of value. He is on the threshold of that supreme sphere reserved for the elect, in which the artist lives only for his own consummation.

Titian's
assistants

But these years of inner loneliness were also those in which Titian most systematically perfected the apparatus of his external effectiveness. We have seen—and Ridolfi saw it, too, long ago—how mythological paintings were duplicated in his workshop and how, even of the religious works, several versions of very unequal quality often exist. Many of these can be traced back to later imitators, but the bulk of these replicas was produced by Titian's workshop, under his supervision and on his responsibility. Like every other great master, Titian always had assistants. In the first document concerning him, the contract for the decoration of the Sala del Gran Consiglio in 1513, two young men who helped him are mentioned. Girolamo da Tiziano, who remained with him for several decades, was a witness at his marriage in 1525, when he was only sixteen years old. Later Orazio became his father's right hand. Various other names

DETAIL FROM THE PORTRAIT OF IPPOLITO RIMINALDI
(so-called 'Young Englishman'). Florence, Palazzo Pitti.

are mentioned as having a similar relationship to Titian. In his late period, when his own capacity for work began to decline and the demand for replicas of his popular subjects to increase, Titian seems to have exploited his assistants systematically. In a letter of 1568 to Emperor Maximilian II, Titian offered him replicas of all the *poesie* which he had delivered to the Emperor's Spanish cousin in the course of many years.

The models for such replicas—and also for the engravings after originals which had long since gone abroad—must have been kept in the workshop. That they were drawings is improbable, on account of the similarity of the colouring and Titian's general principles of work. They must have been painted replicas or elaborated sketches, preserved in great numbers in Titian's house and workshop. On the occasion of his visit in 1566, Vasari noted numerous pictures, some of them still in process of completion, some of them older works, and he also makes a summary mention of 'many less important works', probably those very sketches for pictures, which to him must have seemed to be mere daubs. On the other hand, it was these sketches which aroused the interest of Tintoretto, who purchased several of them after Titian's death—a 'Christ Crowned with Thorns' (now in Munich), a 'Flagellation', 'Diana and Callisto', 'Venus and Adonis'. Other sketches were sold by Titian's son Pomponio to the Barbarigo family, from whose possession they later passed to the Hermitage in Leningrad and to other collections. These broadly executed *modelli* have had a profound influence on our ideas of Titian's style in his old age.

Modelli

Ridolfi tells a curious anecdote about the procedure in Titian's workshop: 'When Titian went out, he put his keys away; but as soon as he had gone, his pupils began to copy his best things, one of them always standing sentry. When Titian after some time looked through the pictures in stock, he also took these pupils' copies and touched them up a little, after which they were sold as by his own hand. And that is why so many works of his pupils go under his name.' This piece of atelier gossip does not make it quite clear whether Titian's pupils on their own initiative sold as originals these replicas which had been foisted upon the old man, or whether Titian himself was a party to this procedure. In any case, contemporary art-lovers were well aware that works of very unequal quality came out of Titian's workshop. On receiving in 1568 the offer of the series of mythological pictures, the Emperor Maximilian II instructed his legate to find out whether the paintings were of the same quality as those Titian had painted in his younger days when his sight was better. In the same year the art dealer Niccolò Stoppio wrote to Max Fugger: 'All say that he can no longer see what he is doing and that his hand trembles so much that he cannot finish anything, but leaves it to his assistants. He has a German named Emanuel in his house, an excellent fellow who does the greater part of the painting, and then he adds a few strokes and sells them as by his own hand.' Certain of his works aroused similar criticism. In 1564 Titian undertook to paint three ceiling pictures for the town hall in Brescia, but when they were delivered in 1569, those who had commissioned them refused to recognize that they were by his hand.

Replicas

Vasari was not the only one to think that Titian would have done better to lay aside his brush much earlier, because what he was producing was liable to ruin his reputation. His own pupils seem to have shared this opinion. An old story which was probably circulating in Venetian ateliers is reproduced in his quaint old fashioned style by that wandering virtuoso, Joachim von Sandrart, who writes: 'In general it was believed by many that his first manner was his best, but when he had reached a great age he denied this and by his alterations spoilt in his old age several good pieces which he had painted in his youth. Wherefore his pupils, whenever he wished to alter such a work, mixed olive oil among his colours, which, because it does not dry, could be washed out again in the absence of Titian, whereby many good pieces were preserved.' The unique, the divine, the immortal Titian, as he was described by his contemporaries, appeared to his entourage as a childish old man and the last height to which he ascended seemed to them to be physiological decay. The solitude of his last years was not only the apotheosis of a genius, but the destitution of a man who had grown so old as to outlive his fame.

Thus we see this admirable artist's life following two tendencies as it draws near its end. Between the two extremes, the works created in his old age to satisfy his own ideas and the mass production serving commercial interests, there are a hundred intermediary and transitory stages. Just as Titian, to the dismay of his entourage, revised unfinished works by his own hand, so, too, he did not hesitate to ennoble a workshop replica by adding a few masterly strokes. A mythological composition, which had been standing unfinished in his workshop since the days of his activity for Alfonso d'Este and which Vasari saw in this condition in 1566, became in 1575 a Christian allegorical composition entitled 'Spain coming to the Rescue of Religion' and was delivered to King Philip, and despite all the reminiscences of earlier times it is an unexceptionable work. To oblige an old friend, Paolo da Ponte, Titian added a few strokes to the portrait, painted by one of his imitators, G. P. Pase, of Ponte's granddaughter Irene di Spilimbergo. External evidence, which is available in this case and is so often of assistance to art historians, is not altogether reliable. In 1573 Titian delivered to the Duke of Urbino a 'Mater Misericordiae', which he had promised to paint himself despite the Duke's assurance that he would be satisfied with a workshop production. The picture is now in Palazzo Pitti and has never been considered as anything but a workshop production. Elsewhere we find obvious traces of Titian himself in works which on the basis of documentary evidence have been assigned to others. To Orazio Vecelli's battle picture of 1564 (since destroyed) in the Ducal Palace in Venice, Titian, according to Vasari, contributed a man on horseback, for which the drawing in Munich may be a preparatory study. And the fresco round the tomb of Jacopo de' Cavalli in Santi Giovanni e Paolo, painted by Lorenzino, whom tradition describes as a pupil of Titian, but who is not known by any other works, is so outstanding in conception and in many details so thoroughly Titianesque, that we are bound to admit that this somewhat crude decorative painting may have been inspired by something of which the Venetian climate has robbed us, namely by Titian's style of fresco-painting.

Attribution of the late works In such circumstances it is bound to remain a matter of opinion to what extent one is willing to attribute to Titian works lying on the periphery of his late production. Neither the opinion of contemporaries nor flawless proof of their having originated in Titian's atelier is decisive evidence, as is shown by the case of the 'Mater Misericordiae' in Palazzo Pitti. Even the versions which were sent to King Philip II may not necessarily have ben the best in every case. The large 'Last Supper' in the Escorial, which incidentally was mutilated immediately after its arrival in 1564 in order to adapt it to the wall of the convent refectory, is dull in its conception and flat in its execution. The 'Adoration of the Magi', two out of the four versions of which are in Spain, has been the subject of much conflicting criticism. The versions in the Prado and in an American private collection, which were successively considered to be the original, might both be Spanish copies of the version in the Escorial, the superiority of which has been affirmed, after some hesitation, by A. L. Mayer. 243 242

In considering many of the late pictures, we must not forget the circumstances under which they originated. The 'Fede', Titian's last work for the Venetian Government, suffered badly from the great delay in execution. In 1555 Francesco Venier commissioned this votive painting in memory of his predecessor, Antonio Grimani, who had died in 1523. In the following year the final payment was made to Titian, but the picture was neither delivered nor finished, and it was not until after the fire of 1574, which it thus escaped, that it was hung in the Ducal Palace. It was completed by pupils, in the opinion of many scholars by Marco Vecelli, a son of Titian's cousin Tito Vecelli and one of his assistants in his later years. Still less of Titian's own hand can be discerned in the painting with which he closed his official activity for the Spanish court. 'Titianus Vecelius Aeques Caes. Fecit', runs the inscription on the 'Allegory of the Victory of Lepanto', but his share in it was certainly very small. This picture, the measurements of which are almost exactly the same as those of the equestrian portrait of Charles V, may have been intended as a pendant to the latter, the one picture representing the victory over the infidels and the other the victory over the heretics, and it may have been for this reason that Philip resorted to the master who had created such an incomparable monument to his father. But Philip at the same time made Titian adhere to a conventional programme, and the much too extensive overpainting by Vicente Carducho in 1625 gave the picture the finishing stroke. When Titian appended that proud signature in 1574, he had nothing more to give to the court of Madrid. In the same year he handed over a list of the works which he had dispatched in the course of twenty-five years. It is pathetic that this retrospect had to serve to make more effective his plea for the final payment of all old arrears, a subject which was the main theme of all his correspondence with Spain. 271 277 183

The latest works Titian was now very old. As so often happens in old age, youthful memories awoke in him and penetrated later layers of experience. Several compositions dating from this time can be traced back, directly or indirectly, to older conceptions. Originality of conception had never been one of Titian's special ambitions, and now the only thing of importance seemed to him to be the realization of his dreams of colour. The 'Magdalen' in the Hermitage in Leningrad, of which several other versions exist, is an elaboration of the 'Magdalen' in Palazzo Pitti, just as the 'Christ Crowned with Thorns' in Munich is an elaboration of the version in the Louvre. The 'Martyrdom of St. Lawrence' in the church of the Gesuiti in Venice was the model for the altar-piece painted in 1564—1567 for the Escorial, and that old masterpiece, 'The Murder of St. Peter Martyr' served as basis for a picture of the same subject which he presented to Pope Pius V in 1567 and which has been preserved only in the form of an engraving. The 'Annunciations' in San Domenico at Naples and San Salvatore at Venice derive from the composition created for the Empress Isabella in 1537. But none of these works can be called a repetition of the earlier version; in each case the new version is a simplification and an intensification of the old, while the transformation of the colouring imbues it with a deeply affecting grandeur.

The 'Christ Crowned with Thorns' in Munich comes closest to being a replica of the Paris version. But whereas in the latter the clarity and solidity of the architecture and the stocky figures combine to form an avowal of physical and moral strength—Christ suffers his martyrdom like a hero—in Munich means and effect are quite different. The architectural setting has almost disappeared, the figures have become more slender and more vague and melt into the spatial background. Everything materially palpable and measurable is eliminated and a mood of gentle resignation is thereby created. In the same way, the 'Martyrdom of St. Lawrence' in the Escorial represents an advance on the version in Venice. The exhibition of refined cruelty has given way to intense spiritual concentration. What is here shown is an act of faith, an inner rather than an external process, set in a nocturnal atmosphere which is a spiritual rather than a physical phenomenon. The older composition provided the material for a new construction; negligently Titian inserts at the top (but reversed) the two flying putti from his old version of the 'Murder of St. Peter Martyr'.

Another example of this retrospective trend in the style of Titian's late period is the 'St. Sebastian' in Leningrad. It goes back to the figure which in the woodcut after the altar-piece of the six saints, in the Vatican, replaces the original more Giorgionesque figure; probably there also existed an older painted version of this figure. In the 'Fall of Man' in the Prado, each of the figures can be traced back to early sixteenth-century Venetian art. Still more instructive as regards Titian's creative procedure during these years is the 'Nymph and Shepherd' in Vienna, likewise dating from about 1570, which is also known as 'Luna and Endymion' or 'Angelica and Medor'. Here we can point out the elements which re-emerge out of the depths of the past. Several scholars have noticed that the recumbent nymph is very similar to a figure in an engraving by Giulio Campagnola, that faithful disciple of Giorgione. In the relationship of the two heads to each other and in the appearance of one hand on the far side of the body, we find reminiscences of the 'Satyr' drawing of

253
274
258
314
231, 256
274
258
265
270
279
7

Titian's Giorgionesque period. Moreover, in that remarkable picture, created in the midst of the Counter-Reformation and of a fervid revival of religious feeling, there is an echo of the mood of the early Renaissance, the mood of Titian's youth. The juxtaposition of the clothed man and the nude woman recalls similar arrangements by Giorgione and his entourage. But instead of direct enjoyment, we find a memory of it, a melancholy retrospect on a long life.

Compared with the mythological paintings of the 1550's, in which we discerned for the first time a similar mood of resignation, the works produced during the last fifteen years of Titian's painting career represent a new, the ultimate climax. It is as if his return to his youthful ideas had released youthful forces in him, so that as an old man he achieved a final monumentality. This was not, as in the corresponding earlier stages, based on an exaltation of the human figure to a heroic degree, but on a freedom from everything disturbing and degrading. Everything smacking of arbitrariness, experiment, ambition, concession to popular taste, is suppressed; the accumulated experience of a long life is used to give reality to an inner vision in its purest form.

The ultimate climax

This spiritualization is so intensive that it inspires even those pictures which, on account of the extensive collaboration of less gifted assistants, do not evoke the same serene impression as the last great masterpieces. In the 'Transfiguration' in San Salvatore at Venice a certain carelessness of execution is noticeable, attributable in part to the fact that the picture was designed as a cover for the silver altar of the church. The conception is conventional, the composition somewhat theatrical, and yet it is difficult not to be impressed by the solemnity of the picture. Concerning the 'Annunciation' in the same church, dating from about the same period and in any case from before 1566, there is an anecdote which bears testimony to the doubts aroused by these late works of the master. The signature, 'Titianus Fecit Fecit', the most plausible explanation of which is that it is due to some early tampering, has been interpreted as a protest by Titian against the rumours which were circulating that most of the painting was due to his pupils. In the 1935 exhibition, this picture was acclaimed as one of the great masterpieces of the late period, although it was hard to overlook certain cruel mutilations, such as the insertion of the angel flying horizontally at the top of the picture. An admirable feature of this work is the way in which Titian returns to the time-honoured harmony of red and blue, the colours of the Madonna, which he first used in his early heroic period, but to which he now gives an even greater intensity. In the early pictures, the effect of this was reminiscent of painting on glass, but now the colour, freed from all material associations, has become a purely spiritual element.

235

256

A masterpiece of religious painting dating from this period is the 'St. Margaret' in the Prado. I agree with Gronau in thinking that this is not the 'portrait' of this saint which Titian sent to King Philip in 1552. The Madrid picture displays that dematerialization of colours which is characteristic of Titian's last period, to which period belong also the two main colours of the picture, the moss-green of the saint's robe and the tender brown of the landscape.

254

233   Similar in character is the full-length 'Madonna and Child' in Munich, which also possesses the solemn severity of Titian's last years.

A similar lofty mood, which in a way is a mood of farewell, is found in the mythological or classical antique subjects painted during this period, and even in the portraits. The most important composition in this category is the *246*   so-called 'Education of Cupid' in the Galleria Borghese in Rome, which as regards subject-matter is as obscure as the famous early work in the same gallery, in the inventories of which it appears for the first time in 1613 under the title of 'The Three Graces'. Lionello Venturi has recently made a somewhat ineffective attempt to defend this title. Unique is the charming colour effect produced in this picture by the contrast between the warm golden-brown and bluish-red in the right half and the cooler white and blue in the left. The seemingly unfinished state of certain portions of the picture heightens the impression of lively directness.

276   In an even more unfinished condition is the 'Lucretia and Tarquin' in the Academy at Vienna, which is not, as has been supposed, a fragment of a larger composition, but an incredibly light version, concentrating on the essentials, of a *275*   picture, a larger edition of which is to be found in the Fitzwilliam Museum at Cambridge. Cort's engraving of 1567 confirms that this is the official version. Here the figures are shown full-length, with the addition of one extra figure, set in a rationalized spatial background. Certain Northern European elements in the execution point to participation of the workshop, perhaps of that Emanuel of Augsburg who was one of its mainstays, while the Vienna picture would appear to be the model by Titian's own hand.

The sketching style and the style of Titian's old age are fused into one. Our ideas of the latter are based mainly on the pictures which were left unfinished *274*   at the time of his death—the ' Christ Crowned with Thorns ', the works which *280*   Pomponio sold to the Barbarigo family, the 'Pietà' in the Academy at Venice which was completed by Palma Giovine. There are also other works in which *273*   we can detect a similar style, e. g. the 'Ecce Homo' in St. Louis (U.S.A.). They cannot all date from Titian's very last years. Whereas the stock-in-trade works produced by the workshop were probably quickly disposed of to customers, these models were intended to serve as the basis for future production. Because they were not for sale, they anticipated to a certain extent that unrestrained boldness which appeared in the late masterpieces and even to the members of the workshop it appeared that they were in need of correction and completion.

Titian's technique   To Titian's mind they were completed. For him each picture grew out of stages, each one of which was complete in itself and at the same time provided the stimulus for further work. According to his technique, this conception created the mode of expression appropriate to it. Palma Giovine, who completed the 'Pietà', has left us an expert analysis of his technical procedure: 'Titian began his pictures with a mass of colour which served as a bed or foundation for what he wished to express. I myself have seen such vigorously applied underpainting in pure red ochre, which was meant to give the half-tone, or in white lead. With the same brush, which he dipped in red, black or yellow, he created the plastic effect of the light portions. With four strokes he was capable of indicating a magnificent figure. Sketches of this kind were of the greatest interest to connoisseurs, because they showed the way to true painting. After he had thus applied this important foundation, he turned the pictures to the wall and left them, without looking at them, sometimes for months. When he afterwards returned to them, he scanned them with a concentration as severe as if they had been his mortal enemies, in order to find faults in them; and if he found something which was not in accord with his intentions, he went to work like a surgeon who ruthlessly removes a tumour, or sets an arm, or brings a displaced foot into the correct position. Thus, by repeated revision, he brought the skeleton of his figures to the highest degree of perfection and, while one picture was drying, he turned to another. This quintessence of a composition he then covered with many layers of living flesh, until the figure seemed to lack only breath. He never painted a figure *alla prima*, and was wont to say that he who improvises can never fashion a perfect line of poetry. He gave the last touch to his pictures by adjusting with his fingers the transitions from the highest lights to the half-tones, or he would apply with his fingers a spot of black in one corner or heighten with a dab of red, like a drop of blood, the liveliness of the surface; and thus he gradually brought his figures to completion. In the last stages of the work, he painted more with his fingers than with the brush...'

This description reminds us of Blaise de Viginières' astonishment when he came across the eighty-year-old Michelangelo hewing the marble with such fury that sparks flew from it. The supreme exertions of these old men enabled them, despite their failing strength, to work in a way which put their juniors to shame. Direct contact with the element to which they had been accustomed all their lives seems to have been the mystic source of an abnormal strength; from Titian's finger-tips power of expression streamed directly on to his last canvases. But such concentration was naturally not continuous. It seems incredible that Titian can have applied the technique as described above to all those huge pictures and replicas which were put into circulation under his name. With them he must have limited himself to giving to the works produced by his assistants that external hall-mark which then and now satisfied the purchasers of 'Titians'. Both the stories which are told of his last years may be true: Titian, as the zealous agents reported, was no longer capable of working, and Titian was creating his purest masterpieces.

His farewell to mythology was the 'Marsyas' in Kremsier; his last word in religious art the 'Pietà' in Venice. The authenticity of the 'Marsyas', which came to light again only a few years ago, but which can be traced back under Titian's name to 1670, is supported by the influence which this composition had on later Venetian painting and by various individual links with other pictures by the master. The actual close of his artistic career was the unfinished 'Pietà', originally intended for the Frari, completed by Palma Giovine and by him donated to the church of Sant' Angelo. The long Latin inscription states the main facts: 'What Titian began and left behind, Palma reverently completed and dedicated to God.' The share of each artist in the work was probably

The 'Marsyas' and the 'Pietà'

280, 281

as follows: the left half—with the Magdalen, the putto beside her, the statue of Moses and the architecture pertaining to it—must be mainly Titian's work, while the statue of the Sibyl and the kneeling Joseph of Arimathea must have been finisheed by Palma. In this picture, too, we find an abundance of earlier motives and reminiscences, and here, too, they are fused into one entity by the originality of the conception and the boldness of the colouring. In no other figure does the passionate and vigorously affirmative temperament of Titian find such triumphant expression as in this Magdalen, crying out in anguish and rushing forward to the edge of the tomb, completely given to God.

The 'Pietà' became Titian's memorial, either because—as Ridolfi tentatively suggests—he could not make up his mind to finish it, or else because the Frari would not accept it. Titian painted his last works for himself. This is *Latest portraits* true, in part, of the portraits produced during these last years. Titian was no longer the official portraitist he had once been; instead of princely patrons, he painted members of his own circle. These late portraits are naturally closer to his earlier methods than free compositions. The so-called portrait of Fran-
238
240 cesco Salvaresio in Vienna, almost completely ruined, is dated 1558, the unknown
241 man in Baltimore 1561, the same year as the 'Man with the palm-branch' in
251 Dresden. To the same period belongs the St. Vincent Ferrer in the Galleria Borghese in Rome, under whose features an individual member of some order may be hidden. What connects these portraits with Titian's style in his old age is the broadness and simplicity of the representation and the renunciation of all formal obligations. The sitters are seen objectively, but with an objectivity which is neither cruel nor kind, but is a simple statement of the artistic possibilities.

268 Only one of these portraits has a right to a special place, that of the imperial antiquary Jacopo Strada, in Vienna, for which we have an unusually large amount of documentary evidence. The circumstantial reports of the sitter and of his competitor Stoppio enable us almost to see Titian painting it in 1568, and yet in many respects it differs from the rest of his œuvre. The tension of the attitude, the abundance of accessories and wealth of detail, reminiscent almost of a still-life, the complicated spatial construction of the background, all these things are quite un-Titianesque, but entirely in harmony with the general development of portrait-painting in Italy. That many alterations have been made to the picture is obvious, but it keeps its place within the framework of Titian's style during his last years by the harmony of its colouring and the subdued mood. This portrait was painted by the master who created the 'St. Margaret' and the 'Education of Cupid', and who about the same time
267 recorded his own features in the self-portrait in Madrid. It is unlikely that this self-portrait is the picture of 1562 which Vasari saw four years later in Titian's workshop. One is tempted to assign this spiritualized portrait, in which the pallor of the complexion is almost fused with the yellowish white of the beard, to the very last period of Titian's life, even at the risk of having to accept the participation of Palma or of some other finisher. Apart from this, such a pure profile for a self-portrait is not very convincing. But the demate-

SHEPHERD AND NYMPH. About 1570. Vienna, Kunsthistorisches Museum.

rialized head, with the eyes looking beyond this world, is Titian as he saw himself and as he compelled others to hand him down to posterity.

And that means Titian as we, too, see him, not as he may have actually looked during the last years of his life. In Cort's engraving of 1566 after the 'Gloria', he appears far more decrepit, and completely so in Van Dyck's strange etching, which shows him caressing the belly of a pregnant woman with his hand, and in the etching by Thomas based on it. The physical decay which the foreign correspondents reported to their courts, may actually have been a fact. Titian had become a very old man who was prudently making his last dispositions. His chief concern was the transfer of his fixed revenues—his broker's patent, his Milanese pension—to Orazio. In 1574 he made his final settlement with the Spanish court and about the same time he was shown to King Henri III of France as one of the sights of the city. His official duties had long since been taken over by others, above all by Jacopo Tintoretto.

Titian died on 27 August 1576, during one of the worst of the epidemics *Titian's death* of plague which periodically afflicted Venice. He does not seem to have died of the plague, as his son Orazio did shortly afterwards, for his remains were carried in solemn procession from the Birri Grande to the Frari and interred in that church. The painters of Venice planned solemn obsequies for him which were to have been a faithful copy of those celebrated in San Lorenzo in Florence for Michelangelo. The plan did not materialize, but it shows that even after his death Titian was the symbol of Venetian art, in contrast to the plastic art of Central Italy.

Colour is, in fact, the keynote of Titian's art. From first to last colour *Titian's colour* was for him an element of goodness, of health and naturalness. He never tortured or forced it, but let it stream out free and unfettered. Titian was the first painter to entrust his power of expression almost entirely to colour.

This pictorial conception is the basis of Titian's significance for posterity. No great painter of the succeeding centuries has failed to feel the need of studying him and finding in the model he provides the touchstone of his own requirements. Titian's influence is due not so much to formulas or technical devices which might be copied from him, as to the example of his logical transformation into pure colour of everything visible. His immediate pupils hardly went further than a feeble imitation of his work, but his real followers—Tintoretto, Rubens, Velazquez, Poussin, Van Dyck, Watteau and the French Impressionists—have successfully preserved and enriched his inheritance. The painting of the three centuries which follow Titian is unthinkable without him.

Together with the other great masters of the High Renaissance he founded the age of 'fine arts', and with them he built that realm of art which is independent of reality and superior to it by its beauty and impressiveness. Since, however, his particular share in this raising of art to a higher and more dignified level was based on the strength of his perceptions and the naturalness of his vision, he, more than any other, has made the conception of artistic beauty a general intellectual need. It was no mere chance that he became the favourite painter of courts and the personal painter of an emperor; through Titian art became a mark of social distinction, a part of general culture, a substitute for other spiritual forces which were disappearing. This conception of art prevailed far into the nineteenth century, and its last offshoots have carried on its influence down to our own times. The man who realized it in the transitory moment of his own existence and artistic achievement has a right to claim a high place in the history of the development of the human mind. Titian is not only a great painter, but he is also, because he never tried to be anything but a great painter, a historical manifestation of the highest importance.

Dal disegno originale di Tiziano posseduto dal Sig Carlo Bianconi in Bologna.

Eighteenth-century engraving after a drawing by Titian

THE PLATES

THE PLATES

1. VOTIVE PICTURE OF JACOPO PESARO. About 1506. Antwerp, Museum. ⟨57¼ × 72¼ inches⟩

2. PORTRAIT OF A MAN. About 1508. Washington, National Gallery of Art (Kress Collection). ⟨29³/₄ × 24⁷/₈ inches⟩

3 PORTRAIT OF A WOMAN (the so-called Schiavona.) About 1508. London, National Gallery. ⟨46¹/₈ × 38¹/₄ inches⟩

4. PORTRAIT OF A MAN (the so-called Ariosto). About 1508. London, National Gallery. ⟨32 x 25¼ inches⟩

5. PORTRAIT OF A BEARDLESS MAN. About 1513—1514. Copenhagen, Statens Museum for Kunst. (32 x 26¼ inches)

6. LANDSCAPE WITH TWO YOUTHS. About 1510. Pen drawing. Vienna, Albertina. ⟨9¼ x 8⅝ inches⟩

7. LANDSCAPE WITH SATYRS. About 1512. Pen drawing. E. and A. Silberman, New York. ⟨9³/₈ x 6¹/₄ inches⟩

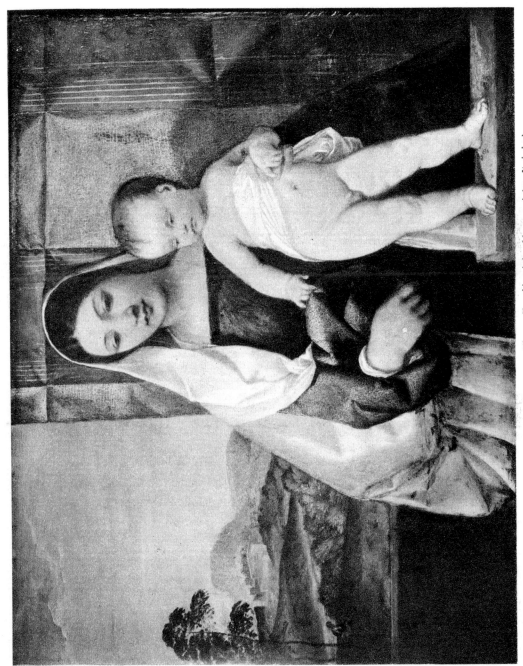

9. THE GIPSY MADONNA. About 1510. Vienna, Kunsthistorisches Museum. ⟨26 x 32³/₄ inches⟩

10. SKETCH FOR THE "JEALOUS HUSBAND" IN THE SCUOLA DEL SANTO. About 1510. Pen drawing.
Paris, École des Beaux-Arts. ⟨7³/₈ x 6⁷/₈ inches⟩

11. THE JEALOUS HUSBAND. 1511. Fresco. Padua, Scuola del Santo

12. MIRACLE OF THE YOUTH'S LEG. 1511. Fresco. Padua, Scuola del Santo

13. TOBIT AND THE ANGEL. About 1510—1514. Venice, Santa Caterina. ⟨68¹/₄ x 58 inches⟩

14. **ST. MARK WITH SAINTS SEBASTIAN, ROCH, COSMAS AND DAMIAN.** About 1511.
Venice, Santa Maria della Salute. ⟨89 × 45¹/₂ inches⟩

15. SALOME WITH THE HEAD OF JOHN THE BAPTIST. About 1512—1515. Rome, Galleria Doria. ⟨31¹/₂ × 28¹/₂ inches⟩

16. HEAD OF SALOME. Detail from Figure 15

17. YOUNG WOMAN AT HER TOILET. About 1512—1515. Paris, Louvre. ⟨38 × 30 inches⟩

18. VANITY. About 1512—1515. Munich, Ältere Pinakothek. (⟨39 × 31³/₄ inches⟩)

19. FLORA. About 1515. Florence, Uffizi. ⟨31¹/₈ × 25 inches⟩

21. HANDS OF THE SO-CALLED "MONK". Detail from Figure 20

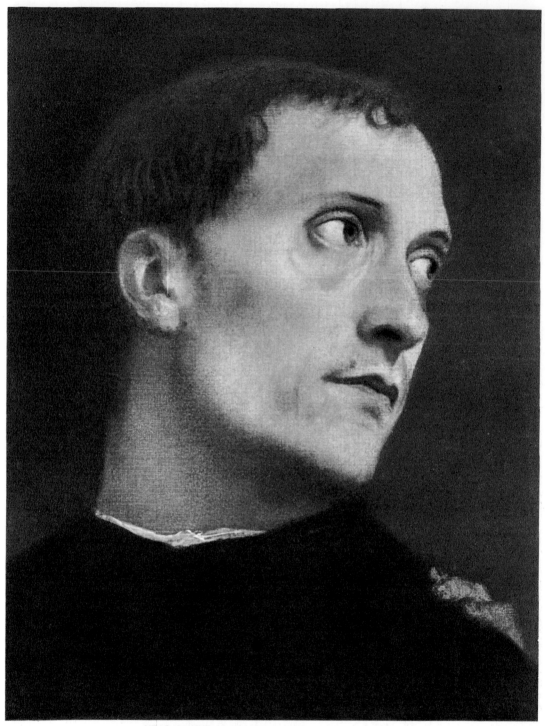

22. HEAD OF THE SO-CALLED "MONK". Detail from Figure 20

23. FORTRAIT OF LUDOVICO ARIOSTO. About 1516. Indianapolis, U. S. A., John Herron Art Institute. ⟨23¹/₂ x 18¹/₂ inches⟩

24. BAPTISM OF CHRIST. About 1516. Rome, Pinacoteca Capitolina. ⟨45¹/₈ × 35¹/₁₆ inches⟩

25. THE TRIBUTE MONEY. About 1518. Dresden, Gemäldegalerie. ⟨29¹/₂ x 21³/₄ inches⟩

26. LANDSCAPE WITH CASTLE. About 1510—1520. Bayonne, Musée. Bonnat

27. THE THREE AGES OF MAN. About 1515. London, Bridgewater House. ⟨42 × 72 inches.⟩ By permission of Lord Ellesmere

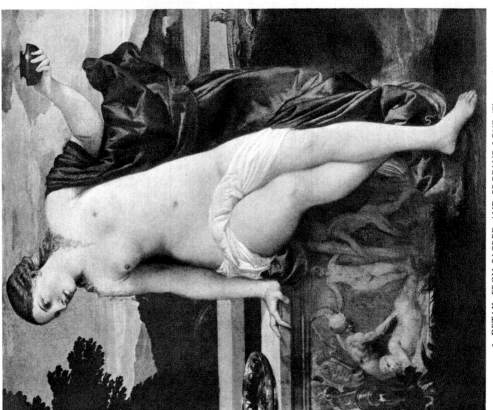

28. DETAIL FROM SACRED AND PROFANE LOVE (Figure 30)

29. GIORGIONE (?) : Detail from the Pastoral Concert

30. SACRED AND PROFANE LOVE. About 1515—1516. Rome, Galleria Borghese. (46³/₄ × 111 inches)

31. LANDSCAPE FROM "SACRED AND PROFANE LOVE" (Figure 30)

32. HEAD FROM "SACRED AND PROFANE LOVE" (Figure 30)

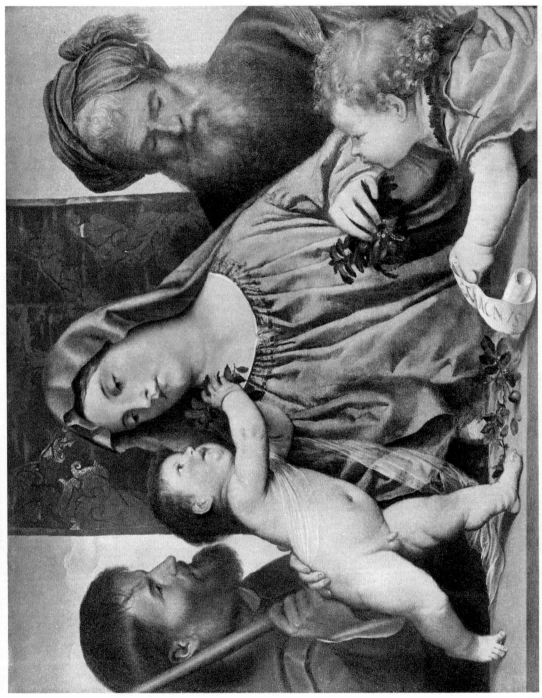

34. THE MADONNA WITH THE CHERRIES. About 1515. Vienna, Kunsthistorisches Museum. ⟨31³/₄ x 39³/₈ inches⟩

35. ASSUMPTION OF THE VIRGIN. 1516—1518. Venice, Santa Maria dei Frari. ⟨272 x 142 inches⟩

36. HEAD OF THE VIRGIN. Detail from the Assumption (Figure 35)

37. HEADS OF ANGELS. Detail from the Assumption (Figure 35)

38. STUDY FOR THE ST. PETER IN THE ASSUMPTION. 1516—1518. Crayon drawing. London, British Museum.
(6¼ x 5½ inches)

40. POLYPHEMUS. About 1515. Pen drawing. Lille, Musée Wicar. ⟨5 × 5¹/₈ inches⟩

41. THE WORSHIP OF VENUS. About 1518. Madrid, Prado. ⟨68 x 68³/₈ inches⟩

42. DETAIL FROM PLATE 41

44. BACCHANTES. Detail from the Bacchanal (Figure 43)

45. LUCRETIA STABBING HERSELF. Hampton Court. ⟨42¹⁵/₁₆ × 25 inches⟩
Reproduced by gracious permission of His Majesty the King

46. VENUS ANADYOMENE. About 1520. London, Bridgewater House. ⟨29 x 23¹/₈ inches.⟩ By permission of Lord Ellesmere

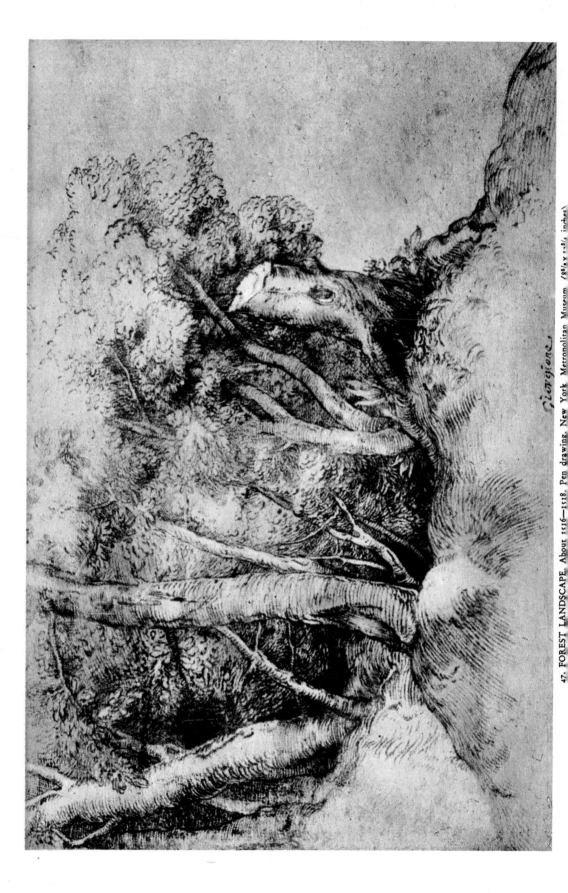

Giorgione

47. FOREST LANDSCAPE. About 1516—1518. Pen drawing. New York Metropolitan Museum. (8⅝ x 13¾ inches)

48. DETAIL FROM MADONNA AND CHILD (Figure 49)

49. MADONNA AND CHILD; BELOW, TWO SAINTS AND A DONOR. 1520. Ancona, Museo Civico. ⟨122 x 84³/₄ inches⟩

50. ST. GEORGE. 1517—1522. London, Messrs. Thomas Agnew's. ⟨49¼ x 26 inches⟩

51. STUDY FOR THE ST. SEBASTIAN IN BRESCIA. About 1518. Pen drawing. Frankfurt a. M., Staedelsches Kunstinstitut. ⟨7¼ x 4¾⟩

52. ST. SEBASTIAN. From the Altar-piece of the Resurrection (Figure 54).
1518. Brescia, SS. Nazaro e Celso. ⟨66 x 25 inches⟩

53. SKETCHES FOR THE ST. SEBASTIAN IN BRESCIA. About 1518. Pen drawing. Berlin, Cabinet of Engravings.
⟨6²/₈ x 5⁵/₈ inches⟩

54. ALTAR-PIECE OF THE RESURRECTION. 1518—1522. Brescia, SS. Nazaro e Celso

55. ANGEL OF THE ANNUNCIATION, FROM THE ALTAR-PIECE OF THE RESURRECTION (Figure 54). ⟨31½ × 25 inches⟩

56. VIRGIN OF THE ANNUNCIATION, FROM THE ALTAR-PIECE OF THE RESURRECTION (Figure 54). ⟨31½ x 25 inches⟩

57. PORTRAIT OF THE DONOR, ALTOBELLO AVEROLDO, FROM THE ALTAR-PIECE OF THE RESURRECTION (Figure 54

58. PORTRAIT OF TOMMASO MOSTI. About 1520. Florence, Palazzo Pitti. ⟨33³/₈ × 26 inches⟩

59. PORTRAIT OF A MAN. About 1520. Paris, Louvre. ⟨16³/₄ × 38 inches⟩

60. PORTRAIT OF A MAN. About 1520. Munich, Ältere Pinakothek. ⟨35 x 29¹/₄ inches⟩

61. PORTRAIT OF A YOUNG MAN. About 1520. London, Lord Halifax. ⟨39¹/₂ × 33 inches⟩

62. THE MAN WITH THE GLOVE. About 1520 Paris, Louvre. ⟨39½ × 35 inches⟩

63. HEAD, DETAIL FROM "THE MAN WITH THE GLOVE" (Figure 62)

64. HAND, DETAIL FROM "THE MAN WITH THE GLOVE" (Figure 62)

65. ANNUNCIATION. 1520—1522. Treviso, Cathedral. ⟨83 x 69¹/₄ inches⟩

66. BACCHUS AND ARIADNE. 1523. London. National Gallery. ⟨69×75 inches⟩

67. ST. CHRISTOPHER. Pen drawing. About 1520. Stockholm, Private Collection. ⟨13 x 7⅞ inches⟩

68. ST. CHRISTOPHER. About 1523. Fresco. Venice, Ducal Palace. ⟨118 x 70½ inches⟩

69. MADONNA OF THE PESARO FAMILY. 1519—1526. Venice, Santa Maria dei Frari. ⟨191 x 106¹/₂ inches⟩

70. MADONNA AND CHILD. Detail from the Pesaro Madonna (Figure 69)

71. BENEDETTO PESARO. Detail from the Pesaro Madonna (Figure 69)

72. FAMILY PORTRAITS. Detail from the Pesaro Madonna (Figure 69)

73. JACOPO PESARO. Detail from the Pesaro Madonna (Figure 69)

74. THE MAN WITH THE FALCON. About 1525. Omaha, Nevada, Museum of Fine Arts. ⟨43¹/₄ × 37¹/₄ inches⟩

75. PORTRAIT OF THE DUKE ALFONSO I OF FERRARA. About 1522. New York, Metropolitan Museum. (50 x 39¹/₂ inches)

76. PORTRAIT OF FEDERIGO GONZAGA OF MANTUA. About 1525. Madrid, Prado. ⟨49¹/₄ × 39¹/₄ inches⟩

77. HEAD OF A MOOR. About 1525. Crayon drawing. Florence, Uffizi. ⟨21¹/₈ × 12⁷/₈ inches⟩

78. STUDY FOR THE HORSEMAN IN THE LEFT BACKGROUND OF THE BATTLE OF CADORE. About 1525. Crayon drawing. Florence, Uffizi. ⟨21¹/₂ x 12⁷/₈ inches⟩

79. HEAD OF ST. CATHERINE FROM PALMA VECCHIO'S "SANTA CONVERSAZIONE", COMPLETED BY TITIAN.
About 1528. Venice, Accademia

80. LANDSCAPE WITH FLOCK OF SHEEP. About 1530 (?). London, Buckingham Palace. ⟨46¹/₄ × 39¹/₈ inches⟩
Reproduced by gracious permission of His Majesty the King

81. ST. JOHN ELEMOSINARIUS. About 1530. Venice, San Giovanni Elemosinario. ⟨104¹/₂ x 58³/₄ inches⟩

82. ASSUMPTION OF THE VIRGIN. About 1530. Verona, Cathedral. ⟨154 × 85 inches⟩

84. MADONNA WITH THE RABBIT. About 1530. Paris, Louvre. ⟨27³/₄ x 33 inches⟩

86. MADONNA AND CHILD WITH ST. CATHERINE AND ST. JOHN. About 1530. London, National Gallery. ⟨39¹/₄ x 55¹/₂ inches⟩

87. LANDSCAPE WITH FLOCKS. Detail from Figure 86

88. LANDSCAPE WITH SATYRS. About 1530—1540. Pen drawing. Bayonne, Musée Bonnat. (10⅝ x 16½ inches)

90. REPOSE DURING THE FLIGHT INTO EGYPT. About 1535—1540. Madrid. Prado. ⟨61 x 127¹/₄ inches⟩

91. SO-CALLED ALLEGORY OF ALFONSO D'AVALOS. About 1532. Paris, Louvre. ⟨48 x 42¹/₂ inches⟩

92. LA BELLA. About 1536. Florence, Palazzo Pitti. ⟨39¹/₂ × 29¹/₂ inches⟩

93. PORTRAIT OF CARDINAL IPPOLITO MEDICI IN HUNGARIAN COSTUME. 1533.
Florence, Palazzo Pitti. ⟨54½ x 42 inches⟩

94. PORTRAIT OF THE EMPEROR CHARLES V WITH A DOG. 1533. Madrid, Prado. ⟨75 × 44 inches⟩

97. IMAGINARY PORTRAIT OF CATERINA CORNARO.
About 1542. Florence, Uffizi. ⟨30 x 29¼ inches⟩

96. GIRL IN A FUR. About 1534. Vienna,
Kunsthistorisches Museum ⟨37¾ x 24⅞ inches⟩

95. PORTRAIT OF ISABELLA D'ESTE. 1534. Vienna,
Kunsthistorisches Museum. ⟨40½ x 25⅜ inches⟩

99. PORTRAIT OF AN OLD WARRIOR, PERHAPS TITIAN'S FATHER. About 1535. Milan, Ambrosiana. ⟨25¹/₄ x 23 inches⟩

98. PORTRAIT OF GABRIELE TADINO, COMMANDER OF CHARLES V's ARTILLERY. About 1538. New York, L. Bendit Collection. ⟨46¹/₄ x 52⁵/₈ inches⟩

100. STUDY FOR THE ST. BERNARDINO IN THE VOTIVE PICTURE OF DOGE GRITTI. About 1535.
Chalk Drawing. Florence, Uffizi. ⟨15¼ × 10⅝ inches⟩

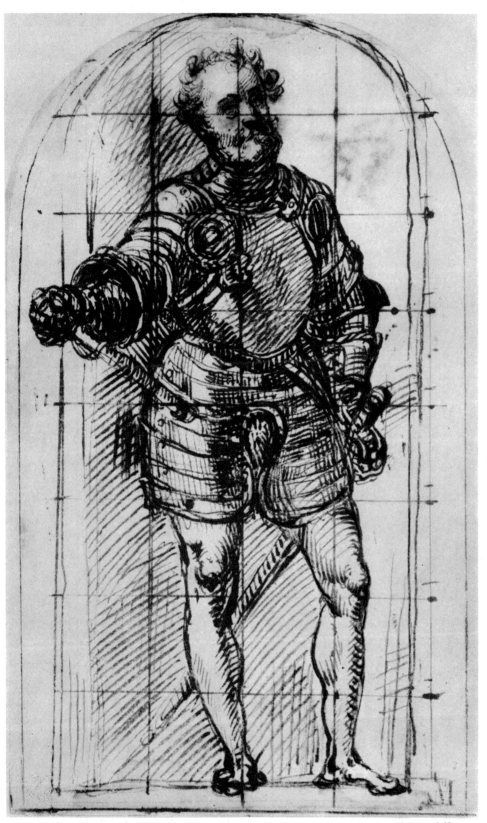

101. DESIGN FOR THE PORTRAIT OF THE DUKE OF URBINO. 1536. Pen drawing. Florence, Uffizi.
⟨9¹/₂ x 5⁷/₈ inches⟩

102. FRANCESCO MARIA DELLA ROVERE, DUKE OF URBINO. 1536—1538. Florence, Uffizi. ⟨45 × 39¹/₂ inches⟩

103. ELEONORA GONZAGA, DUCHESS OF URBINO. 1536—1538. Florence, Uffizi. ⟨45 × 40¼ inches⟩

104. DOG. Oil sketch. Stockholm, National Museum. ⟨8³/₄ x 11¹/₂ inches⟩

105. SKETCH FOR THE "BATTLE", SO-CALLED OF CADORE. Black chalk on blue. Paris, Louvre. ⟨6¹/₄ × 7¹/₈ inches⟩

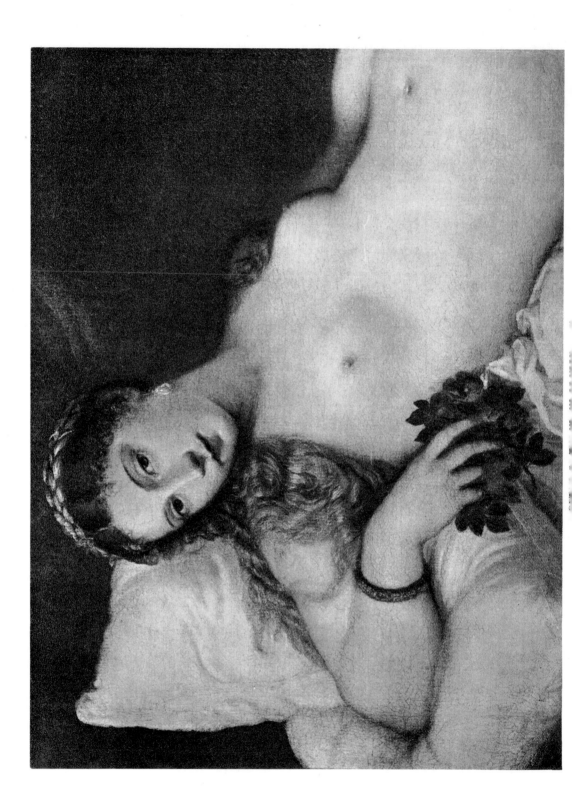

107. THE VENUS OF URBINO. About 1538. Florence, Uffizi. (47¼ x 65 inches)

108. PRESENTATION OF THE VIRGIN. About 1534—1538. Venice, Accademia. (136 x 295 inches)

109. THE VIRGIN ON THE STEPS. Detail from the Presentation (Figure 108)

110. DETAIL FROM THE PRESENTATION OF THE VIRGIN (Figure 108)

111. WOMAN WITH BASKET OF EGGS. Detail from the Presentation (Figure 108)

112. DETAIL FROM THE PRESENTATION OF THE VIRGIN (Figure 108)

113. DETAIL FROM THE PRESENTATION OF THE VIRGIN (Figure 108)

114. GROUP OF SPECTATORS FROM THE PRESENTATION OF THE VIRGIN (Figure 108)

115. ANNUNCIATION. About 1540. Venice, Scuola di San Rocco. ⟨65¹/₂ x 105 inches⟩

116. THE PARDO VENUS. About 1535—1540. Paris, Louvre. (77½ x 151½ inches)

117. DETAIL FROM THE PARDO VENUS (Figure 116)

119. DETAIL FROM THE PARDO VENUS (Figure 116)

120. HEAD OF A GIRL. Detail from the Pardo Venus (Figure 116)

121. ST. MARY MAGDALEN. Florence, Palazzo Pitti. ⟨33³/₈ x 26⁷/₈ inches⟩

122. PORTRAIT OF ALFONSO D'AVALOS, MARQUES DEL VASTO. 1538. Paris, Comtesse de Béhague. ⟨43¹/₄ x 33⁸/₈ inches⟩

123. KING FRANCIS I OF FRANCE. 1538. Paris, Louvre. ⟨43¹/₄ × 35 inches⟩

124. PORTRAIT OF ANTONIO PORCIA. About 1540. Milan, Brera. ⟨45¹/₂ × 35¹/₂ inches⟩

125. PORTRAIT OF BISHOP CRISTOFORO MADRUZZO OF TRENTO. 1542. New York,
Heirs of J. Stillmann. ⟨83 x 43³/₄ inches⟩

127. PORTRAIT OF FILIPPO STROZZI (?). About 1540. Vienna, Kunsthistorisches Museum. ⟨44⁷/₈ x 35¹/₄ inches⟩

126. PORTRAIT OF MONSEIGNEUR D'ARAMONT. About 1540. Milan, Castello Sforzesco

129. PORTRAIT OF GIACOMO DORIA. About 1540. London, Collection of Lady Ludlow.
(45⅝ x 39 inches)

128. PORTRAIT OF ADMIRAL GIOVANNI MORO. About 1540. Berlin,
Kaiser Friedrich Museum. (25³/₁ x 23 inches)

131. DOGE NICCOLÒ MARCELLO. About 1540. Rome, Vatican Gallery. ⟨40⅞ x 31½ inches⟩

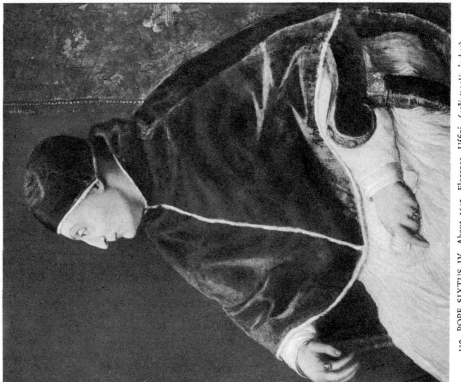

130. POPE SIXTUS IV. About 1540. Florence, Uffizi. ⟨43¾ x 35½ inches⟩

133. PORTRAIT OF CARDINAL PIETRO BEMBO. About 1542. Washington,
National Gallery of Art (Kress Collection). (39½ x 29½ inches)

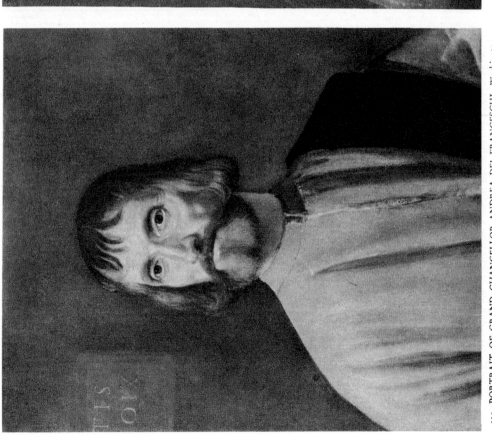

132. PORTRAIT OF GRAND CHANCELLOR ANDREA DE' FRANCESCHI. Washington,
National Gallery of Art (Mellon Collection). (25¾ x 19⅞ inches)

134. PORTRAIT OF IPPOLITO RIMINALDI (the so-called "Young Englishman"). Florence, Palazzo Pitti. ⟨44 × 37 inches⟩

135. PORTRAIT OF A BEARDED MAN. About 1540. Berlin, Kaiser Friedrich Museum. ⟨37¼ x 28½ inches⟩

136. GENERAL DEL VASTO ADDRESSING HIS SOLDIERS. About 1540. Madrid, Prado. ⟨88×65 inches⟩

137. MADONNA WITH SIX SAINTS. About 1542. Rome, Vatican Gallery. ⟨153 × 107 inches⟩

139. ECCE HOMO. 1543. Vienna, Kunsthistorisches Museum. ⟨95 × 142 inches⟩

140. TOBIT AND THE ANGEL. About 1542. Venice, San Marziale. ⟨76 × 51¼ inches⟩

141. HEAD OF THE ANGEL. Detail from Figure 140

142. HEAD OF CHRIST. Detail from Figure 143

143. CHRIST CROWNED WITH THORNS. About 1542. Paris, Louvre. ⟨120×71 inches⟩

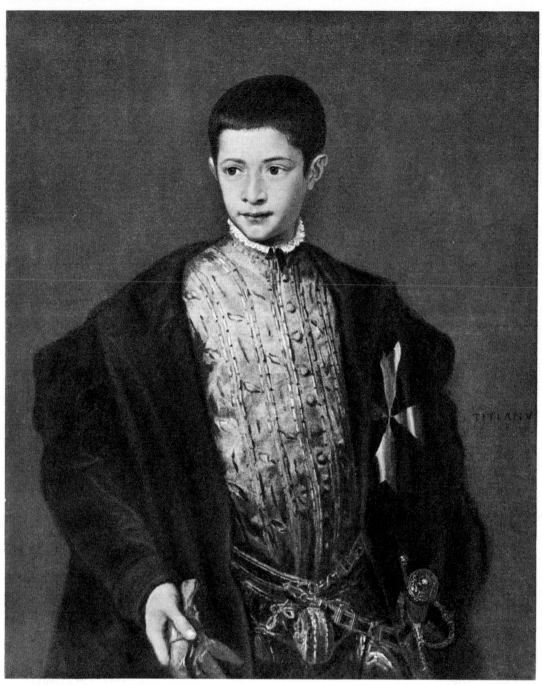

144. PORTRAIT OF RANUCCIO FARNESE. 1542. Richmond, Collection of Sir Herbert Cook, Bart. ⟨36¼ x 29½ inches⟩

145. PORTRAIT OF CARDINAL ALESSANDRO FARNESE. 1543. Rome, Galleria Corsini. ⟨20¾ x 19 inches⟩

146. TEMPTATION OF CHRIST. About 1542. Minneapolis, Art Museum. ⟨36 × 28³/₄ inches⟩

147. ST. JAMES. About 1540—1545. Venice, San Lio. ⟨116³/₄ x 55¹/₂ inches⟩

148. THE EVANGELIST ST. MATTHEW. About 1543/44. Venice, Santa Maria della Salute. ⟨Diameter 28¹/₄ inches⟩

149. THE SACRIFICE OF ISAAC. About 1543/44. Venice, Santa Maria della Salute. ⟨128 x 110½ inches⟩

150. **DAVID AND GOLIATH**. About 1543/44. Venice, Santa Maria della Salute. ⟨110¹/₂ x 110¹/₂ inches⟩

151. CAIN AND ABEL. About 1543/44. Venice, Santa Maria della Salute. ⟨110¹/₂ x 110¹/₂ inches⟩

152. ST. JOHN THE BAPTIST. About 1545. Venice, Accademia. ⟨77³/₄ × 53³/₄ inches⟩

153. LANDSCAPE. Detail from Figure 152

154. THE LAST SUPPER. 1542—1544. Urbino,
Palazzo Ducale. ⟨64¹/₄ x 41 inches⟩

155. MADONNA WITH ST. PETER AND ST. ANDREW.
1547. Serravalle, Cathedral. ⟨179³/₄ x 106³/₄ inches⟩

156. THE RESURRECTION. 1542—1544. Urbino,
Palazzo Ducale. ⟨64¹/₄ x 41 inches⟩

157. CHRIST AT EMMAUS. 1525—1545. Paris, Louvre. ⟨66¾ x 106½ inches⟩

·M·D·XLV·

VBI DILIGENTER INSPEXERIS, ARTEMQVE AC LABOREM
FRANCISCI ET VALERII ZVCATI VENETOR FRATRVM
AGNOVERIS, TVM DEMVM IVDICATO

158. ST. MARK. 1545. Mosaic. Venice, San Marco, Atrium

159. PORTRAIT OF THE LITTLE CLARISSA STROZZI. 1543. Berlin, Kaiser Friedrich Museum. ⟨45¹/₂ × 39 inches⟩

160. PORTRAIT OF POPE PAUL III. 1543. Naples, Museo Nazionale. ⟨42 × 32 inches⟩

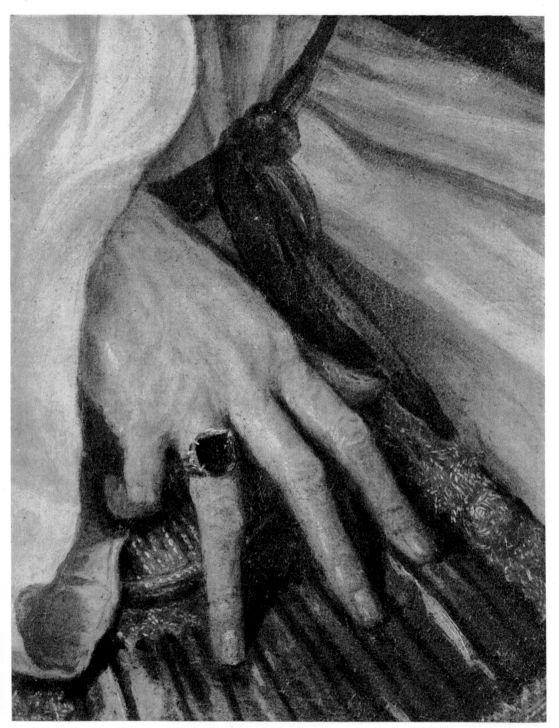

161. HAND OF POPE PAUL III. Detail from Figure 160

162. PORTRAIT OF DANIELE BARBARO. 1544/45. Ottawa, National Gallery of Canada. ⟨32¹/₂ × 27³/₄ inches⟩

163. PORTRAIT OF BENEDETTO VARCHI. About 1543. Vienna, Kunsthistorisches Museum. ⟨46 × 31³/₈ inches⟩

164. X-RAY PHOTOGRAPH OF THE HEAD IN FIGURE 163

165. HEAD OF BENEDETTO VARCHI. Detail from Figure 163

166. PORTRAIT OF PIETRO ARETINO. 1545. Florence, Palazzo·Pitti. ⟨42⁵/₈ x 29³/₄ inches⟩

167. PORTRAIT OF PIETRO ARETINO. About 1545. New York, Frick Collection. ⟨39¼ × 32 inches⟩

168. PORTRAIT OF DOGE ANDREA GRITTI. About 1540. New York, Metropolitan Museum. ⟨40¼ × 31¾ inches⟩

169. PORTRAIT OF DOGE FRANCESCO DONATO. About 1546. Fine Arts Gallery, San Diego, California

170. POPE PAUL III WITH HIS "NIPOTI." 1545/46. Naples, Museo Nazionale. ⟨83 x 68³/₄ inches⟩

171. HEAD OF OTTAVIO FARNESE. Detail from the Family Picture (Figure 170)

172. 'ROGER AND ANGELICA'. About 1515–1545. Pen drawing. Musée Bonnat, Bayonne (10⅝ × 11⅝ inches)

173. DANAË. 1545/46. Naples, Museo Nazionale. ⟨46¹/₄ x 27¹/₄ inches⟩

175. VENUS WITH CUPID AND THE ORGAN-PLAYER. About 1550. Berlin, Kaiser Friedrich Museum. ⟨45¹/₂ x 110¹/₂ inches⟩

176. VENUS WITH THE ORGAN-PLAYER. About 1545 (?). Madrid, Prado. ⟨53³/₄ x 87 inches⟩

177–178. THE ORATOR FRANCESCO FILETTO WITH HIS SON. About 1550. Vienna, Kunsthistorisches Museum. (32¹/₂ x 24¹/₂ inches and 35 x 26¹/₂ inches)

179. PORTRAIT OF A MAN. About 1545. Verona, Museo Civico. ⟨39¾ × 32½ inches⟩

180. PIER LUIGI FARNESE. 1546. Naples, Museo Nazionale. ⟨41¹/₂ × 31³/₄ inches⟩

181. PORTRAIT OF GIOVANNI DA CASTALDO. 1548. New York, Schaeffer Gallery. ⟨44³/₄ × 37³/₄ inches⟩

182. DETAIL FROM FIGURE 181

183. THE EMPEROR CHARLES V AT THE BATTLE OF MÜHLBERG. 1548. Madrid, Prado. ⟨131 x 110¹/₄ inches⟩

184. HEAD OF THE EMPEROR CHARLES V. Detail from Figure 183

185. THE EMPRESS ISABELLA. 1548. Madrid, Prado. ⟨46¼ × 37 inches⟩

186. HEAD OF THE EMPRESS ISABELLA. Detail from Figure 185

187. THE EMPEROR CHARLES V IN AN ARMCHAIR. 1548. Munich, Ältere Pinakothek. ⟨80²/₄ x 48¹/₄ inches⟩

188. PORTRAIT OF A MAN (the so-called Mendoza). About 1545–1550. Florence, Palazzo Pitti. ⟨69¹/₄ × 44¹/₄ inches⟩

189. NICHOLAS PERRENOT GRANVELLA. 1548. Besançon, Museum. ⟨44¼ × 37 inches⟩

190. ANTONIO PERRENOT GRANVELLA, BISHOP OF ARRAS, AFTERWARDS CARDINAL. 1548.
Kansas City, William Rockhill Nelson Gallery of Art. ⟨44¼ × 34½ inches⟩

191. MATER DOLOROSA. About 1548. Madrid, Prado. ⟨26⅞ × 24 inches⟩

192. PORTRAIT OF ANTONIO ANSELMI. 1550. Lugano, Thyssen Collection. ⟨29³/₄ x 25 inches⟩

193. PORTRAIT OF A MONK WITH A BOOK. About 1550. Melbourne, National Gallery of Victoria. ⟨32¹/₄ x 28¹/₂ inches⟩

194. THE ELECTOR JOHANN FRIEDRICH OF SAXONY. 1550. Vienna, Kunsthistorisches Museum. ⟨40³/₄ × 32¹/₂ inches⟩

195. SELF-PORTRAIT. About 1550. Berlin, Kaiser Friedrich Museum. ⟨38 × 29¹/₂ inches⟩

196. PORTRAIT OF A FRIEND OF TITIAN. About 1550. London, Frank Sabin. (34¹/₂ x 27³/₄ inches)

197. THE MAN WITH THE CROSS. About 1550. Madrid, Prado. ⟨48¹/₄ × 39³/₄ inches⟩

198. THE SO-CALLED DUKE OF ATRI. About 1550. Cassel, Gallery. ⟨88 × 59³/₄ inches⟩

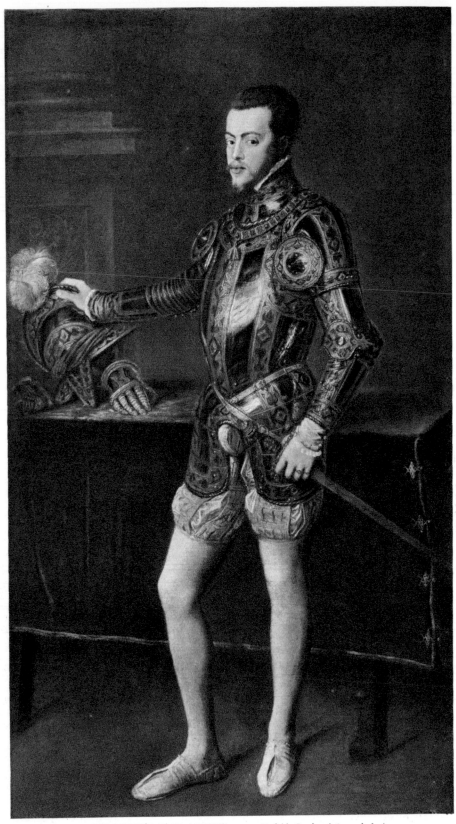

199. KING PHILIP II IN ARMOUR. 1550. Madrid, Prado. ⟨76 × 44 inches⟩

200. KING PHILIP II. About 1550. Naples, Museo Nazionale. ⟨74 × 39½ inches⟩

202. PROMETHEUS OR TITYUS. About 1550. Madrid, Prado. ⟨100 × 85³/₄ inches⟩

201. SISYPHUS. About 1550. Madrid, Prado. ⟨93³/₄ × 85¹/₂ inches⟩

203. VOTIVE PICTURE OF THE VENDRAMIN FAMILY. About 1550. London, National Gallery. ⟨81¹/₂ x 113³/₄ inches⟩

204. DETAIL FROM FIGURE 203

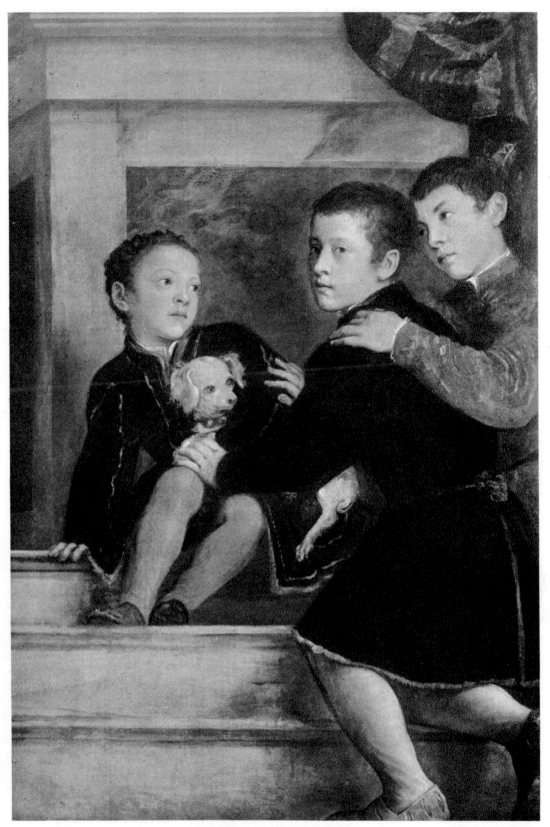

205. DETAIL FROM FIGURE 203

206. ECCE HOMO. 1547. Madrid, Prado. ⟨27¼ × 21 inches⟩

207. MATER DOLOROSA. 1554. Madrid, Prado. ⟨26⁷/₈ × 21 inches⟩

208. STUDY FOR THE MARTYRDOM OF ST. LAWRENCE IN VENICE. About 1550. Charcoal drawing.
Florence, Uffizi. (16¼ x 10 inches)

209. THE MARTYRDOM OF ST. LAWRENCE. About 1550—1555. Venice, Gesuiti. ⟨197½ x 110 inches⟩

210. DETAIL FROM THE MARTYRDOM OF ST. LAWRENCE (Figure 209)

211. ST. JEROME IN THE WILDERNESS. About 1552. Milan, Brera. ⟨93 × 49¼ inches⟩

212. PORTRAIT OF THE PAPAL LEGATE LODOVICO BECCADELLI. 1552. Florence, Uffizi (44×39 inches)

213. PORTRAIT OF MARTINO PASQUALIGO. About 1554—1555. Washington, Corcoran Gallery of Art. ⟨30⅞ x 24⅞ inches⟩

214. KING PHILIP II. About 1554. Stockholm, Hermann Rasch. ⟨38 × 29½ inches⟩

215. KING PHILIP II. About 1554. Cincinnati, Art Museum. ⟨51³/₄×37 inches⟩

216. HALF-FIGURE OF CHRIST. Fragment. About 1553. Madrid, Prado. ⟨26⅝ × 24½ inches⟩

217. CHRIST APPEARING TO THE VIRGIN MARY. About 1554. Medole, Parish Church. ⟨108³/₄ x 78 inches⟩

218. VENUS WITH THE MIRROR. About 1555. Washington, National Gallery of Art (Mellon Collection). ⟨49 × 41¼ inches⟩

219. GIRL WITH DISH OF FRUIT. About 1555. Berlin, Kaiser Friedrich Museum. ⟨40½ × 32 inches⟩

221. VENUS AND ADONIS. 1554. Madrid, Prado. ⟨73½ x 81¾ inches⟩

223. RAPE OF EUROPA. 1559. Boston, Isabella Stewart Gardner Museum. (69¼ x 80¾ inches)

DIANA AND ACTAEON 1559 London, Bridgewater House. By permission of Lord Ellesmere. (74 × 81½ inches)

225. THE PUNISHMENT OF ACTAEON. About 1560. London, Earl of Harewood. ⟨70½ x 78 inches⟩

226. DIANA AND CALLISTO. 1559. London, Bridgewater House. (75 x 81³/₄ inches.) By permission of Lord Ellesmere

227. DIANA AND CALLISTO. About 1560. Vienna, Kunsthistorisches Museum. ⟨72 x 79¹/₂ inches⟩

228. FAUN AND NYMPH. Rotterdam, Boymans Museum

229. LOVERS (JUPITER AND IO?). About 1560. Charcoal drawing, Cambridge, Fitzwilliam Museum. ⟨ 88²/₄ × 104³/₈ inches⟩

230. LA GLORIA. 1554. Madrid, Prado. ⟨136³/₄ × 95 inches⟩

231. ANNUNCIATION. About 1557. Naples, San Domenico Maggiore. ⟨170³/₄ × 75 inches⟩

232. ALLEGORY OF WISDOM. 1559. Venice, Biblioteca Marciana. ⟨66³/₄ x 66³/₄ inches⟩

233. MADONNA AND CHILD IN EVENING LANDSCAPE. About 1560. Munich, Ältere Pinakothek. ⟨68³/₄ × 52¹/₂ inches⟩

235. THE TRANSFIGURATION. About 1560. Venice, San Salvatore. ⟨97 x 116³/4 inches⟩

236. CHRIST ON THE CROSS WITH THE VIRGIN, ST. JOHN AND ST. DOMINIC.
About 1560. Ancona, San Domenico. ⟨130×75 inches⟩

237. DESCENT OF THE HOLY SPIRIT. About 1560. Venice, Santa Maria della Salute. ⟨225 x 102³/₄ inches⟩

238. PORTRAIT OF FABRIZIO SALVARESIO. 1559. Vienna, Kunsthistorisches Museum. ⟨44¼ × 34¾ inches⟩

239, THE MAN WITH THE FLUTE. About 1560. Detroit, Institute of Arts. ⟨39 x 29³/₄ inches⟩

240. PORTRAIT OF A BEARDED MAN. 1561. Baltimore, Md., J. Epstein Collection. ⟨34¼ x 28 inches⟩

241. THE MAN WITH THE PALM. 1561. Dresden, Gallery. ⟨54½ x 34²/₁ inches⟩

244. THE ADORATION OF THE MAGI. About 1560. Madrid, Prado. (55³/₄ x 86½ inches)

243. THE LAST SUPPER. 1564. El Escorial, Monastery of St. Lawrence. (81¾ × 182½ inches)

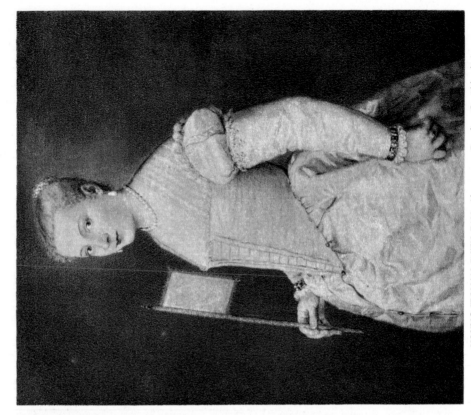

244. TITIAN'S DAUGHTER LAVINIA. About 1565. Dresden, Gemäldegalerie. (40³/₄ x 34 inches)

245. YOUNG WOMAN WITH FAN. About 1555. Dresden, Gemäldegalerie. (40¹/₂ x 34 inches)

246. THE EDUCATION OF CUPID. About 1565. Rome, Galleria Borghese. (46¾ × 73 inches)

247. DETAIL FROM THE EDUCATION OF CUPID (Figure 246)

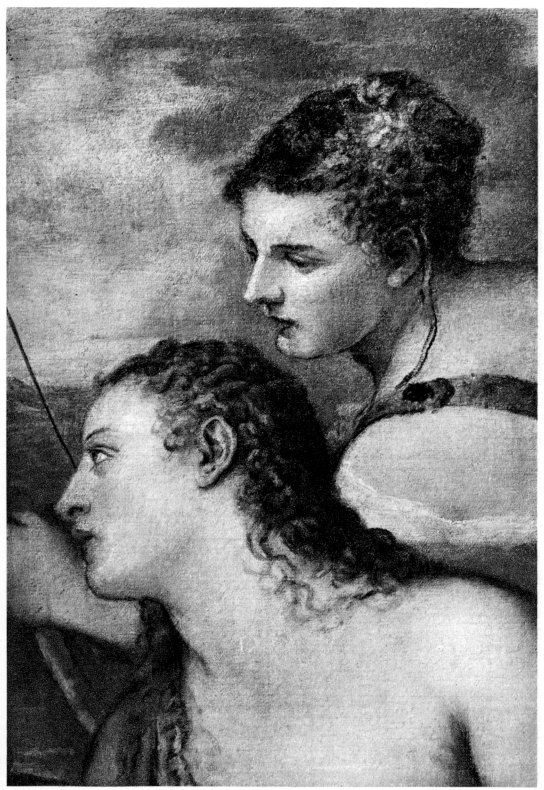

248. DETAIL FROM THE EDUCATION OF CUPID (Figure 246)

250. THE ENTOMBMENT. About 1565. Madrid, Prado (51⅛ x 66⅝ inches)

251. ST. VINCENT FERRER. About 1565. Rome, Galleria Borghese. (38¹/₂ × 31 inches)

252. ALLEGORY. About 1565. London, Francis Howard Collection. ⟨30 × 27 inches⟩

253. ST. MARY MAGDALEN. About 1565. Leningrad, Hermitage. ⟨47 × 39 inches⟩

254. ST. MARGARET. About 1565. Madrid, Prado. ⟨95¾ × 72 inches⟩

255. ANGEL OF THE ANNUNCIATION. About 1565. Crayon drawing. Florence, Uffizi. ⟨16³/₄ x 11 inches⟩

256. ANNUNCIATION. About 1565. Venice, San Salvatore. ⟨162 x 105 inches⟩

257. CHRIST ON THE CROSS. About 1565. El Escorial, Monastery of St. Lawrence. ⟨85 × 43¾ inches⟩

258. MARTYRDOM OF ST. LAWRENCE. 1564—1567. El Escorial, Monastery of St. Lawrence

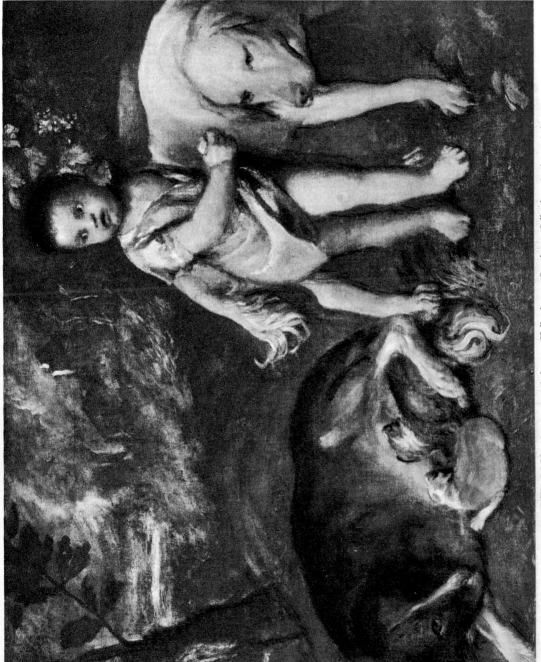

260. BOY WITH DOGS. About 1565. Vierhouten (Holland), van Beuningen Collection. (50½ x 71 inches)

261. ST. NICHOLAS OF BARI. 1563. Venice, San Sebastiano. ⟨67³/₄ x 35³/₄ inches⟩

262. CHRIST ON THE MOUNT OF OLIVES. About 1565. El Escorial, Monastery of St. Lawrence. ⟨69 × 68 inches⟩

263. HORSEMAN FALLING. About 1565. Chalk drawing, Oxford, Ashmolean Museum. ⟨10³/₄ x 10¹/₈ inches⟩

264. HORSEMAN. About 1565. Charcoal drawing. Munich, Graphische Sammlung

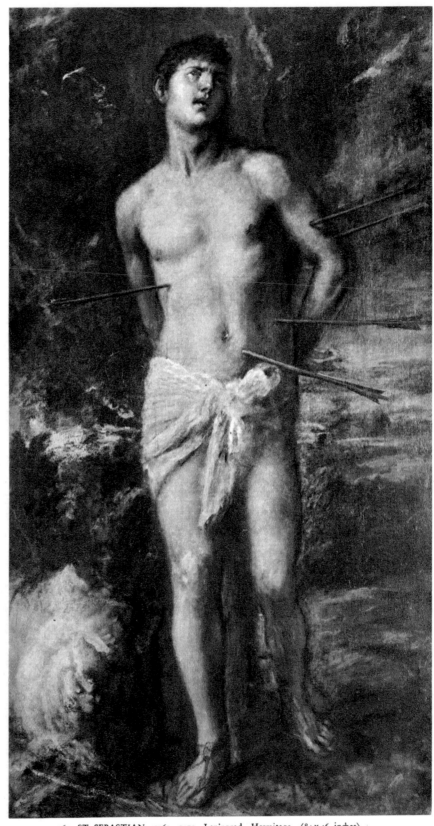

265. ST. SEBASTIAN. 1560—1570. Leningrad, Hermitage. ⟨84 × 46 inches⟩

266. DETAIL FROM THE ST. SEBASTIAN (Figure 265)

267. SELF-PORTRAIT. About 1565. Madrid, Prado. ⟨34 × 25³/₄ inches⟩

268. PORTRAIT OF JACOPO STRADA. 1568. Vienna, Kunsthistorisches Museum. ⟨49¼ × 37¾ inches⟩

269. SPAIN COMING TO THE AID OF RELIGION. About 1570. Madrid, Prado. ⟨66¼ x 66¼ inches⟩

270. THE FALL OF MAN. About 1570. Madrid, Prado. ⟨114¹/₂ × 73¹/₂ inches⟩

272. VIEW OF VENICE. Detail from Figure 271

273. ECCE HOMO. St. Louis, Mo., City Museum

274. CHRIST CROWNED WITH THORNS. About 1570. Munich, Ältere Pinakothek. ⟨110½ x 72 inches⟩

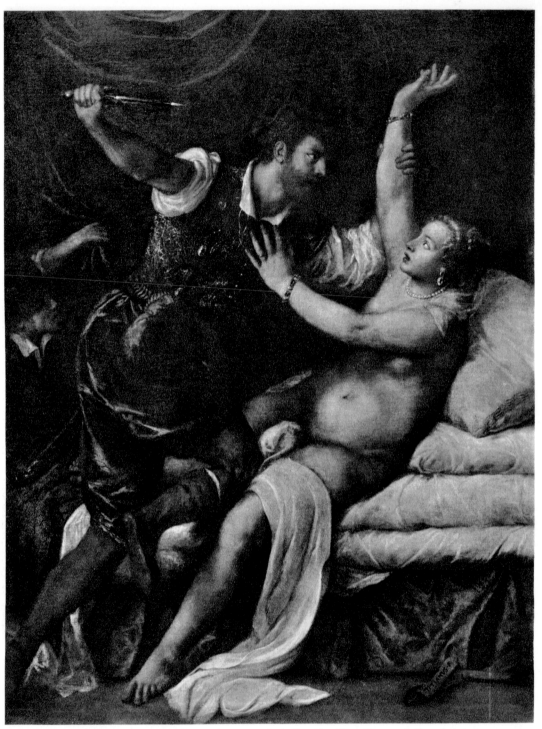

275. LUCRETIA AND TARQUIN. About 1570. Cambridge. Fitzwilliam Museum. ⟨74¹/₈ × 57¹/₄ inches⟩

276. LUCRETIA AND TARQUIN. About 1560—1570. Vienna, Akademie der bildenden Künste. ⟨45 × 39¹/₂ inches⟩

277. ALLEGORY OF THE BATTLE OF LEPANTO. 1571—1575. Madrid, Prado. ⟨132 x 108 inches⟩

278. MADONNA SUCKLING THE CHILD. About 1570—1576. London, National Gallery

280. PIETA. 1573—1576. Venice. Accademia. ⟨138³/₄ x 153³/₄ inches⟩

281. THE FLAYING OF MARSYAS. About 1570. Kremsier, Archiepiscopal Castle. ⟨84 x 81³/₄ inches⟩

282. DETAIL FROM THE FLAYING OF MARSYAS (Figure 281)

283. DETAIL FROM THE FLAYING OF MARSYAS (Figure 281)

APPENDIX

284. CHRIST BEARING THE CROSS. Venice, San Rocco. ⟨27³/₄ x 39¹/₂ inches⟩

285. MADONNA AND CHILD WITH SAINTS. Titian and Francesco Vecelli as donors. 1569. Pieve di Cadore.
⟨40 x 54¹/₄ inches⟩

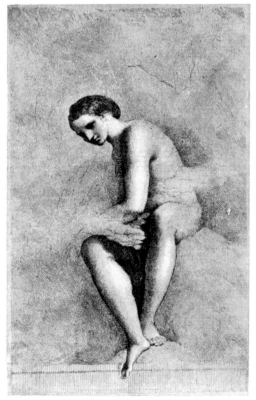

286—289. Copies of mural paintings on the Fondaco dei Tedeschi at Venice. 1508.
GIORGIONE: STANDING WOMAN (Etching by Zanetti)
TITIAN: STANDING WOMAN (Engraving by Jac. Piccino)
TITIAN: SO-CALLED "Calza" friar (Etching by Zanetti)
GIORGIONE: SITTING WOMAN (Engraving by Zanetti)

290—291. Copies of mural paintings on the Fondaco dei Tedeschi at Venice. 1508.
TITIAN: JUDITH (Etching by Zanetti)
TITIAN: SITTING WOMAN (Etching by Zanetti)

292. NOLI ME TANGERE. Painting of Giorgione, finished by Titian. About 1510. London, National Gallery.
(42½ x 35½ inches)

293. DETAIL FROM THE "NOLI ME TANGERE". London, National Gallery (Figure 292)

294. VENUS RECUMBENT. Painted by Giorgione, finished by Titian. About 1510. Dresden, Gemäldegalerie. ⟨43¹/₂ x 70 inches⟩

296. ST. GEMINIANUS. 1535. Mosaic. Venice, Atrium of St. Mark's

295. PORTRAIT OF CARDINAL PIETRO BEMBO. 1542. Mosaic by Francesco and Valerio Zuccato.
Florence, Bargello

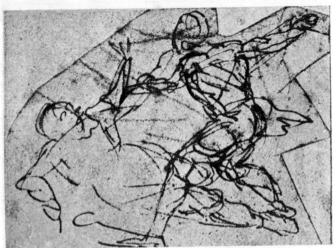

297—299. SKETCHES FOR THE ALTAR-PIECE OF ST. PETER MARTYR
1528. Pen drawings. Lille, Musée Wicar. ⟨2 x 3¹/₈; 2¹/₂ x 3¹/₈; 5³/₄ x 7¹/₈ inches⟩

300 a. TWO DETAILS FROM PLATE 300 (on the next page)

300. TITIAN: MARTYRDOM OF ST. PETER MARTYR. Formerly in SS. Giovanni e Paolo, Venice. Engraving by Martino Rota

301. TITIAN: ANNUNCIATION. 1537. Painted for the Convent of Santa Maria degli Angeli at Murano.
Engraving by G. Caraglio

361 COPY OF TITIAN'S BATTLE OF CADORE formerly in the Ducal Palace at Venice. 1538. Florence, Uffizi

303. VOTIVE PICTURE OF DOGE ANDREA GRITTI. Woodcut after the burnt picture by Titian formerly in the Ducal Palace, Venice (1531)

C. CAESAR CALIGVLA.

IV

Latitiam picto poteris cognoscere vultu
Vera dûm quarta hæc regima incuate fuit.
Venit ad imperium multis fundantibus artes
Sanguine, et immanerâ per fera cæde boûm.

Principis haud melior quisquam, quo denique pessit
Nemo fuit, cecidit cum sibi genitus amor.
Vnam Romani te, qui trucidare cupisti
Ceruicem populi, factio cæcidit onus.

AVLLVS VITELLIVS.

IX

Si te tam voracem factura hæc rapiecina vnde
A te sint regni quod tibi pulsu Othe est.
Mens hominum ivcenas sortis que ignara latentis
Excitea boni tenta celeri pata

Quid tam suspecti his habuit tua cædes honere?
Quid non a potiu turbiu, æque mali.
Te carcer tulit inscia, laqueísque ruinaq?
Fatísque ac tribion, et contigisena mori.

X

Effigiem iam certis boni sura Principis est quam
Luctui obscure sel et ab vmbra vices.
In medium tres, qui tates te, et vencere Neronum.
E medio miseris lis pereire medis.

Te sine quoniam iam tum posseebit erasique.
Principis exemplum sanctè future bom.
Augebis laudes augebis inique retamphes.
Ante voles ô qui vertere incique pium.

D. CLAVDIVS CAESAR.

V

Qui misera tristi nexti imperi mala
Es quanta regni incis deierum capta.
Augusthorum quamque bimi vix offinat
Me redeat, ut domindia dicat vale.
Me læti tulit præcelium ad hos factiges

Exstinmorium pænam ad invontom rapi
Morti metu tremendam, et inde deigt
Discordiarum magnum, et miscikarum agous
Me factioem non punte icuilum
At scelus ad extremom abstude vennfis

304—307. FOUR ROMAN EMPERORS. Engravings by Aeg. Sadeler after Titian's paintings of "Caesars" at Mantua

308. COPY OF TITIAN'S PORTRAIT OF THE DUCHESS GIULIA VARANA OF URBINO, 1546/47.
Florence, Palazzo Pitti. (44 x 33¹/₂ inches)

311. COPY OF TITIAN'S EMPEROR CHARLES V. 1532. Augsburg, Collection of Fürst Fugger-Babenhausen. ⟨47 x 36 inches⟩

312. COPY OF TITIAN'S ELECTOR JOHANN FRIEDRICH OF SAXONY. 1548. Madrid. Prado. ⟨51 x 37 inches⟩

111. RUBENS: COPY OF TITIAN'S DOUBLE PORTRAIT OF THE EMPEROR CHARLES V AND THE EMPRESS ISABELLA, 1548. London. Frank Sabin

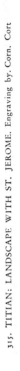

315. TITIAN: LANDSCAPE WITH ST. JEROME. Engraving by. Corn. Cort

TITIANVS VECELLIVS. EQVES. CÆS. PIOV. PONT. MAX. FACIEBAT.

314. TITIAN: ST. PETER MARTYR. Engraving by Luca Bertelli

316. TITIAN: TANTALUS. Ceiling painting for Queen Maria of Hungary.
Engraving by G. Sanuto
317. TITIAN: VULCANS' FORGE. Ceiling painting, formerly in the town hall at Brescia.
Engraving by Melchior Meier or Cornelius Cort

318. TITIAN: VISION OF ST. JOHN THE EVANGELIST. Formerly in the Scuola di San Giovanni
Evangelista at Venice. Engraving by Andrea Zucchi
319. TITIAN: THE SCOURGING OF CHRIST. Engraving by Martino Rota

330 ABRAHAM'S SACRIFICE 1516/18 Woodcut by Ugo da Carpi after Titian. ⟨29¾ x 11½ inches⟩

321. DESTRUCTION OF PHARAOH'S HOST IN THE RED SEA. 1549. Woodcut by Domenico delle Greche after Titian. ⟨47³/₄ x 86¹/₄ inches⟩

322. ADORATION OF THE SHEPHERDS. Woodcut after Titian. ⟨15⅜ × 19¼ inches⟩
323. ADORATION OF THE SHEPHERDS. Copy after Titian. Florence, Palazzo Pitti. ⟨36⅝ × 44⅛ inches⟩

324. LARGE LANDSCAPE WITH ST. JEROME. Woodcut by Boldrini after Titian. ⟨15⅝ × 21 inches⟩
325. ST. FRANCIS RECEIVING THE STIGMATA. Woodcut by Boldrini after Titian. ⟨11¾ × 17¼ inches⟩

326. SAMSON AND DELILAH. Woodcut by Boldrini after Titian. ⟨12¹/₂ x 19⁷/₈ inches⟩

327. CARICATURE OF THE LAOCOÖN GROUP. Woodcut by Boldrini after Titian. ⟨10⁷/₈ x 16¹/₂ inches⟩

CATALOGUE

TITIAN'S PAINTINGS, DRAWINGS AND WOODCUTS

THE REPRODUCTIONS in this volume and the catalogue which accompanies them make no claim to completeness, but are limited to those works that I consider the most important in conveying the achievements of Titian as painter and draughtsman. I have included certain paintings that seem to me of doubtful authenticity but are assigned to the master by well-known scholars: their inclusion and discussion will, I think, clarify our ideas of Titian's work. On the other hand, I have deliberately omitted a number of works commonly assigned to Titian by reason of old tradition or in consequence of more recent attributions. However interesting many of these may be for the expert historian of art, they seem to me to contribute little to the interest which the master arouses among a wider circle of art-lovers. Some paintings have been omitted because they are merely repetitions or variants of pictures reproduced in this volume; a further increase in the material was pointless in view of the fact that Suida's book aims especially at completeness, and in such cases I refer the reader to his book. Some discoveries of recent years have been omitted because they need thorough examination before they can be included in a book that tries to present a general picture of Titian's activity. Experience shows that such finds are apt to dazzle and blind those who unearth them, and also, to some extent, even wider circles. Hence there may be some genuine Titians among the works I have omitted. On the whole, however, I must confess that the majority of the works I have rejected seem to me so remote from Titian in style and quality, or so altered by deterioration or restoration, that I omit them without misgivings. In some cases I have set out my doubts elsewhere and the paintings in public collections in the U.S.A. will be critically examined in a book on Titian in America, which I am preparing together with E. Tietze-Conrat.

The Catalogue on the following pages will serve to supplement the captions of the reproductions and the observations in the text. Abbreviations of literature refer to the short bibliography on pages 363 and 364. Catalogue entries dealing with works no longer preserved in the original are placed in brackets.

BIBLIOGRAPHY

I. SOURCES

Pietro Aretino, Lettere, 6 volumes, Paris 1609.

Marco Boschini, Le Ricche Miniere della Pittura, Venice 1674.

W. Braghirolli, Tiziano alla Corte dei Gonzaga di Mantova. Atti e Memorie della R. Accademia Virgiliana di Mantova, 1881.

G. Campori, Tiziano e gli Estensi. Nuova Antologia XXVII (1874), pp. 571 seqq.

L. Cust, The Chatsworth Van Dyck Sketch-book, London, 1902; New edition, ed. G. Adriani, Vienna 1940.

Lodovico Dolce, Dialogo della Pittura intitolato l'Aretino, Venice 1557. German edition in Eitelberger's Quellenschriften, Vienna II, 1871.

Georg Gronau, Die Kunstbestrebungen der Herzoge von Urbino. Jahrbuch der Preussischen Kunstsammlungen XXV, Supplement.

Georg Gronau, Documenti artistici urbinati. Florence 1936.

G. B. Lorenzi, Monumenti per servire alla Storia del Palazzo Ducale di Venezia, Venice 1868.

Marcanton Michiel (L'Anonimo Morelliano), Notizia d'opere di disegno, Bassano 1800; The Anonimo, edited by George C. Williamson, London 1903.

Carlo Ridolfi, Le Maraviglie dell'Arte della Pittura, Venice 1648. New edition by Detlev Freiherr von Hadeln, Berlin 1914.

A. Ronchini, Delle Relazioni di Tiziano coi Farnesi memoria. Atti e Memorie delle deputazioni di Storia Patria per le Provincie Modenesi e Parmensi, II, Modena 1864.

G. Vasari, Le Vite de' più eccellenti Pittori, Florence 1550. Second edition, Florence 1568. Modern edition by G. Milanesi, VII, pp. 425 seqq., Florence 1881.

Zanetti, Varie Pitture a fresco de' Principali Maestri Veneziani, Venice 1760.

M. R. Zarco del Valle, Unveröffentlichte Beiträge zur Geschichte der Kunstbestrebungen Karls V. und Philipps II. Mit besonderer Berücksichtigung Tizians. Jahrbuch der Sammlungen des a. h. Kaiserhauses VII/II, pp. 221 seqq.

II. GENERAL DESCRIPTIONS (arranged according to year of publication)

Breve Compendio della Vita del Famoso Titiano Vecelli di Cadore, Venice 1622 (the so-called Anonimo del Tizianello).

St. Ticozzi, Vite dei Pittori Vecelli di Cadore, Milan 1817.

Crowe and Cavalcaselle, Life and Times of Titian. 2 vols. London, 1877.

Claude Phillips, Titian, London 1898.

Georg Gronau, Tizian, Berlin 1900. English edition, London 1904.

Charles Ricketts, Titian, London 1910.

V. Basch, Titien, Paris 1918.

L. Hourticq, La Jeunesse de Titien, Paris 1919.

(O. Fischel) Tizian, Des Meisters Gemälde, in Klassiker der Kunst, fifth edition, 1929.

Wilhelm Suida, Tizian, Zürich 1933. French edition 1935.

Theodor Hetzer, Tizian. Geschichte seiner Farbe, Frankfurt 1935.

Hans Tietze, Tizian, Leben und Werk, Wien 1936.

III. SPECIAL WORKS

1. Biographical:

G. Cadorin, Dello Amore ai Veneziani di Tiziano, Venice 1833.

Herbert Cook, Did Titian live to be 99 years old? The Nineteenth Century No. 299 (1902, January).

Herbert Cook, When was Titian born? Repertorium für Kunstwissenschaft XXVII, pp. 98 seqq.

J. Gilbert, Cadore, or Titian's Country, London 1869.

R. L. Douglas, Date of Titian's birth, Art Quarterly 11, 1948, p. 136 ff.

G. Ludwig, Die Hochzeit Tizians, Jahrbuch der Preussischen Kunstsammlungen XXIV, Supplement, p. 114.

Lodovico Foscari, Iconografia di Tiziano, Venice 1935.

2. Style:

E. Tietze-Conrat, Die Linearkomposition bei Tizian, Innsbruck 1915.

E. Tietze-Conrat, Titian's workshop in his late years, Art Bulletin, 28, 1946, 16 ff.

Th. Hetzer, Die frühen Gemälde Tizians, Basle 1920.

Th. Hetzer, Studien über Tizians Stil, Jahrbuch für Kunstwissenschaft 1923.

Fritz Heinemann, Tizian, die zwei ersten Jahrzehnte seiner künstlerischen Entwicklung, Münchner Dissertation 1928.

Pedro Beroqui, Tizian en el museo del Prado, Madrid 1927. Second edition 1946.

L. Hourticq, Le problème de Giorgione, Paris 1930.

3. Drawings and Graphic Art.

W. Korn, Tizians Holzschnitte, Breslau 1897.

Paul Kristeller, Il Trionfo della Fede, Berlin 1906.

Paul Kristeller, Tizians Beziehungen zum Kupferstich, Mitteilungen der Gesellschaft für vervielfältigende Kunst 1911, p. 23.

Detlev Freiherr von Hadeln, Tizians Handzeichnungen, Berlin 1924. English edition (with six additional reproductions), London 1927.

L. Fröhlich-Bum, Studien zu Handzeichnungen der italienischen Renaissance, in Jahrbuch der Kunsthistorischen Sammlungen in Wien, N. F. II, pp. 163 seqq.

Idem, Tizians Landschaftszeichnungen, in Belvedere 1929, pp. 71 seqq.

H. Tietze and E. Tietze-Conrat, Tizian-Studien, in Jahrbuch der Kunsthistorischen Sammlungen in Wien, N. F. X, pp. 137 seqq.

Idem, Tizian-Graphik, Die Graphischen Künste, 1938, p. 8 ff. and 52 ff.

Idem, Titian's Woodcuts, The Print Collector's Quarterly, 1938, p. 332 ff and 464 ff.

Fabio Mauroner, Le Incisioni di Tiziano, Padua, 1943.

IV. GENERAL WORKS ON VENETIAN AND ITALIAN ART

B. Berenson, The Venetian Painters of the Renaissance, New York and London 1897.

B. Berenson, Italian Pictures of the Renaissance, Oxford 1932.

Jakob Burckhardt, Beiträge zur Kunstgeschichte von Italien, Basle 1898.

R. Buscaroli, La Pittura di Paesaggio in Italia, Bologna 1935.

Max Dvořak, Italienische Kunst II, Munich 1928.

Heinrich Kretschmayr, Geschichte von Venedig, III, Gotha 1934.

Giulio Lorenzetti, Venezia e il suo Estuario, Venice 1926.

J. Lermolieff (G. Morelli), Kunstkritische Studien über italienische Malerei, 3 volumes, Leipzig 1890/93.

H. Tietze and E. Tietze-Conrat, The Drawings of the Venetian Painters of the XVth and XVIth centuries, New York, 1944.

Adolfo Venturi, La Storia dell'Arte Italiana, Milan, esp. 9/III, 1928.

Lionello Venturi, Italian Paintings in America, 1933.

E. Zimmermann, Die Landschaft in der venezianischen Malerei, 1893.

PAINTINGS

All measurements are given in inches, first height, then width

ANCONA, MUSEO CIVICO

Madonna and Child ; below, two saints and a donor. On wood. Signed : Aloyxius Gotius Ragusinus Fecit MDXX. Titianus Cadorinus pinxit.—From the church of San Francesco at Ancona. The two saints are St. Francis, and probably not, as is usually assumed, St. Blasius, but the donor's patron saint, Aloysius. In the background lagoon landscape with St. Mark's and the Ducal Palace. The first picture signed by Titian with a date added.
Figure 49 (48).

ANCONA, SAN DOMENICO

Christ on the Cross with the Virgin, St. John and St. Dominic. On canvas. Signed : Titianus Fecit. Mentioned by Vasari in 1567, probably painted during the first half of the sixties.
Figure 236.

ANTWERP, MUSEUM

St. Peter enthroned, with Jacopo Pesaro and Pope Alexander VI. On canvas. Crowe and Cavalcaselle and others doubt whether the inscription is genuine : Ritratto di uno di casa Pesaro in Venezia che fu fatto Generale di Santa chiesa. Titiano F.
The picture was seen by Van Dyck in Venice at the beginning of the 17th century and copied by him in his sketch-book (Chatsworth). At one time in the collection of King Charles I of England, it then passed to Spain, to the convent of San Pasqual in Madrid. In 1823 it was presented by King William I of Holland to the Antwerp Museum. Dated by several critics as late as 1512, or 1520, in my opinion an early production, perhaps finished (in the right half) after an interruption of several years.
Figure 1.

ASCOLI PICENO, MUSEUM

Stigmatization of St. Francis. On canvas. 118 x 69¾ inches. Signed : Titianus Vecellius Cadur. From the church of San Francesco in Ascoli, where Doctor Desiderio Guidone endowed in 1561 the chapel in which it was hung. This date is generally assumed to be that of the painting, the condition of which appears from reproductions to be very unsatisfactory.
Reproduced in Suida, Plate CCIIIa.

⟨AUGSBURG, COLLECTION OF PRINCE FUGGER-BABENHAUSEN

Charles V in armour. On canvas. 47 x 36 inches. Inscription : Carolus V. D. G. Roma, Iper. anno 1548. Copy of a portrait by Titian which, to judge by the Emperor's features, might be the first he painted in 1533 at Bologna. Suida ascribes the copy to a painter of the manner of Moro. The same collection contains a pendant in the portrait of Emperor Ferdinand I, which too is probably derived from an original by Titian (reproduced in Klassiker [5], p. 285).
Figure 311.⟩

BALTIMORE, MD. (U. S. A.), MUSEUM, J. EPSTEIN COLLECTION

Portrait of a Man. On canvas. Signed : Titiani opus MDLXI. Formerly in the following collections : Herman de Zoete ; Pickhurst Mead, Hayes, England ; Charles Brinsley Marlay, Mullingar, Ireland. See A. L. Mayer in Belvedere V, p. 184, and Tatlock in Burlington Magazine XLVII, p. 222.
Figure 240.

⟨BERGAMO, ACCADEMIA CARRARA

Head of a Girl, from the Battle of Cadore. Oil on paper. 14¼ x 12 inches. According to inscription on the back was transferred in 1809 from wood to canvas. Acquired in 1869 from the Lochis Gallery. By O. Fischel in Kunstchronik 1922, p. 411 (with reservations) and by Hourticq, Giorgione, pp. 167 seqq. (more definitely) considered to be a remnant of Titian's picture in the Sala del Gran Consiglio in the Ducal Palace, or of the corresponding cartoon. The style points rather to a copy made after 1550, perhaps by Leonardo Corona.
Reproduced in Klassiker [5], p. 84.⟩

BERLIN, KAISER FRIEDRICH MUSEUM

Girl with dish of fruit. On canvas. Acquired in 1832 from the collection of Abbot Celotti in Florence. The older writers held this to be a portrait of Lavinia and connected i with a letter of Argentina Rangona di Pallavicini written from Modena on April 26th, 1549, in which a portrait of Lavinia by Titian is mentioned. This was refuted by Hadeln, Pantheon 1931, p. 82, who does consider it to be not a portrait, but a late example of the series of female half-figures. Perhaps the information that in 1567/68 Titian presented Jacopo Strada with a " Pomona ", may be connected with this picture. According to Crowe and Caval- caselle the hand of Orazio Vecelli may be detected.
Figure 219.

Venus with Cupid and the Organ-player. On canvas. Signed: Titianus f. Purchased in 1915, apparently from a Bourbon collection. The organ-player has the features of Philip II. See Bode in Berliner Museen XXXIX, p. 93. This version of a subject very much in favour in Titian's circle is superior to most others, but even so hardly a full autograph. In Berliner Museen XLVII, p. 210, Bode published another version of the painting, in a private col- lection, which he considered as good as the one in Berlin.
Figure 175.

Portrait of Admiral Giovanni Moro. On canvas. Inscription (apparently of later date): Joannes Maurus Generalis Maris Imperator MDXXXVII. Purchased in Venice in 1841. A. Venturi (Collezione Crispi) and H. Mendelsohn, Dossi, p. 118, ascribe it to Dosso Dossi. Fischel and Suida think the date in the inscription refers to some event in the life of the Admiral, and date the painting about 1520. Ricketts and others ascribe it to the thirties.
Figure 128.

Portrait of a Bearded Man. On canvas. Signed: Ticianus f. Acquired in 1821 from the Solly collection. Before the signature came to light during cleaning, it was held to be by Tintoretto.
Figure 135.

Self-portrait. On canvas. Formerly in Casa Barbarigo di San Raffaele, Venice, then in the Solly collection; acquired by the Museum in 1821. The picture was dated about 1550 by Gronau and A. Venturi, in consideration of the age of the subject, and was held by them to be unfinished. Ricketts dates it about 1558/60. Suida for stylistic reasons will not admit a date prior to 1560, mentions that in 1566 Vasari saw a portrait of this kind in Titian's house which had been painted four years before, i. e. in 1562, and maintains that this must have been the Berlin picture. The same opinion is held by Foscari, Iconografia, p. 16.
Figure 195.

Portrait of Clarissa, daughter of Roberto Strozzi. On canvas. Signed: Titianus F. Annor. II. MDXLII. Acquired in 1878 from the Palazzo Strozzi in Florence.
The iconography of this picture is dealt with exhaustively by Gronau in the Jahrbuch der Preussischen Kunstsammlungen XXVII, pp. 7 seqq. This, the only portrait of a child by Titian which has been preserved, is described and effusively praised by Aretino in a letter to Titian dated July 6th, 1542.
Figure 159.

BESANÇON, MUSEUM

Portrait of Nicholas Perrenot Granvella. On canvas. The picture was painted at Augsburg in 1548 and remained in the possession of the Granvella family until purchased by the Museum. The pendant portrait of Granvella's wife has disappeared. Despite injuries and overpainting it must, according to Gronau, be considered one of the artist's finest works, whereas Crowe and Cavalcaselle are rather doubtful as to its authenticity, and A. Venturi (9/VII, 766) attributes it to Scipione Pulzone under the influence of Titian.
Figure 189.

BOSTON, MUSEUM OF FINE ARTS

Portrait of a Gentleman holding a book. On canvas. Signed: Ticianus. Coll. C. M. Majorca Montillaro, Conte di Francavilla, Palermo; Frederic D. Pratt, Long Island, N. Y. The identification of the model (in an eighteenth century inscription on the back of the canvas) as Giovanni Paolo Baglione of Perugia has been universally rejected. The attribution to Titian was, however, almost universally accepted, see Edgell in Boston Museum of Fine Arts Bulletin 1943, p. 407. In my opinion the portrait is more probably the work of a follower. The authentic portraits by G. B. Pace show the same characteristics as this picture: the stiff and conventional posture, the petty interest in details of costume and ornaments, the peculiar staring gaze.

BOSTON, ISABELLA STEWART GARDNER MUSEUM

Rape of Europa. On canvas. Signed: Titianus P. Painted for King Philip II. Mentioned in a letter dated June 19th, 1559 as having been begun, and in another dated April 26th, 1562, as having been sent to Spain together with a Christ on the Mount of Olives. In 1623, when plans were being made for a marriage between the Infanta Maria and Prince Charles (afterwards King Charles I) of England, it was intended to present it to the bridegroom, but when the plan came to nothing it remained in Spain and was acquired at the beginning of the eighteenth century by the Duc de Grammont. Subsequently it was in the collection of the Duke of Orleans and several English collections, and was eventually acquired by Mrs. Gardner in 1896 from the Earl of Darnley's collection at Cobham Hall. A popular monograph on the painting was published by Stuart Preston in the Gallery Books, No. 7, London, n. d. Figure 223.

BRESCIA, SS. NAZARO E CELSO

Altar-piece. Centre panel: Resurrection of Christ. At the sides above, Annunciation; below, left, Saints Nazarus and Celsus with the donor; right, St. Sebastian. On wood. Signed: Ticianus faciebat MDXXII. The altar-piece was begun in 1520 by order of the Papal Legate Altobello Averoldo, and the St. Sebastian—as can be gathered from the correspondence between the Ferrarese ambassador Tebaldo and Alfonso d'Este—was finished in the same year. The inscription on the Sebastian side-panel refers to the completion of the whole altar-piece. Drawings for the picture in Berlin and Frankfurt am Main (Figures 51, 53). Figures 54 (52, 55, 56, 57).

(BRESCIA, TOWN HALL

Three ceiling pictures. By contract dated October 3rd, 1564, Titian undertook to deliver three ceiling pictures to the Town Hall of Brescia, the main hall of which was decorated with perspective paintings by Cristoforo Rosa. The detailed programme for this work was sent to Titian in the following year. The paintings were to represent an allegory of Brescia between Mars and Minerva, Vulcan's Forge (a reference to the city's manufacture of arms), and Ceres and Bacchus. In the autumn of 1568 they were brought to Brescia by Orazio. A long-drawn-out dispute over the payment ensued, because the purchasers were not convinced that the paintings were by Titian's own hand. They were destroyed when the Town Hall was burnt on January 18th, 1575. Only the Vulcan's Forge is preserved in an engraving, attributed by Mariette to Melchior Meier. From this engraving we see that Titian adhered literally to the instructions in the programme, which has come down to us in Patrizio Spini's ' Supplemento delle Historie Bresciane di M. Helia Cavriola ', 1744, p. 331. See also Memorie intorno alle pubbliche fabbriche della Città di Brescia, raccolte da Baldassare Zamboni, Brescia 1778, pp. 75 seqq. and 139 seqq. Figure 317.)

BUDAPEST, MUSEUM OF FINE ARTS

Portrait of Doge Marcantonio Trevisan. On canvas. 40¾ x 34 inches. Acquired with the collection of Count Janos Palffy. A portrait of this Doge by Titian is mentioned by Pietro Aretino in November, 1553, and was paid for in the following year. Hadeln in Pantheon 1931, p. 489, doubts its authenticity while Suida accepts it. Hadeln's objections seem to me justified. Reproduced in Suida, Plate CCIIa.

Portrait of Vittoria Farnese. On wood. 31½ x 24¼ inches. From the collection of Count Janos Palffy. B. Berenson, Gazette des Beaux-Arts 1926, and Gombosi, Preussisches Jahrbuch 1928, pp. 55 seqq., claim that this is a Titian and refer to an entry in a Farnese inventory of 1680. Previously attributed to Pulzone, Pontormo or Allori, and by Suida, Pantheon 1936, p. 102, to Salviati. According to A. L. Mayer, Gazette des Beaux-Arts, s. VI, vol. 18, p. 309, the painting may be the copy by a Parmesan painter from Titian. At any rate, the picture is not Venetian and has no connection with Titian. Reproduced in Suida, Plate CXLVIII.

CAMBRIDGE, FITZWILLIAM MUSEUM

Tarquin and Lucretia. On canvas. Signed: Titianus F. A painting of this subject, probably the one engraved by Cornelis Cort in 1571, is mentioned in a letter of Titian dated August, 1571 as having been sent to King Philip II. Until the beginning of the 19th century it remained in Spain; it then came into the possession of Joseph Bonaparte and after passing through a number of English collections was acquired by Fairfax Murray, who presented it in 1918 to the Fitzwilliam Museum. (Another picture of the same subject is mentioned by the Anonimo del Tizianello as belonging to Lord Arundel, who presented it to Charles I; on the sale of the latter's collection it passed in 1649 to Mazarin and then to Louis XIV, and appears in the inventories of royal property until it was ceded to the Museum at Bordeaux in 1802. Florence Ingersoll-Smouse in the Gazette des Beaux-Arts 1926, p. 89, explains how the two pictures were previously confused and mentions that the second copy had always been in bad condition and was further damaged by fire in 1870. It is now no longer in Bordeaux.) Figure 275.

CASTEL ROGANZUOLO, NEAR CENEDA, PARISH CHURCH

Altar-piece (Virgin and Child, with St. Peter and St. Paul at the sides, and above Pietà). This altar-piece, for which payments were made from 1543 to 1560, partly in money and partly in natural produce, was placed in position in 1549. Despite the reliable documentary evidence, Crowe and Cavalcaselle definitely denied that it was a Titian. Gronau accepted Gardin's refutation of this theory (Antonio Gardin, Errori ... nella Storia Critica della Pala di Tiziano a Castel Roganzuolo, Florence 1883). During the war the painting, with the exception of the Pietà, was buried in order to save it from the Austrian troops, and was completely ruined in consequence. A. Moschetti, I Danni ai Monumenti e alle Opere d'Arte delle Venezie, 1932, pp. 321 seqq. (ill.)

CHATSWORTH, COLLECTION OF THE DUKE OF DEVONSHIRE

Portrait of a Young Man. On canvas. 38¹/₄ x 30 inches. Held by some writers to be a Tintoretto. In the appendix to the catalogue of the 1915 Burlington Fine Arts Club exhibition, Suida dates it between 1530 and 1540. After having seen the original I too reject the attribution to Titian, as did also A. L. Mayer in Gazette des Beaux-Arts, s. VI, vol. 18, p. 304.

CHICAGO, ART INSTITUTE

Mythological Group ('The Wemyss Allegory'). On canvas. 51¾ x 61 inches. Earl of Wemyss, Gosford House, Scotland; Wildenstein Gallery, Paris & New York; Thyssen Collection, Munich; Wildenstein Gallery; Ch. Worcester, Chicago.

The painting was highly praised by W. R. Valentiner and L. Venturi, passed over in silence by Suida and myself (first edition, under New York, Wildenstein; at that time I had not seen the original) and emphatically rejected by Crowe and Cavalcaselle, whose judgment is endorsed by Zarnowski in Rivista d'Arte. S. 2, 17, 1935, p. 201, by Panofsky, and by E. Tietze-Conrat, who in Art Bulletin XXVII, 1945, pp. 269 seqq. rediscussed the whole matter in full. Her results, which I accept, were that the invention of the painting (which incidentally is heavily impaired by later restoration, probably made in England in the eighteenth century and possibly by Sir Joshua Reynolds) goes back to one by Titian, which has however been reversed by an imitator. Furthermore, that the imitator in question may be Titian's pupil Damiano Mazza, a corresponding composition by whom was described by Ridolfi (I, 224) as existing in the Palazzo Donà in Venice. The artistic figure of Mazza, most probably the author of the 'Ganymede' in the National Gallery, London, is, however, too uncertain to justify an outright attribution to him of the painting.

CINCINNATI, O. (U. S. A.), MUSEUM

Portrait of King Philip II. On canvas. From the Barbarigo-Giustiniani Collection in Padua, which was derived from Titian's estate. Afterwards Collection Lenbach, Munich, and Mrs. Thomas I. Emery, Cincinnati.

The relationship between this painting and the portrait of the king has been discussed by A. L. Mayer, Münchner Jahrbuch, n. s. II, and again by E. Tietze-Conrat, in the Art Bulletin XXVIII, 1946, p. 82. Mayer dated the portrait around 1556, about three years after the portrait of Philip in the Rasch Collection, Stockholm. It seems however more likely that the canvas in Cincinnati is Titian's modello kept in the studio for further replicas (among them the Rasch portrait) and that it was reworked to look more like a regular portrait, perhaps on the occasion of its passing to the Barbarigo. At that time the clumsy crown was added, which never appears in any of Titian's other portraits of potentates.
Figure 215.

COPENHAGEN, STATENS MUSEUM FOR KONST

Portrait of a Beardless Man. On canvas. 31¹³/₁₆ x 26¹/₄ inches. See Fr. Beckett, Kunst Museets Aarsskrift 1914. This painting, the original of which I saw only after the publication of the first edition of this book, is in my opinion an early autograph by Titian, around 1513/14, as Suida too (pl. XXX) assumes.
Figure 5.

Portrait of a Man with a long Beard. On canvas. 44 x 36³/₄ inches. Published by O. Fischel in Kunst Museets Aarsskrift 1926/28 and Eric Zahle, Italiensk Kunst i Danmark, Copenhagen 1934, 30. The painting impressed me favourably at the Mostra in Venice 1935 (No. 92), but having re-examined it ten years later, I do no longer see Titian's characteristics in it.

DETROIT (U. S. A.), INSTITUTE OF ARTS

Judith. On canvas. 44¹/₄ x 37 inches. Collection Cornwallis West, London. Most critics dwell on the puzzling contrast between the smooth and finished head of Judith and the extremely loose technique in the lower part of the picture. The catalogue of the collection puts this contradictory impression as follows: from the last period of the artist, about 1570, but the figure of the Judith begun earlier, about 1550. And Suida says: late version of a composition from the 1530's. The invention is certified for Titian's circle by Vorsterman's engraving of 1660 and by several paintings using approximately the same composition, though representing Salome. Their style points to the middle of the sixteenth century. The gap between the two halves may best be bridged if we presume that a modello of Titian—of the type of the Lucretia in Vienna—was finished by assistants to make it a complete painting.

Portrait of a Man with a flute. On canvas. Signed: Titianus F.—From the collection of Baron von Stumm, Berlin. First noticed as a late work by Hadeln in Burlington Magazine, 1926, November.
Figure 239.

DETROIT (U.S.A.), EDSEL FORD COLLECTION

Portrait of a Bearded Man. On canvas. 31¼ x 27⅝ inches. Formerly Brownlow Collection, London. Gronau's identification, in Art in America XXV, 1937, p. 93, of the painting as the one mentioned in Ridolfi (I, 201) as existing in the house of C. Orseti seems convincing, not so, however, his identification of the model as Andrea Navagero, who was librarian of the Marciana from 1516 to 1524. At any rate the classification of the portrait as an early work of Titian seems correct.

DETROIT (U.S.A.), EDGAR B. WHITCOMB COLLECTION

Portrait of the Grand Chancellor Andrea de' Franceschi. On canvas. Formerly in the Viardot collection. Of this picture several variants exist, one of them, without the hands, formerly in the Earl of Wemyss Collection, now in the National Gallery, Washington (see there), another showing the same model together with Titian, at Windsor Castle. For the relationship between these paintings, see Washington. The version in Detroit, whose Tintorettesque character was emphasized by Holmes (Burlington Magazine 1929, p. 159), is in my opinion a copy after Titian's original by a painter trained or influenced by Tintoretto. (Even Tintoretto himself occasionally made copies from Titian's portraits, as recorded by Ridolfi.)

DRESDEN, GEMÄLDEGALERIE

The Tribute Money. On wood. Signed: Ticianus F.—Acquired from the art-collections of the Dukes of Modena in 1746.
According to Vasari, the picture was originally on the door of a chest in Alfonso d'Este's palace at Ferrara, but he does not, as several writers have maintained, say that it was painted in 1514. While Crowe and Cavalcaselle, Morelli, Philips and others date it between 1508 and 1514, and Oskar Hagen (Zeitschrift für Bildende Kunst 1918, p. 233), even places it in '1507 rather than 1508', Ricketts suggests a somewhat later date, for which Hetzer (Frühe Gemälde) has given more detailed reasons. The latter places it after 1516, very close to the 'Assunta', and Suida agrees with him in this. A. L. Mayer in Gazette des Beaux-Arts, s. VI, vol. 20, p. 308, points to the fact that the painting has been cut all round, as an old replica in the Accademia di San Luca in Rome confirms.
Figure 25.

Landscape with Venus in repose. On canvas. 29½ x 34 inches. Acquired in 1697 from the French dealer C. le Roy. Morelli identifies it as the Venus which Marcantonio Michiel saw in 1525 at the house of Hieronimo Marcello in Venice and which Boschini and Ridolfi also saw in the Palazzo Marcello. Since Morelli the picture has been generally attributed to Giorgione, but recently this theory has been opposed by Hourticq, Jeunesse, p. 247, and Suida (see also Suida, Giorgione, Nouvelles attributions, Gazette des Beaux-Arts 1935, September-October). For reconstructions of the original appearance of the picture see also Carlo Gamba, Dedalo IX, p. 205, and Hans Posse in Preussisches Jahrbuch LII, pp. 29 seqq., where the X-ray photograph is reproduced. For the previous history of the picture see Fogolari, La Venere di Dresda è quella di Giorgione in Casa Marcello? in Ateneo Veneto 1933/34, p. 232. I myself still believe that it was painted by Giorgione, and that Titian merely finished it (see my Tizian, Leben und Werk).
Figure 294.

The Man with the palm-branch. On canvas. Inscription: MDLXI Anno... Natus aetatis suae XLVI Titianus Pictor et Aeques Caesaris.—Purchased from Casa Marcello, Venice, before 1753. According to Cook (Burlington Magazine vol. 6) the sitter is the painter Antonio Palma, nephew of Palma Vecchio and father of Palma Giovane. Gronau and the catalogue of the 1935 Venice exhibition agree with this supposition, which, however, has been disputed by Tscheuchner (Repertorium XXIV), who thinks that the box on the window-ledge is not a colour-box but a medicine-case, and draws attention to traces of a halo; according to his theory the subject is a apothecary or doctor who caused himself to be painted as a saint in his profession.
Figure 241.

Portrait of Titian's daughter Lavinia. On canvas. Inscription: Lavinia Tit. V. F. Ab. Eo. P.—
Acquired in 1746 from the collection of the Dukes of Modena, who brought it from Ferrara
at the beginning of the 17th century.
The dating of the picture is given with few variations as about 1558. Hadeln, who has made
(Pantheon 1931) the most exhaustive studies of the portraits of Lavinia, thinks that this is her
best documented portrait and dates it in the latter half of the fifties.
Figure 244.

Portrait of a Young Woman (the so-called 'Lavinia as bride'). On canvas. Acquired in 1746
from the ducal gallery in Modena. The identification of the subject with Titian's daughter
Lavinia has been refuted by Hadeln in Pantheon 1931, p. 82; he also corrects the supposition
that the flag-shaped fan is a part of a bride's costume. Some writers consider that the picture is
a copy of a lost original by Titian which also served as basis for the copy by Rubens in Vienna.
Figure 245.

ESCORIAL, MONASTERY OF ST. LAWRENCE

Adoration of the Magi. On canvas. The painting, one of several versions existing, is traceable
in Spain since 1559 and in the Escorial since 1574. A. L. Mayer in Burlington Magazine vol. 71,
p. 178, set forth cogent arguments for considering this the original. Unfortunately no photograph of the painting is available.
Figure 242.

Last Supper. On canvas. Sent to King Philip II in 1564 after seven year's work; a painting of
the same subject which was burnt in 1571 in SS. Giovanni et Paolo was probably a preparatory
work. On its arrival at the Escorial, the painting was found to be too large and was cut in
order to fit it to the wall. Whether a smaller workshop repetition in Milan, which has rich
architectural additions above, justifies assumptions as to the original appearance of the Escorial
picture, is doubtful, as Jan Muller's engraving after Titian's imitator Gillis Coignet shows the
composition without the architectural additions, which may perhaps have been first inspired
by Paolo Veronese's version of the theme. A. L. Mayer in Gazette des Beaux-Arts, s. VI,
vol. 20, p. 299, discusses on the ground of an old copy in the Bridgewater House in London
(ill. l. c., p. 292) the alterations suffered by the painting. The Escorial picture, so far as the
bad state of preservation permits one to form an opinion, is mostly workshop painting.
Figure 243.

Christ on the Mount of Olives. On canvas. 1559/62. With considerable participation of workshop assistants.
Figure 262.

Christ on the Cross. On canvas. A late picture.
Figure 257.

St. Jerome. On canvas. $72^{1}/_{2} \times 67$ inches. A painting of this subject was sent to King Philip on
September 24th, 1575. The composition, a development of the St. Jerome in the Brera, has
been compared by Hetzer with Dürer's woodcut of 1512. The state of the painting does not
allow one to judge whether any part of it is by Titian's own hand.
Reproduced in Suida, CCIIb.

Martyrdom of St. Lawrence. On canvas. Vasari mentions the picture, on which Titian began to
work in 1564, among those which he saw in their preliminary stage at Titian's house in 1566,
and also refers to Titian's intention to send it to the King of Spain. A letter of Titian to
Philip II, dated December 2nd, 1567, proves that it had then been dispatched. It was placed
on the high altar of the old church in the Escorial and is a variant of the painting in the
Gesuiti at Venice. The differences between the latter and the Escorial version are exhaustively
dealt with by E. von Rothschild in Belvedere 1913, II, p. 11. Cornelius Cort's engraving of
1571 does not agree completely with either version.
Figures 258 (259).

FERRARA, CASA ORIANI

Portrait of Lodovico Ariosto. On canvas.—Contemporary sources already mention that a
portrait of Ariosto by Titian remained in possession of the family.
The identity of the subject is proved by the striking likeness between the painting and the
woodcut portrait of the poet, based on a drawing by Titian, which was first published in the
1532 edition of the Orlando. In addition to this a number of repetitions of the portrait have
always been known, and Georg Gronau in Burlington Magazine 1933, II, p. 194, has given an
exhaustive exposition of the reasons for considering this painting as the original on which such
repetitions were based. He also establishes the fact that Titian had frequent opportunities
of painting Ariosto's portrait, specially at the time when he was working in Ferrara on the
mythological paintings for Alfonso d'Este. For stylistic reasons, Gronau places the painting
near the so-called Allegory of Avalos in Paris and the Ippolito de' Medici in Palazzo Pitti.

FLORENCE, MUSEO NAZIONALE

Mosaic picture of Cardinal Pietro Bembo. Signed: Francesco e Valerio Zuccati 1542. In Burlington Magazine 1936, p. 281, Suida emphatically repeats his assertion, previously given in his book, that this mosaic is based on a work by Titian.
Figure 295.

FLORENCE, PALAZZO PITTI

Adoration of the Shepherds. On wood. 37 x 44¼ inches. Brought from Urbino to Florence in 1631 with the inheritance of Vittoria della Rovere. It is usually identified with the painting of this subject which Titian is said to have painted in 1532 for Francesco Maria della Rovere. Mary Pittaluga (Dedalo XIII, p. 297) denies that the composition and execution are Titian's, but Suida assigns both to him. That this is perhaps a smaller repetition by a minor painter after an idea of Titian's in the twenties, is set forth in detail in the Jahrbuch der Kunsthistorischen Sammlungen, N. F. X., 1936. Gronau in Bolletino d'Arte 1936/37, pp. 289 seqq., reiterates his opinion that this is the painting repeatedly mentioned in the correspondence of the Dukes of Urbino to Titian, delivered by him in 1533 and listed in 1631 among the paintings that passed from Urbino to Florence. Another repetition of the composition, much closer to the original version, but also probably not by Titian's own hand, is at Christ Church College, Oxford (see T. Borenius, Pictures by the Old Masters in the Library of Christ Church, Oxford 1916).
Figure 323.

St. Mary Magdalen. On wood. Signed: Titianus. Brought from Urbino to Florence in 1631 with the della Rovere inheritance. Perhaps a second version of the picture which Titian painted in 1531 for Vittoria Colonna (see my Tizian, Leben und Werk). According to E. von Rothschild, Belvedere 1931, I, it must certainly be based on an antique Venus.
Figure 121.

The Concert. On wood. Acquired in 1654 by Cardinal Leopoldo de' Medici in Venice. For the various attributions to Giorgione, Titian, Domenico Campagnola, Sebastiano del Piombo, see Hetzer, Jugendwerke, p. 133, and Heinemann, p. 27. My own belief in Titians's authorship is explained in my book on Titian. E. Tietze-Conrat in Gazette des Beaux-Arts, s. 6, vol. 27, again pleaded for Sebastiano del Piombo, while T. Hetzer in Thieme-Becker, vol. 34, p. 161, called the painting closer to Titian than to Giorgione.
Figures 20 (21, 22).

Portrait of Tommaso Mosti, Secretary to the Duke of Ferrara. Originally on wood, transferred to canvas. Inscription on the back, perhaps copied from an older one: Tommaso Mosti di anni XXV L'anno MDXXVI Titiano de Cadore pittore.
While Gronau and Hetzer date the painting in 1515, the catalogue of the Venice exhibition adheres to 1526. The latter date has been firmly upheld by Wart Arslan, Dedalo 1930, p. 136, who compares the painting with the two early male portraits in Paris, which, like Hourticq, he dates 1527. Ricketts makes the same comparison but places the whole group about 1520.
Figure 58.

Portrait of Cardinal Ippolito de' Medici. On canvas. The cardinal is depicted in Hungarian costume, in remembrance of the fact that in 1532 he was sent as Papal Legate to Vienna with three hundred musketeers, to take part in the campaign against the Turks. The picture was painted in 1532, or more probably at the beginning of the following year.
Figure 93.

Portrait of a man standing, with relief frieze in background. On canvas. The identification of the subject with the Ambassador Diego de Mendoza, whose portrait Titian, according to Vasari, painted in 1540/41 in full length, has no certain foundation, although the catalogue of the recent Venice exhibition considers it probable. On the right of the relief is a figure playing the lyre, probably derived from the same original as the figure below on the right in Marcantonio's engraving 'Quos Ego', B. 352.
Figure 188.

Portrait of Pietro Aretino. On canvas. The picture was sent by Aretino himself to Duke Cosimo I of Tuscany, in 1545, accompanied by a detailed letter. According to a letter from Aretin to Giovio, written in April of the same year, the picture had by then been finished.
Figure 166.

Portrait of the jurist Ippolito Riminaldi. On canvas. For unknown reasons this picture was called the 'Duke of Norfolk', and was later described as the portrait of a young Englishman. The identification of the subject as Ippolito Riminaldi is based on the really convincing remblance to the portrait bearing this name on the back in the Galleria San Luca in Rom (Venturi 9/3, p. 326). The attribution of this second portrait to Titian, proposed by Venturi (loc. cit.) and accepted by Suida and Elena Berti-Tosca (Bollettino d'Arte 1934/35, p. 440), seems unfounded on account of the inferior quality of the painting. The Florentine portrait is usually dated about 1540/45.
Figure 134.

' *La Bella.*' On canvas. Brought from Urbino to Florence in 1631. Thausing's suggestion (Zeitschrift für Bildende Kunst 1878) that this is a youthful portrait of the Duchess Eleanora
Gonzaga is now no longer accepted. Equally improbable is the hypothesis of Ozzola
(Bollettino d'Art II, p. 491), that this might be the picture which Titian painted in
1534/36 of Isabella d'Este. The woman represented is the same who served as model for
the 'girl in a fur' at Vienna, and perhaps also for the Venus of Urbino. In a letter dated
May 2nd, 1536, Duke Guidobaldo speaks of a 'portrait of a lady in a blue dress', which he
wanted Titian to finish perfectly in every way and together with the 'timpano'. The
suggestion that 'timpano' may mean a musical instrument has made identification more
difficult. Hadeln's statement that this word means a cover, such as Titian painted in the
allegorical picture in the Howard collection, eliminates the difficulty.
Figure 92.

⟨*Portrait of a Lady,* perhaps of the Duchess Giulia Varana of Urbino. On wood. 44 x 33¹/² inches.
Discovered by Gronau in the state apartments of the Palazzo Pitti and by him identified as
the portrait of his wife mentioned in 1546/47 in the correspondence of Duke Guidobaldo.
According to Johannes Wilde (Jahrbuch der Kunsthistorischen Sammlungen in Wien, N. F. IV,
p. 261) it is a copy by Rubens of an original by Titian. I too think that the Titianesque
character of the conception and the Flemish execution leave no room for doubt, but
A. L. Mayer in Gazette des Beaux-Arts, s. VI, vol. 18, p. 306, accepts the painting as
Titian's original.
Figure 308.⟩

Madonna della Misericordia. On canvas. Ordered in 1573 by the Duke of Urbino, who declared
that he would be satisfied with getting a picture made by an assistant since he presumed that
the Master himself was no longer working personally; but Titian promised to execute the
painting with his own hands. (See Gronau, Documenti Urbinati, pp. 66 seqq., 107 seqq.) It came
to Florence with the Urbino inheritance, was listed as by Titian in the earliest inventory, but
ever since as a bottega replica or as by Marco Vecelli. A surprising feature of the painting,
which the Duke described simply as ' *una Madonna in piedi che sotto il manto habbi numero
di gente* ', is that the family kneeling at the feet of the Madonna is not the Duke's, as one
would expect, but Titian's own, as already correctly stated by Gronau and more amply
discussed by E. Tietze-Conrat in the Art Bulletin 1946, p. 87. She also pointed out that in
spite of Titian's own protestations to the contrary the painting is a typical bottega production
in which various assistants may have had a share.

FLORENCE, UFFIZI

Madonna and Child, with St. John the Baptist und St. Antony Abbot. On wood. Signed:
Ticianus F. Formerly in the gallery of Archduke Leopold Wilhelm; sent from Vienna to
Florence in 1793 in exchange for another picture. Variously dated between 1505 and 1530.
The autograph character of the painting was rejected by Hetzer (Frühe Gemälde, p. 88), who
in his article in Thieme-Becker most emphatically reiterates his opposition to the attribution
to Titian.
Figure 85.

St. Margaret. On canvas. 46 x 39 inches. The picture, formerly attributed to Palma Giovane,
was claimed as a late work of Titian by R. Longhi (L'Arte XXVIII), and Suida supported
this opinion. Nevertheless the name of Palma seems appropriate to this coarse and at
the same time smooth painting, in which the technique of Titian's late period has been made
use of. For the resemblance confirming the ascription to Titian's bottega of the female type
with one of the women in the Madonna della Misericordia in the Palazzo Pitti, see E. Tietze-
Conrat in Art Bulletin 1946, p. 91.
Reproduced in Suida, Plate CCLXVII b.

⟨*Battle of Cadore.* On canvas. Copy in reduced dimensions of the mural painting by Titian in
the Sala del Gran Consiglio of the Ducal Palace in Venice. destroyed by fire in 1574. That
this copy, and not the engraving by Giulio Fontana (which is extended towards the right),
preserves the original composition, has been proved by E. Tietze-Conrat in Mitteilungen der
Gesellschaft für vervielfältigende Kunst 1925, p. 42.
Figure 302.⟩

Flora. On canvas. Sold by Don Alfonso López, Spanish ambassador in Amsterdam, to the
Grand Duke Leopold Wilhelm; sent in exchange from Vienna to Florence in 1793.
The woman depicted is described by Burckhardt (Kulturgeschichte der Renaissance[9] II, p. 87,
note 1), on grounds derived from books on costume and from Sansovino, as being in bridal
dress. The costume is, however, probably one of fantasy, and the painting is the last of the
series of early female half-figures. Gronau dates it as such about 1515, Spahn 1516/18, Crowe
and Cavalcaselle and Hetzer (Frühe Gemälde) shortly after 1520. A. L. Mayer in Gazette
des Beaux-Arts, s. VI, vol. 20, p. 308, expresses the opinion that the painting has been cut

all round although he admits that Sandrart's engraving, to which he refers, may have widened the composition according to the taste of the Baroque age.
Figure 19.

The Venus of Urbino. On canvas. Brought to Florence in 1631 with the Della Rovere inheritance. Mentioned in 1538 in the correspondence of Duke Guidobaldo II of Urbino, who was at that time Duke of Camerino, as a "naked woman". In March of that year he sent a messenger to Venice to fetch the picture.
Figure 107 (106).

Venus and Cupid. On canvas.—Presented by Paolo Giordano Orsini to the Grand Duke Cosimo II in 1618; later in Antonio de' Medici's collection and bequeathed with his other pictures to the Uffizi in 1632.
Figure 174.

Pope Sixtus IV. On canvas. Came from Urbino to Florence in 1631 with the Della Rovere inheritance. Closely related to the portrait of Julius II in Palazzo Pitti, with the same broad Venetian conception. See Gronau in Preussisches Jahrbuch XXV, supplement, and L. Burchard, ibid., XLVI, p. 121.
Figure 130.

Portrait of the Papal Legate Lodovico Beccadelli. On canvas. Inscription: Julius P. P. III. Venerabili frati Ludovico Episcopo Ravellen. apud Dominum Venetorum nostro et apostolicae sedis Nuntio, cum annum ageret LII, Titianus Vecellius faciebat Venetiis MDLII mense Julii.—Acquired from the collection of Cardinal Leopoldo de' Medici in 1675.
Figure 212.

Portrait of Francesco Maria della Rovere, Duke of Urbino. On canvas. Signed: Titianus F.— Came to Florence in 1631 with the Della Rovere inheritance.
From the correspondence of the Dukes of Urbino we learn that the picture was begun in 1536 and finished in 1538 (Gronau, Preussisches Jahrbuch 1904, supplement, p. 79). From the drawing in the Uffizi (Figure 101), we see that the portrait was originally conceived as a full-length figure and afterwards cut to make it a pendant to the portrait of the Duchess.
Figure 102.

Portrait of Eleanora Gonzaga, Duchess of Urbino. On canvas.—Came to the Uffizi in 1631 with the Della Rovere inheritance. Painted in 1538. See above, under Portrait of Duke Francesco Maria, to which that of his wife is now a pendant (Figure 102).
Figure 103.

Imaginary portrait of Caterina Cornaro. On canvas. Inscription on the back: Titiani Opus 1542, which according to a document of 1773 was copied from another inscription that had become difficult to read. From the inheritance of Don Antonio de' Medici, 1632. Generally supposed to be an old copy of an original Titian.
Figure 97.

HAMPTON COURT, H. M. THE KING

Lucretia stabbing herself. On canvas. 42¹⁵/₁₆ × 25 inches. Mentioned in the inventory of Charles I Collection as "a Mantua piece by Titian" and in Mazarin's inventory of 1661; published in Apollo VII, p. 47, and in Burlington Magazine 80/81, p. 185, accepted also by Berenson (as early and in great part authentic) and Suida. In my opinion too an early production.
Figure 45.

INDIANAPOLIS (U. S. A.), JOHN HERRON ART INSTITUTE

Portrait of Lodovico Ariosto. On canvas. 23¹/₂ × 18¹/₂ inches. First traceable in Sotheby Sale, January 29, 1930, No. 52 A; later collection Mr. and Mrs. Booth Tarkington, Indianapolis. The literature on the painting is listed in Wilbur D. Peat's article in the Bulletin of the Art Institute of Indianapolis, 1947, April, on the occasion of the acquisition of the painting. The identification of the sitter as Lodovico Ariosto first suggested in the Catalogue of the Exhibition "Four Centuries of Venetian Painting", Toledo, 1940, 65, is based on the resemblance to the portrait in the Casa Oriani, Ferrara (see there) and the woodcut, probably after a drawing by Titian, in the 1532 edition of the Orlando Furioso. Both, however, represent the poet at a considerably older age. The identification is further supported by Ridolfi's description (I, 162) of a portrait of Ariosto by Titian, then owned by the painter Niccolo Renier and probably our picture: "He painted the poet in a grand pose, wearing a coat lined with lynx and cut out at the breast so that folds of the shirt are shown with charming carelessness". Stylistic considerations, first of all the relationship with the portrait of Tommaso Mosti in the Palazzo Pitti, point to an origin of the painting around 1516, the year in which Titian's relations with Ferrara started.
Figure 23.

KANSAS CITY (U. S. A.), WILLIAM ROCKHILL NELSON GALLERY OF ART

Portrait of Antonio Perrenot Granvella, Bishop of Arras, afterwards Cardinal. On canvas. Signed: Titianus de Cadore. This picture had been lost for many years and came to light again in 1934 from the collection of R. A. Tattorn. It was evidently painted in the autumn of 1548, probably in Augsburg, and this is further proved, according to Gronau (Das unbekannte Meisterwerk I, p. 33) by the Augsburg clock on the table.
Figure 190.

KASSEL, GEMÄLDEGALERIE

Supposed portrait of Giovanni Francesco Aquaviva, Duke of Atri. On canvas. The subject, formerly held to be Alfonso d'Avalos, Marquis of Vasto, was identified as the Duke of Atri by Justi, Preussisches Jahrbuch XV, pp. 160 seqq., but this is disputed by Hadeln, Pantheon 1934, I, p. 16, who bases his argument on a recently discovered portrait of the Duke bearing the name in full. The date suggested on the basis of the earlier identification, 1552, is not very far from that of 1550 proposed by Crowe and Cavalcaselle on stylistic grounds. The same dog with scarcely any difference occurs again in the picture of a child with dogs in the van Beuningen collection at Rotterdam (Figure 260).
Figure 198.

KENOSHA, WIS. (U. S. A.), HEIRS OF NATHAN ALLEN

Portrait of Doge Andrea Gritti. On canvas. 33 x 26 inches. Formerly belonged to Gilbert Elliot, then to John Ruskin, London, and then to Trotti, Paris.
Reproduced in Suida, Plate LXXIII.

KREMSIER, ARCHIEPISCOPAL GALLERY

The Flaying of Marsyas. On canvas. First mentioned in 1670 on the occasion of an auction-sale in Vienna, purchased in 1673 by the Bishop of Olmütz. Has always been attributed to Titian (Eugen Dostal, Studien aus der Erzbischöflichen Galerie in Kremsier, Brünn, 1924; Anton Breitenbacher, Geschichte der Erzbischöflichen Galerie in Kremsier, 1925). The picture was mentioned by Frimmel, Blätter für Gemäldekunst 1909, supplement V, and given publicity by Benesch, Pantheon I, 1928, and Eugen Dostal, Das unbekannte Meisterwerk, I, Plate 26.
Figures 281 (282—283).

LENINGRAD, HERMITAGE

St. Mary Magdalen. On canvas. Signed: Titianus P.—Acquired in 1850 from Palazzo Barbarigo, where the picture must have come after Titian's death. According to a letter from Hernández to King Philip II, dated November 20th, 1561, Titian was then working on a Magdalen which went to Spain in December of the same year. The best specimen of the Magdalen, of which a number of repetitions were made, is said to have been that in the possession of Silvio Badoer. Of those still extant, that in Leningrad is generally considered to be the best.
Figure 253.

St. Sebastian. On canvas.—Acquired in 1850 from Casa Barbarigo, to which it came as part of Titian's estate.
Figures 265 (266).

Danaë. On canvas. 47¹/₄ x 74 inches. Workshop repetition of the Madrid picture. The old woman is very reminiscent of Palma Giovane. See Venturi, Storia dell'Arte 9/VII, p. 192.
Reproduced in Suida, Plate CCXIV b.

Portrait of Paul III. On canvas. 39 x 31¹/₄ inches. Acquired in 1850 from Casa Barbarigo-Giustiniani, Padua. The painting was rather unfavourably judged by Crowe and Cavalcaselle and by Ricketts, which seems in part justified by the heavy overpainting it has suffered. This may have taken place when Titian's modello kept in his studio was ceded to the Barbarigo. Compare E. Tietze-Conrat in Gazette des Beaux-Arts, s. VI, vol. 29, p. 77.

The Flight into Egypt. Formerly in the imperial castle of Gatchina and published by Baron Liphart in Starye Gody 1915, January-February, p. 10, as by Paris Bordone, an attribution also accepted by Berenson, Lists, p. 431. In Gatchina the painting was attributed to Titian and it is now exhibited under this name in the Hermitage. In Art in America 1941, pp. 144 seqq., E. Tietze-Conrat identified the painting with one described by Vasari (VII, 429), as a work from Titian's Paduan period preserved in the house of Andrea Loredan and more fully described by Ridolfi (I, 155) as follows: "... an oil painting of the Madonna with the Child in her arms who is travelling to Egypt, followed by Saint Joseph, with an angel guiding the beast of burden; and through the leafy landscape many animals pass, making obeisance to their Lord; and there is also a very naturalistic background (curtain) of trees and in the distance a soldier and shepherds.' To support her identification E. Tietze-Conrat pointed to similarities in the rendering of the figures to those in Titian's woodcut of c. 1515, the Sacrifice of Abraham. No adequate photograph was available.

Portrait of a Young Woman with feather hat and fur. On canvas. 38¹/₂ x 29¹/₂ inches. Formerly in the Crozat collection, 1772. Variant of the girl in a fur in Vienna (Figure 96), but later; according to Fischel, Klassiker, by Padovanino.
Reproduced in Suida, Plate CLXXXII.

LONDON, THOMAS AGNEW AND SONS LTD

St. George. On wood. Formerly Sir Audley Neeld Collection. Exhibited in the Burlington Fine Arts Club 1915, Titian and his Contemporaries, as 'Ascribed to Giorgione', but ascribed to Titian by Roberto Longhi. In my opinion Longhi is right and the painting which evidently is not a complete composition, can be identified as a fragment of the painting repressenting St. Michael, St. George and St. Theodore, which Titian executed between 1517 and 1522 as a present of the Venetian Government to Odet de Foix, Vicomte de Lautrec, Marshall of France and Governor of Milan. The documents referring to this long drawn-out affair are published in Sanudo, Diarii, vol. XXIV, pp. 303, 326, 364.
Figure 50.

LONDON, BRIDGEWATER HOUSE

The Virgin and Child with St. John Baptist and the Donor. On canvas. 35¹/₂ x 47¹/₂ inches. In their comments on the painting Crowe and Cavalcaselle hesitated between Palma Vecchio, Bernardo Licinio and Polidoro Lanzani; Morelli (München und Dresden, p. 26), on the other hand, accepted it as an early work by Titian executed probably 1510/12. Ricketts and A. L. Mayer, Gazette des Beaux-Arts, s. VI, vol. 18, pp. 305 seqq., place it in approximately the same period, while Suida (pl. LXXIX, p. 26) dates it somewhat later. Hetzer's sharp criticism of the painting, which he ascribes to an artist in the 1530's under Titian's influence, is in my opinion not outweighed by the contrary opinion of the other critics. Hetzer also considered the version in Glasgow, which Suida calls a bottega replica, certainly closer to Titian than the Bridgewater House painting. Ill. Suida, pl. LXXIX.

The Three Ages of Man. On canvas. Perhaps the picture which Vasari saw at Faenza in the house of Giovanni da Castel Bolognese, for whose father-in-law Titian painted it; afterwards in Augsburg, acquired in the latter half of the seventeenth century by Queen Christina of Sweden, sold in 1722 by the Princes Odescalchi to the Duke of Orléans, in whose gallery the picture remained until 1798. Among the slightly varying versions mentioned by Hetzer, Frühe Gemälde, pp. 49 seqq., the present picture is held to be the original, although Hetzer, as earlier Burckhardt, Beiträge², p. 466, note 1, considers it to be a copy. A. L. Mayer, Gazette des Beaux-Arts, s. VI, vol. 18, p. 305, insists on the autograph character of the painting, which he dates no later than 1512.
Figure 27.

Diana and Callisto. On canvas. Painted in 1559 for King Philip II, presented by Philip V in 1704 to the Marquis de Grammont, who took it with him to France. Remained until 1798 in the Galerie d'Orléans. Signed: Titianus F. After cleaning, the picture was reproduced with many details and discussed by Roger Fry and Kennedy North in Burlington Magazine, 1933. On its relationship to the replica in Vienna, see A. Stix in Jahrbuch der Kunsthistorischen Sammlungen in Wien XXXI, p. 335.
Figure 226.

Diana and Actaeon. On canvas. Sent to King Philip II in 1559 together with the Diana and Callisto, and presented with the latter in 1704 by King Philip V to the Marquis de Grammont. The latter presented it to the Regent and after the dispersal of the Galerie d'Orléans it went to England. Both pictures were to have been given to Charles I of England, on the occasion of his marriage to the Spanish Infanta, which, however, did not take place. The connection with the Callisto picture, whose subsequent destinies it shared, is only in the subject. The conception of the two pictures was not contemporaneous. Recently Roger Fry has written on the artistic character and Kennedy North on the technical elements of the picture (Burlington Magazine, 1933).
Figure 224.

Venus Anadyomene. On canvas.—Formerly in the collections of Queen Christina and the Duke of Orléans. Gronau dates this picture 1515/20 and identifies it with the picture of a 'bagno' mentioned in the correspondence between Titian and Alfonso d'Este in 1517. Most other writers date it later, as do Crowe and Cavalcaselle, while Phillips places it between the Bacchus and Ariadne and the Venus of Urbino. On the present state and technique of the picture see Kennedy North in Burlington Magazine, 1932/I; from the X-ray photograph it is clear that originally the head was turned in the other direction.
Figure 46.

LONDON, BUCKINGHAM PALACE

Landscape with Shepherd. On canvas. Gilbert, in Cadore or Titian's Country, London 1869, p. 352, tried to identify the landscape with the view from the Palazzo Pilloni in Belluno. Most writers doubt that this is an original Titian ; Wickhoff (Kunstgeschichtliche Anzeigen I, p. 116) assigns it to Domenico Campagnola, as does Zimmermann (Venezianische Landschaft, p. 127) ; L. Fröhlich-Bum (Jahrbuch der Kunsthistorischen Sammlungen in Wien XXXI, p. 199) gives it to Andrea Schiavone, Constable (Dedalo X) to Cariani ; R. Buscaroli, La pittura di paesaggio in Italia, Bologna 1935, thinks that it was executed by a pupil after a drawing by Titian. These negative opinions reflect the feeling that so pure a landscape lies outside Titian's limits, but the same might be said of the other painters suggested. The noticeably high format tempts one to think that this is only a fragment of a larger picture, in which the landscape with the flock of sheep would have occupied the same proportion of space as that in the similar representation in the Madonna with St. Catherine in the National Gallery. A comparison with the detail of the latter picture here reproduced (Figure 87) shows a stylistic difference which excludes Titian. The conception of the shepherd and flock is most akin to that of the Holy Family with the child John bringing the lamb in the Louvre (Klassiker[5], p. 259), which is usually attributed to Domenico Campagnola.
Figure 80.

LONDON, LORD HALIFAX

Portrait of a Beardless Man. On canvas. Formerly at Temple Newsam. First assigned to Titian by Gronau, Repertorium XXXI, p. 514, which is disputed by Hetzer, Frühe Werke, p. 127, and Fischel, in Klassiker ; attributed to Lorenzo Lotto by Hugo de Brunner, Burlington Magazine vol. 53, pp. 116 seqq. ; Heinemann, Ricketts and Suida attribute it to Titian about 1515. I am inclined to agree with them.
Figure 61.

LONDON, EARL OF HAREWOOD

Death of Actaeon. On canvas. Formerly in the collection of Archduke Leopold Wilhelm ; mentioned in 1559 in the correspondence between Titian and King Philip, but perhaps never sent to Spain. Was later in the Galerie d'Orléans, and recently in the possession of Sir Abraham Hume, Earl of Brownlow. (According to Klassiker[5] there were two versions of the same composition.) Hetzer, in Thieme-Becker vol. 34, p. 166, questions the authenticity of the painting.
Figure 225.

LONDON, FRANCIS HOWARD COLLECTION

Allegory. On canvas. Painted as a 'timpano' and first published by Hadeln in Burlington Magazine 1924, p. 179, as a work of Titian. There is an exhaustive iconographic study on the picture by Erwin Panofsky, Herkules am Scheidewege, Studien der Bibliothek Warburg 1930.
Figure 252.

LONDON, LADY LUDLOW

Portrait of Giacomo Doria. On canvas. Signed : Ticianus. Inscription : Giacomo Doria q(uondam) Augustini. Acquired by the previous owner, Sir Julius Wernher, from a private collection in Naples. First noticed by H. Cook, Burlington Magazine vol. 1, p. 185. Constable's description of the painting as undoubtedly by Titian's own hand, but a lifeless and superficial work, seems correct to me.
Figure 129.

LONDON, NATIONAL GALLERY

The Tribute Money. On canvas. 48 x 40½ inches. Signed : Titianus F. Formerly in the Soult collection, perhaps identical with the picture painted in 1568 which Titian mentions in his list of 1574 as having been dispatched. Attributed by Crowe and Cavalcaselle to Palma Giovane. Suida's warm support of its authenticity has recently been seconded by Sir Kenneth Clark, who had the painting thoroughly cleaned and put on exhibition as a work by Titian. Nevertheless in my opinion it still lacks the marks of an autograph and in the National Gallery too it is again listed as a bottega production.
Reproduced in Suida, Plate CCLXXI.

Christ appearing to Mary Magdalen. On canvas. 42½ x 35½ inches. From the Muselli collection, Verona. From 1727 to 1792 in the Galerie d'Orléans, since 1855 in the National Gallery. The objections to the attribution to Titian have been reviewed by Hetzer, Jugendwerke, p. 107, the relationship to Giorgione by G. M. Richter, Burlington Magazine 1934, II, pp. 4 seqq. I agree with the latter's opinion, that it is a picture begun by Giorgione and finished by Titian between 1511 and 1515. The group of houses on the hill to the right corresponds exactly with that in Giorgione's Dresden Venus (Figure 294).
Figures 292 (293).

The Holy Family, with worshipping Shepherds. On canvas. 41½x56 inches. Until 1810 in Palazzo Borghese, since 1831 in the National Gallery. Is noticed in Van Dyck's sketch-book. The authenticity of the picture, in which the Palmesque elements have often attracted attention, is doubted by many writers, especially by Hetzer, Frühe Gemälde, p. 110. Heinemann, p 14, suggests that the picture was begun by Titian in his early period, but left unfinished, that he returned to it again between 1517 and 1519, then definitely abandoned it, and that it was finished by some minor artist. More convincing is the comparison by Öttinger (in Magyar Müvészet 1931, IV) with Paris Bordone's Crema altar-piece, now in the Galleria Tadini at Lovere, in consequence of which he ascribes the London picture to Bordone.
Reproduced in Suida, Plate LXXVIII.

Madonna and Child with St. John and St. Catherine. On canvas. Perhaps identical with the picture mentioned in Malatesta's letter to Federigo Gonzaga, 1530. Later in the sacristy of the Escorial, in 1720 in the collection of the Duke de Noailles in Paris. Weaker version in Palazzo Pitti ; a copy, with slight variations, in the Vienna gallery, see Fröhlich-Bum in Jahrbuch der Kunsthistorischen Sammlungen in Wien XXXI.
Figures 86 (87).

Madonna suckling the Child. On canvas. Formerly in the Dudley and Mond collections. In Burlington Magazine 1928, p. 55, Hadeln discusses a Holy Family in the Henniker-Heaton collection, in which the central group is very similar to the National Gallery picture. He considers the former to be a preliminary study for the latter. As, however, the Joseph is taken from Raffael's Family of Francis I in the Louvre, one has the impression that it is not a sketch, but rather a composition by a later hand.
Figure 278.

Study for 'La Gloria'. On canvas. 51¾x39½ inches. Till 1808 in Madrid, then in the collections of Samuel Rogers, Lord Henry Vane and the Duke of Cleveland. Described by Crowe and Cavalcaselle as a copy of the Madrid picture. First claimed for Titian after cleaning by Hadeln and more fully discussed by Holmes in Burlington Magazine I, pp. 53 seqq. In this article the variations from the definite version and from Cornelis Cort's engraving of 1566 are fully set out. Palma Bucarelli in Gazette des Beaux-Arts 1935, II, 247, and A. L. Mayer in Bolletin de la Sociedad espagnola de excursiones 1935, XLIII, call the painting a pasticcio executed by Francisco Rizi.

Bacchus and Ariadne. On canvas. Signed : Ticianus F.—Painted in 1523 for Duke Alfonso d'Este of Ferrara ; went to the Aldobrandini family in 1598, and later to the Ludovisi collection in Rome. Came to the National Gallery in 1886. The correct interpretation of the subjectmatter and discovery of the literary source (Ovid combined with Catullus) are due to E. Wind, Giovanni Bellini's Feast of the Gods (Cambridge, Mass., 1948, p. 56 f.).
Figure 66.

Venus and Adonis. On canvas. 69x72 inches. Formerly in Palazzo Colonna, Rome, then in the Angerstein collection, London, and purchased together with the latter in 1824. The position of this version among the numerous other repetitions of the same composition is discussed by Holmes, Burlington Magazine XLIV, 1924, pp. 16 seqq., and A. L. Mayer in Münchner Jahrbuch, n. s. 4, 1925, pp. 16, 21 seqq. According to them the version in London which belongs to the larger and earlier type of this composition is perhaps the *modello* that remained in Titian's studio and after his death was acquired by Tintoretto, while the version in the Prado would be an autograph replica.

Votive picture of the Vendramin family. On canvas. According to the legacy inventory of 1641 once belonged to Van Dyck, since 1656 in the possession of the Dukes of Northumberland, from whom the National Gallery acquired it in 1929.
In Apollo II, September 1925, pp. 126 seqq., Gronau identified all the figures as members of the Vendramin family ; previously they were held to be of the Cornaro family ; as Gabriel Vendramin died in 1552, Gronau dates the picture about 1550. Others, however, date it in the early forties (Klassiker der Kunst), or about 1560 (Crowe and Cavalcaselle and Phillips). It has also been assigned by some to Tintoretto, a theory which has been refuted emphatically by Ricketts. According to A. L. Mayer, Gazette des Beaux-Arts, s. VI, vol. 18, p. 304, the painting was not completely finished and was restored by Sir Joshua Reynolds.
Figures 203 (204, 205).

Portrait of Man (the so-called Ariosto). On canvas. Signed : Titianus T. V.—Acquired in 1904 from Lord Darnley's collection at Cobham Hall.
The old traditional identification of the subject has been accepted by some writers but denied by several. Recently Gronau in Burlington Magazine 1933, II, p. 194, has reassembled all the arguments in refutation of this theory. Another identification, namely with the nobleman of the Barbarigo family whom Titian, according to Vasari, painted in a manner which might easily be confused with Giorgione, was first suggested by J. P. Richter, Art Journal 1895, p. 90. All those who believe that it is an authentic Titian place it at the beginning of his series of

portraits. These include, in addition to Crowe and Cavalcaselle and Gronau, Fry, Ricketts, A. Venturi, Heinemann and Suida. In Art Bulletin 1934, Cook and G. M. Richter favour the attribution to Giorgione, while L. Justi leaves the question open whether it is by Titian or Giorgione. Wickhoff, Gazette des Beaux-Arts 1904, p. 114, assigns it to Sebastiano del Piombo, a theory supported in general by Th. Hetzer, Die frühen Gemälde, 117. Recent thorough cleaning which rectored the light blue color of the doublet adds in my opinion to the Titianesque character.

It is worth noting that Rembrandt, as is proved by his 1640 self-portrait in London and also by the etched self-portrait of 1639, knew this picture, of which Sandrart also made a sketch when he was in the Netherlands. It may be identical with the picture called 'L'Ariosto Poeta' which according to the inventory of his estate in 1644 once belonged to Van Dyck. According to a letter from Vignon to François Langlois dated 1641 (Bottari IV, p. 303) it was at one time in the possession of the Ambassador López.
Figure 4.

Portrait of Doge Andrea Gritti. On canvas. Formerly in the Otto Gutekunst Collection. First noticed by Hadeln, Dogenbildnisse von Titian, in Pantheon 1930, p. 489, who, because it coincides with Tintoretto's substitute for Titian's votive picture of Andrea Gritti which was burnt in 1574, deems it to be a fragment or a repetition by the painter's own hand of the Titian picture. Nevertheless his votive picture must have had the simple composition shown in the woodcut made from it (Figure 303), in which the only difference is that the figure of Gritti is replaced by that of the next Doge but one, Francesco Donato, i. e. the Doge is kneeling in the usual way and is seen in sharp profile. This is confirmed by the drapery studies on the back of the drawing, related to this composition, of St. Bernardino in the Uffizi (Hadeln, Zeichnungen Titians, Plate 23), which correspond to the profile attitude of the Doge. There is consequently no reason to connect the portrait which Fiocco ascribes to Pordenone and Dussler rejects altogether, with Titian's votive painting. It may however go back to another representation of Gritti painted by Titian in the chapel of the Ducal palace and, in view of its entirely different colorscale, be a copy made by a member of the older generation (Catena?). Another version in Cambridge, Fitzwilliam Museum.

Portrait of a Woman (so-called Schiavona). On canvas. Signed: T... V... Acquired by the Gallery from the Sir Herbert Cook Collection, in Richmond, in 1945. In 1641 this picture had belonged to the Martinengo Colleoni family in Brescia and was described as by Titian: later it was in the Galleria Crespi at Milan. It was formerly ascribed to Giorgione and Licinio, but is nowadays considered by the great majority of writers to be a work of Titian. It is closely related to the so-called Ariosto in the National Gallery, London (Figure 4), and the young man in the Goldman collection in New York (Figure 2). The resemblance of the woman depicted to the young woman in the fresco of the newborn child in the Scuola del Santo (Figure 9) has often been remarked. The identification of the woman as Caterina Cornaro, suggested by Herbert Cook, Giorgione, pp. 74 seqq., is generally disputed.
Figure 3.

LONDON, FRANK SABIN

⟨*Double Portrait of the Emperor Charles V and the Empress Isabella.* On canvas. A picture of this kind is first mentioned in Titian's letter to Granvella of September 1st, 1548; it was one of the works which Charles V took with him in 1556 to Yuste (Pinchard in Revue Universelle des Arts III, p. 219), is mentioned in the Madrid inventories and was probably destroyed in the fire at the summer palace there in 1734; in any case since then it has disappeared. The present picture came to light a short time ago, and was described as a copy by Rubens after the lost original of Titian, by Alfred Scharf, Burlington Magazine 1935, I, p. 259.
Figure 313.⟩

Portrait of a friend of Titian. On canvas. Inscription: Di Titiano Vecellio singolare amico.— From the Lansdowne collection, London. Dated by Suida about 1530, by Wilde, Jahrbuch der Kunsthistorischen Sammlungen 1934, about 1540.
Figure 196.

LONDON, WALLACE COLLECTION

Perseus and Andromeda. On canvas. From the collection of King Philip II of Spain. Later perhaps belonged to Van Dyck, then to the Duc de la Vrillière, the Duc d'Orléans, Sir G. Page Turner, the Marquis of Hertford. Titian promised this picture to Philip II in a letter written in 1553, and it was probably dispatched in 1556. Dolce, whose Dialogue appeared in 1557, includes it among the paintings sent to Spain. Ricketts thinks the style too advanced for so early a date and suggests that it is a copy painted about 1565 of the picture painted for Philip. No other version, however, is known; a contemporary copy under the name of Tintoretto is in the Hermitage.
Figure 222.

LUCERNE, JULIUS BÖHLER

Portrait of a Young Man, supposed to be Titian's son Pomponio. On canvas. 41 x 34 inches. First brought to notice by Gronau in Zeitschrift für Bildende Kunst 1922, p. 67. The identification of the subject as Pomponio is based on the name inscribed on a later copy of the picture on copper. Gronau dates it about 1550, which may seem a little late.
Reproduced in Suida, Plate CCVIII b.

Portrait of Giovanni Francesco, Duke of Aquaviva. On canvas. 55¹/₂ x 40¹/₂ inches. Signed: *Titianus F.* Inscription giving name of subject and year 1551. A portrait of Aquaviva is mentioned in a letter from Pietro Aretino to the Duke in August 1552 (Lettere VI, fol. 89 verso). The picture was first brought to notice by Hadeln in Pantheon 1934, I, p. 16. The authenticity was most emphatically rejected by Hetzer (Thieme-Becker 34, 166), and not having seen the original I now prefer to leave the painting among the doubtful works.

LUGANO, BARON HEINRICH THYSSEN (SCHLOSS ROHONCZ DONATION)

Portrait of Antonio Anselmi. On canvas. On the back an old inscription, not in Titian's writing: (Ant)onius Anselmus Ann. 38 1550 (T)itianus F. Formerly in the Diercksen collection, Berlin. Discussed by Rintelen in Preussisches Jahrbuch XXVI, p. 202.
Figure 192.

MADRID, PRADO

The Fall of Man. On canvas. Signed: Titianus F.—Not mentioned in the correspondence between Titian and King Philip, and first heard of in the chapel of the Alcazar at Madrid, in the burning of which in 1734 it was much damaged, being afterwards extensively restored by Don Juan de Miranda. The dating of the picture varies in the different writers between 1560 and 1570; all draw attention to the fact that both figures are derived from much older motives.
Figure 270.

Salome holding the salver up. On canvas. 34¹/₄ x 31¹/₂ inches. Acquired in 1665 from the estate of the Marquis de Leganes and first mentioned in the inventory in 1666. A workshop repetition, with variations, of the girl with a dish of fruit in Berlin (Figure 219).
Reproduced in Suida, Plate CCXXVI a.

Adoration of the Magi. On canvas. 55¾ x 86¹/₂ inches. A picture of this subject is mentioned as having been dispatched in a letter from Titian to King Philip II dated April 2nd, 1561, but the version in the Prado, according to Beroqui, is not heard of before 1818. A. L. Mayer in Burlington Magazine 71, p. 178, considers it a copy, perhaps by Luca Giordano, of the original in the Escorial. It is certainly not an autograph by Titian.
Figure 242.

Rest on the Flight into Egypt. On canvas. Presented to Philip IV in 1644 by Don Ramiro Felipe de Guzman, Duque de Medina de las Torres, and mentioned in 1657 as being in the Escorial. A picture corresponding to this is described by Vasari as being in the collection of Titian's legal friend Assonica. Whether the latter is the Madrid version has not been definitely proved. On the one hand Assonica's picture is mentioned in Ridolfi's book of 1646 as still being in his possession, and the volume of engravings, Tabellae selectae et explicatae, by Carola Caterina Patina, 1691, states that this much-admired picture was lost in a shipwreck during the crossing to Spain. Lastly, a painting of this subject, likewise described as an 'Opera celebre', is mentioned as being in the monastery church of Montalto at Messina (Guida per la Città di Messina scritta dall'autore delle Memorie dei Pittori Messinesi, Messina 1826, p. 22). The high quality of the Madrid version made it seem probable to me that it is either the original, or a very exact replica. A. L. Mayer, Gazette des Beaux-Arts, s. VI, 18, p. 309, and Hetzer (Thieme-Becker 34, 163), however, reject the attribution to Titian and the identification with the Assonica painting. Another version, in a private collection in Austria (reproduced in Suida, Plate CCLVIII), might be the copy by Padovanino mentioned in the Platina book of engravings.
Figure 90.

Christ on the Mount of Olives. On canvas. 69¹/₄ x 53³/₄ inches. A painting of this subject was promised to King Philip by Titian in a letter dated June 19th, 1559. To which of the two versions traceable in the possession of the Spanish royal family from 1574 onwards this notice refers, is doubtful. In my opinion that in the Escorial (Figure 262) is much closer to Titian, whereas the Madrid version, in which the chief emphasis is laid on the huge figures of soldiers in the foreground, while the painting is a coarse imitation of Titian's late style, might be the work of a Spanish imitator. The Martyrdom of St. Lawrence by El Mudo (Francisco Navarete) in the Escorial betrays a similar style.
Reproduced in Suida, Plate CCLV.

Ecce Homo. On slate. Signed: Titianus. Perhaps the picture which Titian brought to Charles V at Augsburg in 1548 and which the latter took with him to Yuste; in 1574 in the Escorial,

in 1600 at the Alcazar, Madrid. Titian presented a repetition to Aretino at Christmas 1547. Repetitions at Chantilly and in the Ambrosiana.
Figure 206.

Ecce Homo. With three figures. On canvas. 39½ x 39½ inches. Comes from the Escorial, where it was held to be by Titian as early as 1574. According to Berenson an imitation of Titian by Jacopo Bassano in his youthful period; according to Madrazo by Leandro Bassano. Recently reclaimed for Titian by Suida in Vita Artistica II, 1928. In my opinion a typical imitation, because the style is reminiscent of Titian's at various periods. Repetition in Dresden and Burgos Cathedral.
Reproduced in Suida, Plate CCLXXI b.

Christ and Simon of Cyrene (full-length). On canvas. Signed: J. B. Titianus (?).—Not mentioned in Titian's list of the pictures delivered to Philip, 1574. First appears in the inventory of the Escorial in the same year. Most writers date the picture about 1560, only Ricketts places it in the forties while admitting retouches in the fifties. Wickhoff holds it to be a work of Palma Giovane (Kunstgeschichtliche Anzeigen 1904, p, 116); to me appears to be the work of a Spanish imitator of Titian.
Reproduced in Suida, Plate CCLXXII b.

Christ and Simon of Cyrene (in half-figure). On canvas. Signed: Titianus Aeques F.—According to Beroqui first mentioned in the inventory in 1666.
Dated by Fischel about 1560, by Suida about ten years later. According to Wickhoff it is, like the full-length composition, by Palma Giovane.
Figure 234.

Entombment. On canvas. Signed: Titianus Vecellius Aeques Caes. The picture was sent to King Philip II in 1559, to replace one of the same subject sent by Titian in 1556 which had been lost in transit. Unlike this picture, the earlier version was in half-figure. According to Foscari, Iconografia 19, Titian has painted himself as Joseph of Arimathea. Wickhoff is alone (Jahrbuch der Z. K. 1909, p. 24) in doubting the authenticity of the picture and attributing it to Palma Giovane.
Figure 249.

Entombment. On canvas. Signed: Titianus f.—From the Escorial. This picture, which Crowe and Cavalcaselle thought might be by a Spaniard, e. g. del Mazo, was claimed for Titian with particular emphasis and dated about 1570 by Roberto Longhi, Arte 1925, p. 40. Before this Charles Ricketts had already raised the question whether this might not be the picture which Vasari saw in Titian's house in 1566. Eugen von Rothschild advances the same suggestion in Belvedere 1931, p. 202, and draws attention to the fact that Bonasone's engraving of 1567 is not based on the lost version of the Entombment, as is suggested in Klassiker⁵, p. 205; the engraving merely varies the height of the Prado picture by the addition of the wall of rock. He therefore dates it about 1566.
Figure 250.

Christ appearing to Mary Magdalen (fragment). On canvas.—This fragment was found by Pedro de Madrazo in the Escorial; when and why the picture was dismembered is not known. The picture, of which the original composition has been preserved in a copy attributed to A. S. Coello in the Escorial, was painted by Titian in the summer of 1553 for Queen Maria of Hungary and sent to her in the Netherlands in the autumn of the following year. Another version, probably the modello, appears to have remained in the atelier, as Vasari mentions it on the occasion of his visit to Titian in 1566 and describes it as unfinished. This is confirmed by the fact that Van Dyck noted the composition in his Italian sketch-book.
Figure 216.

Mater Dolorosa with folded hands. On wood. Probably brought to the Emperor at Augsburg in 1550; from Yuste it passed to the Escorial.
Figure 191.

Mater Dolorosa with raised hands. On marble. Signed: Titia..s. Conceived as a pendant to the Ecce Homo (Figure 206) and sent to the Emperor in Flanders in September, 1554, together with the Gloria. There is a variant of this picture in the Carvallo collection in Paris.
Figure 207.

Madonna and Child with St. Anthony of Padua and St. Roch. On canvas. 36½ x 52½ inches. The picture is mentioned in 1657 as being in the sacristy of the Escorial, by the 'mano del Bordonon'. Since Morelli it has been generally assigned to Giorgione and still bears his name in the gallery. In more recent times it has been assigned by L. Venturi, L. Hourticq, R. Longhi and W. Suida to Titian. Crowe and Cavalcaselle included it among Pordenone's works, but also thought of Francesco Vecelli; Hetzer also (Frühe Gemälde, p. 24) denies the attribution either to Giorgione or Titian for reasons of quality. In any case it cannot, in my opinion, be by Titian, for both the conception of the heads and the arrangement of the figures are contrary to his. The comparison with the 'Gipsy-Madonna' and the picture of St. Mark in

the Salute, of which one or two motives remind us, only serves to emphasize the contrast with Titian's manner. Hourticq (Jeunesse, p. 118) claims to recognize a self-portrait of Titian in the St. Roch.
Reproduced in Suida, Plate XIII.

St. Margaret. On canvas. Signed: Titianus.—Sent by Philip II to the Escorial, mentioned in 1666 in the inventory of the Alcazar at Madrid.
Since Crowe and Cavalcaselle this picture has often been identified with that mentioned by Titian in a letter dated October 11th, 1552, as having been sent shortly before to Spain. As, however, the letter speaks of a portrait (ritratto) of St. Margaret, Gronau thinks that it must have been a half-figure, and he dates the Prado picture on stylistic grounds about fifteen years later, which seems to me evident. A. L. Mayer in Gazette des Beaux-Arts, s. VI, 18, p. 309, who too questions the earlier origin, identifies the painting with one in the collection of King Charles I and later sold to the King of Spain.
Figure 254.

'La Gloria' (Adoration of the Holy Trinity). On canvas. Signed: Titianus P.—Begun in 1551 and according to a letter of Titian dated September 10th, 1554, sent to the Emperor Charles V in the Netherlands. Two other versions of this composition are extant: a large copy, which Holmes in Burlington Magazine I, pp. 53 seqq., maintains to be a preliminary sketch for the Madrid picture (see London, National Gallery) and the engraving by Cornelis Cort of 1567, for the publication of which Titian obtained a privilege from the Venetian senate. In the picture appear portraits of Emperor Charles V, his wife Isabella, King Philip, Queen Maria of Hungary, and of Titian himself.
Figure 230.

Spain coming to the aid of Religion. On canvas. Signed: Titianus F. Sent to Philip II in 1575. A picture begun for Alfonso d'Este and left unfinished in the atelier after his death in 1534 was transformed into this allegory by Titian after 1566. The detailed description which Vasari, on the occasion of his visit in the above-mentioned year, gives of the picture then representing a mythological subject, makes the identification certain. In 1625 it was extensively restored by Vicente Carducho (see the Allegory of the Battle of Lepanto), but this hardly altered the composition; this is clear from the practically identical copy in the Galleria Doria, Rome. The meaning of the original composition as 'Capitulation of Vice before Virtue' was discussed by R. Wittkower in Journal of the Warburg Institute III, 138, where also the condition of the painting is circumstantially described by Neil MacLaren. Both statements, as well as the addition to the iconography in E. Wind, Bellini's Feast of the Gods, 1948, p. 38, note need checking.
Figure 269.

Allegory of the Battle of Lepanto. On canvas. Signed: Titianus Vecelius eques Caesaris fecit. In September, 1575, the Spanish Ambassador Guzman de Silva informed the King of the dispatch of this picture. Apparently Titian had been sent a general sketch by Coello and a picture of the King as basis for the portrait. The personal participation of Titian in the painting is small; Ricketts has drawn attention to the beautiful invention of the large angel swooping down from above, which is derived from Tintoretto. In 1625 Vicente Carducho received a thousand reals for the enlargement and overpainting of this picture (and also of the 'Spain coming to the aid of Religion'); according to J. Moreno Villa in Archivo Español de Arte y Arqueología No. 26 (May-August 1933) the slave with the part surrounding him is probably an addition by Carducho.
Figure 277.

The Worship of Venus. On canvas. Painted for Alfonso d'Este in 1516/18. Brought to Rome in 1598 by the Cardinal Legate Aldobrandini, remained until 1638 in Palazzo Ludovisi, Rome, then consigned to the Viceroy Count Monterey as a present for King Philip IV. There is a copy by Padovanino in Bergamo. The copy by Rubens in Stockholm (reproduced in Cicerone XIV, 1922, and in the 1928 catalogue), which, according to Roosval (Konsthistoriska Sallskapets Publikation 1915) is a late work of Rubens, shows, among other variations from the Madrid picture and the old engraving of the latter, at the top in the sky a chariot drawn by swans and containing a divinity, a compositional motive which occurs in a similar form in the Farewell of Adonis. As, however, in Rubens's copy of the Bacchanal, similar variations occur, it might be that Rubens copied a second, no longer traceable, version of the composition. The iconographical interpretation from the Amores of Philostratus was already known to Ridolfi.
Figures 41 (42).

Bacchanal. On canvas. Signed: Ticianus F. Inscription on the sheet of music: Qui boit et ne reboit, ne sais que boire soit. The origin and history of the picture are the same as for the Worship of Venus. Copies by Padovanino and Rubens as of the latter picture. In Rubens' picture the river-god pressing grapes on the hill to the right is missing, and instead of him there is a shepherd, a characteristic motive of Titian's early period; this likewise points to the existence of a second version. The iconographical interpretation from Philostratus was first given by Wickhoff in Jahrbuch der Preussischen Kunststammlungen XXIII. Figures 43 (44).

Venus with the Organ-player. On canvas. A picture of Venus is mentioned by Titian in December, 1545, in a letter to Charles V; this is probably the picture which he brought to Augsburg three years later. It is improbable that our picture is identical with the latter, as the mode of painting points to a later period. The subject was often treated by Titian with the help of his workshop, and our version appears for the first time in the inventory of the Alcazar in 1666. Hadeln (Pantheon 1931, II, p. 275) suggests that it is the version painted for Francesco Assonica and acquired by King Philip IV from the collection of Charles I of England after the latter's death. The composition is noted in Van Dyck's sketch-book at Chatsworth (Plate 39). Contrary to Suida, who considers the picture entirely or mainly by Titian's own hand, I think that the workshop elements predominate. Figure 176.

Venus with the Organ-player and a putto. On canvas. 58¾ x 85¾ inches. Signed : Titianus F. According to the Madrid catalogue, this may be the picture in the possession of Granvella which was declined by Rudolf II and then sent to Philipp III of Spain. Whereas Suida considers it to be entirely or mainly by Titian's own hand, this is doubted by most other writers. Gronau thinks that at least the landscape is perhaps by Titian. In my opinion the workshop elements predominate throughout the whole picture, though it is true that it has suffered greatly through restoration. Reproduced in Suida, Plate CCXVIII.

Danaë. On canvas. Sent in 1553 to the later King Philip II. Figure 220.

Venus and Adonis. On canvas. Mentioned by Titian in 1553 in a letter to King Philip II and sent in the following year to London, where it arrived in bad condition. There are many other versions, see A. L. Mayer, Tizianstudien, in Münchner Jahrbuch 1925, p. 274. Figure 221.

Tityus (Prometheus). On canvas. For Queen Maria of Hungary Titian made four pictures of the Damned in Hell, of which three were painted in 1549 and sent to the Queen's summer palace at Binche in the Netherlands, while the fourth followed in 1553. During the sixteenth century they hung in the Pieza de las Furias in the Madrid Alcazar. Only our picture and the Sisyphus are still extant, the Tantalus being preserved in an engraving. The fourth (Ixion) has vanished completely. But even the two extant pictures were held by the older Spanish writers to be copies by Alonso Sanchez Coello. Their deplorable state of preservation makes it difficult to decide this question. The description of the picture as Prometheus is disputed in the Prado catalogue, which maintains that the subject is Tityus, who was punished for the rape of Latona in a similar manner to Prometheus. The latter had nothing to do with Hades. Figure 202.

Sisyphus. On canvas. For the history of this painting and opinions thereon see the preceding picture. Figure 201.

Portrait of Daniele Barbaro. On wood. 31¾ x 27 inches. Appears for the first time in the inventory of the Alcazar in 1666. A second version is in the gallery at Ottawa (Figure 162). Whereas the Prado catalogue states that the latter is a copy of the Madrid picture, Beroqui (p. 99) maintains that the Madrid picture was painted five years later than the Ottawa version. In my opinion the Ottawa picture is the original, and the Madrid version a repetition. Reproduced in Suida, Plate CLXXXIII.

Portrait of Federigo II Gonzaga, Margrave of Mantua. On wood. Signed : Ticianus F. Appears for the first time in the Spanish inventories in 1655 and came from the collection of the Marqués de Leganes. Was once held to be a portrait of Alfonso d'Este, the subject being first correctly defined by Gronau. Several repetitions exist. Figure 76.

So-called Knight of Malta. On canvas. Mentioned in the inventories from 1666 on as a Tintoretto, from 1747 as a Titian. J. Babelon (Revue de l'Art ancien et moderne 1913, p. 269) has attempted to identify the subject as Gianello della Torre, clockmaker to Charles V and Philip II. Allende Salazar and F. X. Sanchez Cantón, Retratos del Museo del Prado 1919, have demonstrated the invalidity of this supposition and also mention that the cross is not that of the Order of Malta. They suggest a member of the Cuccina family, but according to Beroqui, Tizian en el Museo del Prado, this too is uncertain. Figure 197.

Self-portrait. On canvas. The picture is sometimes identified with that painted in 1562, which Vasari saw in 1566 in Titian's atelier; there is no proof that it was sent as a present to Philip II, as Foscari assumes (Iconografia di Tiziano, p. 18). It first occurs in the inventories in 1666, and is perhaps the picture acquired for 400 Gulden from the estate of Rubens. Figure 267.

The Elector Johann Friedrich of Saxony in armour. On canvas. A portrait af the Elector of Saxony in the armour which he wore at the battle of Mühlberg came to Spain with the pictures of Queen Maria of Hungary in 1556 and is described in detail in the inventory of 1600. Cesare Vecellio, who in his work on costumes written in 1590 definitely states that he saw Titian working on this picture, took the armour as a model for a courtly warrior in his book. The picture was damaged in the fire at the Alcazar in 1734. This may be the reason why it is now so hard to say with certitude whether the Prado picture is the original or a copy.
Figure 312.

Portrait of Charles V with a dog. On canvas. Painted in Bologna between December, 1532, and February, 1533; can be traced in Spain from 1600 on; sent to England in 1623 as a present to King Charles I, and returned to Spain after his death. On the relationship of the picture to its model, a portrait of the Emperor by Jakob Seisenegger, see Gustav Glück, in Festschrift für Julius Schlosser, Vienna 1927, p. 46.
Figure 94.

Portrait of Charles V on horseback. On canvas. Painted in Augsburg between April and September, 1548. Went to Spain with the other pictures from the estate of Queen Maria of Hungary. As B. Beinert made known in Archivo Español de Arte 1946, pp. 1 seqq., the painting was damaged immediately after completion in Augsburg and repaired by C. Amberger. Later on, the lower parts of the picture were damaged in the fire of the Alcazar at Madrid.
Figures 183 (184).

Portrait of Philip II in armour. On canvas. Painted in 1550 at Augsburg and sent on May 16th, 1551, to Queen Maria of Hungary in the Netherlands. After her death it went to Spain. Several repetitions are known.
Figure 199.

General del Vasto addressing his soldiers. On canvas. Mentioned several times in 1540 in Aretino's letters. On November 20th Aretino sent the Marchese del Vasto a detailed description and the picture itself was delivered in 1541. In February, 1541, Titian suggested to Girolamo Martinengo of Brescia that he would paint his portrait, if Martinengo in return would place at his disposal a complete set of armour, to serve as model for the picture of the marquis (Aretino, Lettere II, p. 193 v). The picture first appears in the inventories in 1666; it may in the meantime have been in Mantua and then in the possession of Charles I of England. Old copies exist in the museum at Naples and in the Prado.
Figure 136.

Portrait of the Empress Isabella. On canvas. According to the investigations of Gustav Glück in Jahrbuch der Kunsthistorischen Sammlungen, N. F. VII, and of Beroqui, this is not the picture which Titian painted in 1543/44 at the emperor's command and on the basis of a portrait by another hand (according to Roblot de Londre, Gazette des Beaux-Arts 1905, May, pp. 455 seqq., by A. S. Coello) and which the Spanish Ambassador Don Diego de Mendoza dispatched in 1545, but that which Titian painted at Augsburg in 1548 and which then came into the possession of Queen Maria. See also Gronau, Titian's Portrait of the Empress Isabella, in Burlington Magazine vol. 2, p. 281.
Figures 185 (186).

⟨*Annunciation.* Painted for the convent of Santa Maria degli Angeli at Murano, but not accepted by the nuns, whereupon Titian sent it to the Empress Isabella. In a letter of November 9th, 1537, Aretino writes at length of this picture, which in 1794 was still in the chapel of Aranjuez and has now disappeared. The composition has been preserved in an engraving by Caraglio (Figure 301). The painting in San Domenico Maggiore at Naples (Figure 231) is clearly derived from this older version.⟩

⟨MANTUA, PALAZZO DUCALE

The twelve Roman Emperors. This series of portraits of Emperors was created between April, 1537, and the end of 1538. According to tradition, the twelfth—probably Domitian—was painted by Giulio Romano. In 1628 the series came into the hands of Charles I of England and in 1652 it went to Spain. Since then it has vanished, but several series of painted copies are extant. See Gronau, Münchner Jahrbuch III. One series has been for the last few years in the original position at Mantua. I reproduce in this volume examples from the engravings made by Aeg. Sadeler. In Titian's own time the originals were reckoned among his finest works; attention was drawn to the fact that antique works, partly busts and partly medals, were used as models for the iconography of the Emperors. In a letter of July 7th, 1587, the exceptionally high price which Duke Federigo paid for these pictures is explained as being

due to the special erudition which was needed for them (A. Luzio, La Galleria dei Gonzaga, Milan 1913, p. 89).
Figures 304—307.⟩

MEDOLE, PARISH CHURCH

Christ appearing to the Virgin. On canvas. Painted in 1554, in connection with Titian's efforts to have the canonry of Medole transferred from his son Pomponio to his nephew. The picture was much damaged during the Napoleonic wars.
Figure 217.

MELBOURNE, NATIONAL GALLERY OF VICTORIA

Portrait of a Monk. On canvas. Acquired by the Felton Bequest Committee. First brought to notice by Hadeln in Burlington Magazine 1924, and by him dated not long before 1550, which seems more likely than the dating in the sixties of Klassiker[5]. I know the picture only from photographs.
Figure 193.

MILAN, AMBROSIANA

Adoration of the Magi. On canvas. Mentioned in 1618 in the inventory of the Ambrosiana. According to a somewhat doubtful tradition, a repetition painted for the Cardinal of Ferrara (Ippolito d'Este) of the picture sent to the king of Spain; it is assumed that it was intended for King Henri II of France, for which reason to King's initials and those of Diane de Poitiers appear on the frame. The divergences from the other versions of the composition are considerable. Fischel (Klassiker[5], p. 322) is reminded of Titian's followers, but in fact the picture is a typical workshop production. A replica of this version in the D'Atri Collection was published by A. L. Mayer in Burlington Magazine LXXI, p. 178.
Portrait of an Old Man in armour. On canvas. As early as the beginning of the 17th century this picture was connected with the fact that Titian was said to have painted his father in armour (Inventory of the museum of Cardinal Federigo Borromeo, 1618). On the other hand Gronau (Di due quadri del Tiziano poco conosciuti, in Rassegna d'Arte VII, p. 135) suggested that it is a portrait of Giangiacomo de' Medici (1498—1555), because it resembles the likeness on the latter's tomb in Milan Cathedral. This is contradicted by the fact that the style of the picture points to a date not later than 1540, at which time Giangiacomo was only forty years old, and also that the man depicted can scarcely have been a professional Condottiere such as Giangiacomo. His appearance points rather to the traditional identification. Cavalcaselle included the picture in the postscripts to his book (Archivio Storico dell'Arte IV, pp. 1 seqq.).
Figure 99.

MILAN, BRERA

St. Jerome in the Wilderness. On canvas. Signed: Titianus F. From Santa Maria Nuova at Venice. The semicircular top is a later addition, as is proved by the rectangular copy in San Luca at Rome and by several drawings.
Figure 211.

Portrait of Antonio Porcia. On canvas. Signed: Titianus. Brought from the Castello Porcia near Pordenone in 1891 or 1892. In consequence of the appearance of the subject, who was born in 1508, and the manner of painting, the picture is unanimously assigned to the latter half of the thirties. First discussed by G. Frizzoni in Archivio Storico dell'Arte 1892, p. 20.
Figure 124.

MILAN, CASTELLO SFORZESCO

Portrait of Monseigneur d'Aramont. On canvas. Signed: Titianus F. Inscription: Mons[or] de Aramont Imbasator de ... a Constantinopoli. From the collection of Prince Trivulzio. Suida, who first brought the picture to notice in Belvedere 1929, pp. 7 seqq., also discusses the life of the adventurer and diplomat depicted; his stay in Venice from 1541 to 1543 enables us to date the picture.
Figure 126.

MINNEAPOLIS, MIN. (U. S. A.), INSTITUTE OF ARTS

Temptation of Christ. On wood. Formerly in the Galerie d'Orléans. According to the catalogue painted about 1530, according to Suida about the end of the fourth decade, according to Klassiker[5] begun about 1540 and continued in the sixties. To me it seems quite possible that it was created in the early forties.
Figure 146.

⟨MODENA, GALLERIA ESTENSE

Portrait of a Lady with Moorish slave (supposedly Laura de' Dianti). On canvas. Signed: Ticianus. In Münchner Jahrbuch 1911, Hadeln attempted to prove that this is the original and the version in Richmond a copy. But probably both are merely copies of a lost original. Figure 309.)

MUNICH, ÄLTERE PINAKOTHEK

Christ crowned with thorns. On canvas. A late picture, perhaps the version described by Boschini as a sketch, which after Titian's death passed to Tintoretto, and was sold by the latter's son Domenico to a buyer from the North. A comparison with the older version in the Louvre (Figure 143) is instructive.
Figure 274.

Madonna and Child in evening landscape. On canvas. Signed: Titianus Fecit. Comes from the sacristy of the Escorial, where it was described in 1605 by Siguenza. In 1810 came into the hands of General Sebastiani, from whom the gallery acquired it in 1815. According to Morelli a workshop picture finished by the master, but otherwise generally held to be an important work of the late period. According to Fischel, Klassiker[5], derived from a drawing by Raffael, which is not convincing. Repetition in Stockholm (Sirén, Dessins et Tableaux Italiens en Suède, 1902 p. 94). The halo is noteworthy.
Figure 233.

Jupiter and Antiope. On canvas. 24×20 inches, oval. Described as a Titian in the older inventories, now attributed to Paolo Veronese. In more recent times Voll (Alte Pinakothek, p. 230), A. Venturi, (Studi dal Vero, 1927) and Suida (Vita Artistica II) have gone back to the attribution to Titian. On the other hand Morelli rightly remarked: 'Neither Titian, nor Giovanni Contarini (as in Crowe and Cavalcaselle), and still less Paolo Veronese; pictures of this kind are as fatherless as foundlings.' Date of creation and manner are best illustrated by the close resemblance to Bart. Spranger's Mars and Venus in Vienna (reproduced in Gustav Glück, Gemäldegalerie in Wien, plate 158).
Reproduced in Suida, Plate CCXXXII a.

Vanity. On canvas. From the collection of Rudolf II. Formerly ascribed to Salviati, Palma, Giorgione and also Pordenone. The invention points to the half-figure pictures of Titian's early period, about 1515, but the painting is perhaps only a copy, as Hetzer also thinks (Jugendwerke, p. 58).
Figure 18.

Portrait of a Man. Canvas gummed on to wood. From the Electoral gallery in Düsseldorf. Generally dated between the end of the Giorgionesque period and the beginnings of Titian's personal style, that is to say about 1520.
Figure 60.

Portrait of Charles V. On canvas. Signed: Titianus F. and MDXLVIII. Painted at Augsburg. Crowe and Cavalcaselle admit collaboration of Cesare Vecellio, while Ricketts (p. 118) detects extensive overpainting by a Northern artist and thinks that in the main it is a work of Rubens.
Figure 187.

NAPLES, SAN DOMENICO MAGGIORE

Annunciation. On canvas. Signed: Titianus Fecit. First mentioned in D'Eugenio, Napoli Sacra, 1623, p. 287, where 1557 is given as the date of the consecration of the chapel. De Dominici (Vite, 1742, I, p. 290) states that the original was removed and replaced by a copy by Luca Giordano. The correctness of this information has been disputed by R. Longhi (Giunte al Tiziano, Arte 1925, p. 40), who rediscovered the picture. In fact the style corresponds to that of Titian in the late fifties, while the composition employs many elements from the older version (see the engraving by Caraglio, Figure 301). The attribution to Titian was rejected by Hetzer, Thieme-Becker, vol. 34, p. 166, who ascribes the painting to the unknown artist who, in his opinion, painted also the Death of Actaeon in the collection of the Earl of Harewood.
Figure 231.

NAPLES, MUSEO NAZIONALE

Danaë and Cupid. On canvas. According to Vasari, painted in 1545/46 in Rome for Ottavio Farnese. For the other versions of the subject, see Hadeln, Burlington Magazine 1926, vol. 48, pp. 78 and 82 seqq.
Figure 173.

Portrait of Cardinal Alessandro Farnese. On canvas. 39×29½ inches. Titian painted the cardinal's portrait in 1543 at Bologna or in 1545 at Rome. That the picture in question is the original is doubted by most writers (Crowe and Cavalcaselle, p. 447, Ricketts, p. 108, Klassiker[5], Serra in Bollettino d'Arte 1934/35, p. 549, Dussler, Zeitschrift für Kunstwissenschaft 1935, p. 238).
Reproduced in Suida, Plate CL b.

Portrait of Pier Luigi Farnese. On canvas. Painted about 1546.
Figure 180.

Portrait of Charles V. On canvas. 39¹/₄ x 29¹/₄ inches. According to Crowe and Cavalcaselle
perhaps the picture which Titian sent to the imperial governor in Milan in 1549; this is
doubted by Fischel, Klassiker, as the features of the subject point to a much earlier period;
he thinks it might be a portrait of Ferdinand I, a supposition which the catalogue of the 1935
exhibition in Venice also finds not unfounded. As Dussler emphasizes in Zeitschrift für Kunstwissenschaft 1935, p. 238, the present state of the picture makes it difficult to ascertain
whether it is the original or a copy, but it is more probably the former.
Reproduced in Suida, Plate CLV.

Portrait of Paul III (with biretta). On canvas. 42¹/₂ x 32¹/₂ inches. In spite of its lesser brilliancy
the painting is in its general conception and colouristic treatment closer to Titian than the
more famous bareheaded portrait of the Pope. It may be one of the two portraits of the
Pope which Titian painted in Bologna in 1543 and which Vasari saw in the houses of two
cardinals in Rome. The other would be the one represented by the version in Vienna, while
the one in the Hermitage might be the modello (later on brought to completion in the
bottega) which Titian kept in his studio for later use.
Reproduced in Suida, Plate CLII.

Portrait of Paul III (bareheaded). On canvas. The problem of this famous portrait, of which
numerous replicas exist, has recently been re-investigated by E. Tietze-Conrat in Gazette des
Beaux-Arts, s. VI, vol. 29, pp. 73 seqq., who emphasized the striking discrepancy, also noticed
by F. Wickhoff, A. Venturi and others, between the heroic appearance of the Pope here and
his frailty and physical decay as stressed by all the contemporary witnesses and also
represented by Titian himself in his other portraits of the Pope. She drew the conclusion that
this portrait was not painted from life, but rather, if not by Sebastiano del Piombo, was
done by Titian on the basis of a portrait by Sebastiano.
Figure 160 (161).

Portrait Group of Paul III with his Nipoti Ottavio and Cardinal Alessandro Farnese. Painted
at Rome in 1546. Some parts of the picture are unfinished.
Figures 170 (171).

Portrait of Philip II as Prince. On canvas. Signed: Titianus Eques Caes. F. About 1553. This
version is considered the best workshop repetition of an original painted by Titian for Spain,
which has now disappeared. On the portraits of Philip see A. L. Mayer in Münchner Jahrbuch 1925, p. 267.
Figure 200.

Portrait of a Lady. On canvas. From the Palazzo del Giardino in Parma and probably depicting
a member of the Farnese family or of their court. In bad state of preservation. According
to Dussler in Zeitschrift für Kunstwissenschaft 1935, p. 238, a modest atelier version.

NAPLES, CASTELLO REALE

Portrait of Pier Luigi Farnese. On wood. 39 x 29¹/₂ inches. First claimed for Titian by Longhi,
Giunte al Tiziano, Arte 1925, an opinion which Suida accepted in his book, though in his
article on the 1935 exhibition in Venice, Pantheon 1936, p. 102, he retracts this statement,
and is inclined to attribute it to a painter of Parma (Girolamo Bedoli, Mazzuola). Dussler,
Zeitschrift für Kunstwissenschaft 1935, p. 238, admits the proximity to Parmigianino, but
also notices reminiscences of Fra Sebastiano. In any case the picture has nothing to do with
Titian.
Reproduced in Suida, Plate CLIII.

NEW YORK, H. C. FRICK COLLECTION

Portrait of Pietro Aretino. On canvas. From Palazzo Chigi in Rome. Much praised by Cavalcaselle in his postscripts in Archivio Storico dell'Arte IV, p. 1, but definitely rejected by
A. Venturi in Arte VIII, p. 286. In Burlington Magazine vol. 7, pp. 344 seqq., Roger Fry
discusses the picture in detail and brings it into relationship with Titian's other portraits
of Aretino. A. L. Mayer, Gazette des Beaux-Arts, s. VI, vol. 18, p. 307, suggests a somewhat
later date because of Aretino's beard being grey, while, according to a letter, Aretino had
stopped dyeing his beard only in 1548.
Figure 167.

NEW YORK, METROPOLITAN MUSEUM

Venus with the lute-player. On canvas. 62 x 80³/₄ inches. Formerly Earl of Leicester, Holkham
Hall. According to G. M. Richter, Burlington Magazine, vol. 59, p. 58, painted about 1560;
according to Hadeln, Pantheon 1932, p. 237 seq., begun in the forties and finished c. 1560.
The problem of this painting, which was called by Hetzer (Thieme-Becker 34, p. 164)
the one most remote from Titian of all the Venuses connected with him, was thoroughly

discussed by E. Tietze-Conrat in Art Bulletin, vol. 26, 1944, 266 seqq. She took as her point of departure the unequivocal statement by Joachim von Sandrart, the German painter and connoisseur of the seventeenth century, describing the painting, then his property, as a work of Jacopo Tintoretto's son. One or two attempts to disprove this statement (in Art Bulletin, vol. 27, 1945, p. 82; vol. 29, 1947, p. 123), have failed to impugn the trustworthiness of the contemporary witness. Though the ascription to Domenico Tintoretto remains difficult to prove in view of our insufficient knowledge of his style in his early years, and though Tintoretto's second son, Marco, too may be taken into consideration, the elimination from Titian's œuvre seems irrefutable. The reclassification explains stylistic contradictions which had called forth some sophistry from Hadeln and other advocates of Titian's authorship. O. Brendel in Art Bulletin 1946, p. 61, has dealt with the neo-platonic ideas in his opinion reflected in the painting.

Portrait of Duke Alfonso d'Este. On canvas. Formerly belonged to the Comtesse de Vogué, Dijon. Discussed by A. L. Mayer in Münchner Jahrbuch, N. F. II, 1925, and exhaustively by Gronau in Jahrbuch der Kunsthistorischen Sammlungen in Wien, N. F. II, p. 233. According to the latter this is the first portrait of Alfonso which he presented to Charles V through the mediation of Covos, who brought it to Spain where it disappeared after 1686. The second version, which was painted in 1536 to replace the first, is preserved in copies only; one, which at that time I thought to be possibly the lost original, was included in the Exhibition ' Four Centuries of Venetian Painting ', Toledo, O., 1940, No. 63, another, by Dosso, in the Palazzo Pitti, is reproduced in Klassiker der Kunst, 5th edition, p. 72. Whether the painting in the Metropolitan Museum is the original or a copy is difficult to decide, owing to the extensive restoration.
Figure 75.

Portrait of Doge Gritti. On canvas. $41^{1}/_{2} \times 31^{1}/_{2}$ inches. Formerly in the Friedsam collection and before that in Palazzo Barbarigo, Venice. Accepted by Hadeln in his grouping of Doges' portraits in Pantheon 1930, and also by Berenson, L. Venturi and A. L. Mayer; the two last named place the painting in Titian's late years long after Gritti's death. As E. Tietze-Conrat pointed out in Art Bulletin 1946, p. 81, the portrait is a preparatory sketch painted by Titian and turned into a regular painting, perhaps when Pomponio sold it to the Barbarigo. The character of a sketch is still recognizable in the negligently painted hands. A version based on this sketch is the one owned by the heirs of Nathan Allen in Kenosha, Wisconsin, ill. Suida pl. LXXIII.
Figure 168.

NEW YORK, L. BENDIT COLLECTION

Portrait of Gabriel Tadino, Commander of Charles V's Artillery. On canvas. Formerly Collection Baron Heyl, Darmstadt. Inscription naming the model and giving the date of 1538, which may be correct, though the inscription seems to be a later addition. First published by A. L. Mayer in Pantheon 1930, p. 482.
Figure 98.

NEW YORK, A. SACHS COLLECTION

Adoration of the Magi. On canvas. Discussed by A. L. Mayer in Pantheon 1930, pp. 60 seqq., in connection with the other versions of the same subject; see above, under Madrid. He thought it possible that this is the version painted for Philip II in 1559, which disappeared from Spain at the time of the Napoleonic wars; in any case he found the treatment so advanced that he is prepared to believe it a late work. Venturi also, in Italian Paintings in America, p. 526, emphasizes the late character of the picture. Having studied the painting thoroughly on the occasion of the Exhibition ' Four Centuries of Venetian Painting ', Toledo, O., 1940 (No. 60), I now consider its colour scale different from Titian's and the painting a (Spanish?) copy from Titian's original, possibly the one in the Escorial, which A. L. Mayer changing his former opinion is inclined to rate highest among the existing versions (see Burlington Magazine, vol. 71, p. 178).

NEW YORK, SCHAEFFER GALLERIES

Portrait of Giovanni de Castaldo. On canvas. The identification of the sitter rests on his close resemblance to the portrait of the general in P. Totti's Ritratti ed Elogi di Capitani Illustri, Rome 1632, and on Leoni's medal. The medal dangling from the chain presents the portrait of F. F. d'Avalos, who had been Castaldo's commander in the Battle of Pavia in 1525. Castaldo's portrait is mentioned by Vasari (VII, 450) as one of those which Titian painted in Augsburg in 1548. The style of the painting confirms this date.
Figures 181 (182).

NEW YORK, HEIRS OF J. STILLMANN

Portrait of Bishop Christoforo Madruzzo of Trento. On canvas. Belonged formerly to Baron Valentino de' Salvadori and before that to the Roccabruna and Gaudenti della Torre

families. Signed: Titianus fecit. The history of its creation was expounded by Lodovico
Oberziner, Il Ritratto di Cristoforo Madruzo di Tiziano, Trento 1900; according to this, it
was painted at Venice between February 15th and March 15th 1542, when Madruzzo was
the Emperor's representative there. Ricketts, p. 100, thought that it was a late Moroni.
Figure 125.

OMAHA, NEVADA, MUSEUM OF FINE ARTS

The Man with the Falcon. On canvas. Signed: Titianus F. Formerly in the collections of the
Prince of Carignano, Louis François de Bourbon; Lord Carlisle, Castle Howard; Eduard
Simon, Berlin; A. W. Ericson, New York. The proposed identifications of the model as
Giorgio Cornaro, brother of Caterina Cornaro, as Francesco Maria della Rovere, or as
Federigo Gonzaga, cannot be maintained. The heavy repaint makes it difficult to judge this
brilliant painting, whose style offers some puzzling features.
Figure 74.

OTTAWA, NATIONAL GALLERY OF CANADA

Portrait of Daniele Barbaro. On canvas. The picture was purchased directly from the Giovio
family at Como, and can therefore be safely identified with the picture which Titian sent
in 1544 or 1545 to Bishop Paolo Giovio and which is referred to in a letter of Aretino
(Lettere III, p. 104). I agree with L. Venturi, Arte 1932, p. 482, that this version is superior
to that in the Prado.
Figure 162.

PADUA, SCUOLA DEL SANTO

Three frescoes with scenes from the life of St. Anthony. The subjects are: St. Anthony healing
a new-born child, The healing of the youth's leg, The jealous husband. Titian's receipt for
payment received is dated December 2nd, 1511. According to Francesco Zanoni's report
in 1748, the frescoes, which he had undertaken to restore, were in a very bad state of
preservation even at that time.
Figures 8, 11, 12.

PADUA, SCUOLA DEL CARMINE

The meeting at the Golden Gate. Fresco. First attributed to Titian by Brandolese, Pitture di
Padova 1795, p. 190. This is supported by Hourticq and Suida, who also assign to Titian
the Annunciation to Joseph in the same building. Crowe and Cavalcaselle believe that in the
execution the hand of Domencio Campagnola predominated; others, such as Heinemann,
p. 69, ascribe the fresco to an anonymous pupil of Titian. I agree with Hetzer that emphasis
should be laid on the fact that the whole conception is contrary to the spirit and style of
Titian, as are also the treatment of the figures and the details. The paintings are works of
the local Paduan school.
Reproduced in Suida, Plate VII.

PANSHANGER, LORD DESBOROUGH

Group of three children of King Ferdinand. On canvas. In his letter of October 20, 1548, to
King Ferdinand I, Titian reports that he was taking along designs or sketches of the three
princesses in order to have them finished in Venice. As for the painting in Panshanger,
which this author has not seen in the original and apparently no recent writer has studied,
Crowe and Cavalcaselle attributed the main part of the work to Cesare Vecelli. It seems
to be an arrangement made in the workshop, perhaps on the ground of Titian's above-
mentioned sketches. The fact that in the inventory of the paintings in the estate of Charles V,
of February 26, 1561 a corresponding group portrait is listed without naming Titian as the
author (Jahrbuch der Kunsthistorischen Sammlungen in Wien, vol. XII, part 2, p. CLXXVI,
no. 254) is a further argument against the attribution to Titian.

⟨PARIS, MUSÉE DES ARTS DÉCORATIFS

Portrait of Queen Maria of Hungary. On canvas. 25³/4 x 34 inches. Copy of a lost original
which Titian painted at Augsburg in 1548. See G. Glück in Jahrbuch der Kunsthistorischen
Sammlungen in Wien 1934, and Suida in Burlington Magazine 1934, LXIV.
Reproduced in Suida, French edition, Plate CCCXXVI.⟩

PARIS, LOUVRE

Christ crowned with thorns. On wood. Signed: Titianus F. Painted for the Capella della
Santa Corona in the church of Santa Maria delle Grazie at Milan. Removed from the church
in 1797. In the Louvre since the beginning of the 19th century.
Figure 143 (142).

Entombment. On canvas. Sold from Mantua in 1628 to Charles I of England; probably painted for the Margrave Federigo of Mantua or his mother Isabella d'Este; later passed to Jabach and then to Louis XIV. There is an old replica in the Manfrin gallery.
Figure 83.

Christ at Emmaus. On canvas. Signed: Tician... Sold from Mantua in 1627 to Charles I of England, probably painted for the Margrave Federigo of Mantua; later passed to Jabach and Louis XIV. Before Titian went to Augsburg in 1548, Alessandro Contarini purchased another version and presented it to the Signoria. The latter is perhaps the picture formerly in the church of the Pregadi in Venice and now belonging to the Earl of Yarborough; it was refered to by Wilczek, Preussisches Jahrbuch 1928, pp. 159 seqq., in an attempt to reconstruct the Louvre picture, which has been mutilated at the top. The main part of the Louvre picture was painted at the end of the twenties and it was finished later. Hourticq, Jeunesse, p. 235, endeavours to prove that the heads are portraits of members of the Gonzaga family, but A. L. Mayer in Gazette des Beaux-Arts, s. VI, vol. 20, p. 299, made it seem probable that the canvas was originally painted for a member of the Maffei family in Verona and only later on passed to the Gonzaga collections.
Figure 157.

Madonna with the Rabbit (La Vierge au Lapin). On canvas. Signed: Ticianus F. First heard of as belonging to Louis XIV, often identified as the picture painted for Federigo Gonzaga described in a letter of his agent dated February 5th, 1530, as the Madonna with St. Catherine.
Figure 84.

Madonna and Child with Saints Stephen, Jerome and Maurice. On canvas. $42^5/8 \times 52$ inches. Presented by Lord Carlisle to King Charles I of England, then sent to Louis XIV in exchange. Considered by some writers to be a workshop repetition of the Vienna picture (see below), by others as the original. Probably (as stated by Heinemann, p. 40) both it and the Vienna picture are repetitions of a lost original, painted about 1520 at the earliest; Hetzer, Frühe Gemälde, p. 86, is likewise of this opinion.
Reproduced in Suida, Plate LXXXIV b.

St. Jerome in landscape. On canvas. First heard of as belonging to Louis XIV. Dated by Fischel, Klassiker[5], about 1558/59 and assigned to the same period by Philips, Late Works, p. 14; Ricketts, however, dates it at the beginning of the thirties and identifies it with a St. Jerome painted for Federigo Gonzaga in 1532. The same observation is made by Gronau and accepted by Suida, Hourticq and L. Venturi. (L'Arte 1932, p. 490). The last-named mentions a replica in Gatschina, which was sold in Berlin on June 4th, 1929 (see Starye Gody 1915, January/February).
Figure 89.

Young Woman at her toilet. On canvas. Formerly in the gallery of Charles I of England, where it was called: La Maîtresse du Titien. Other attempts to identify the subject as Alfonso d'Este and Laura de' Dianti, Francesco Covos and Cornelia, Federigo Gonzaga and his mistress Isabella Boschetti, are equally unfounded, and in part in contradiction with the period of its creation, which is almost universally recognized to be that of the Giorgionesque half-figure paintings, i. e. 1512/15, between the Salome and the Flora. In the 17th century it suffered considerably from restoration; Heinemann, p. 50, raises the question whether this picture—together with a replica in the Nemes collection, Munich, considered by some to be superior—is not derived from a lost original by Titian.
Figure 17.

Fête Champêtre. On canvas. $43^3/4 \times 54^1/2$ inches. Sold in 1627 from the Gonzaga gallery to Charles I of England; later passed to Jabach and from him to Louis XIV. The picture, which was formerly considered almost universally to be by Giorgione (only Wickhoff and Seidlitz attributed it to Domenico Campagnola and A. Venturi to Sebastiano del Piombo), has now been assigned to Titian by Hourticq, R. Longhi (Vita Artistica II) and Suida. I myself consider that the Giorgionesque character is undeniable, and I believe Heinemann, pp. 34 seqq., is right in stating that it may be a Giorgione finished by Sebastiano del Piombo.
Reproduced in Suida, Plate XXIV.

The Pardo Venus. On canvas. Until 1624 in the Palacio del Pardo in Madrid. Then presented to Charles Stuart, the subsequent King Charles I of England; later sold to Jabach and by him to Louis XIV. In all probability may be identified with the picture which Titian mentions in his Memorandum of 1574 as 'La Nuda con il Paese e con il Satiro' which he sent to King Philip in 1567. Suida, who connects this entry with the Munich Jupiter and Antiope, quotes with reference to the Pardo Venus a passage from Lomazzo, Idea del Tempio, 1590: 'Una Venere che dorme con satiri che gli scoprono le parti più occulte, ed altri satiri intorno che mangiano uva e ridono come ubbriachi e lontano Adone in un paese che segue la caccia. La qual pittura è restata a Pomponio suo figliolo dopo la sua morte.' Whether this description refers to the Louvre picture or to a version on a similar theme which was in the atelier, is

doubtful. It is impossible that the Pardo Venus could have originated in 1567, as both the individual elements and the grouping point to a much earlier date; it may be the picture was gone over again at a later period.
Figures 116 (117—120).

So-called Allegory of Alfonso d'Avalos. On canvas. Passed from the collection of Charles I of England to Louis XIV. It is now agreed that this picture, which was formerly supposed to represent Alfonso d'Avalos, Marquess del Vasto, bidding farewel to his wife Maria of Aragon, has nothing to do with Charles V's army commander. Equally unconvincing is Hourticq's suggestion that it depicts Titian's farewell to his wife, who died in 1530. More probably it is a representation of allegorical character. The composition was repeated in the workshop several times, there being two versions in Vienna (Suida, Plate CCXXII a, b), one in Munich (Suida, Plate CCXV b), in the Galleria Borghese in Rome.
Figure 91.

Portrait of Francis I. On canvas. Painted in 1538/39, as was already deduced by Mariette, from a medal. Other portraits of the king by Titian, authenticated by documents, have been preserved; one of them, without a cap, but corresponding to the Paris picture in the posture, is in the possession of the Earl of Harewood, London, and is reproduced in Suida, Plate CCIII a.
Figure 123.

Portrait of a Young Man (L'homme au gant). On canvas. Signed: Ticianus F. Sold to King Charles I of England with the Gonzaga collection in 1627, then to Jabach and from him to Louis XIV. In recent times Hourticq has made the interesting suggestion that the subject is to be identified as Girolamo Adorno, the picture being that which Pietro Aretino sent to Federigo Gonzaga in 1527 together with his own portrait (see below, next paragraph). As Adorno was already dead in 1523, the picture must have been begun earlier and merely completed in 1527. A. L. Mayer, Gazette des Beaux-Arts, s. VI, vol. 20, p. 289 seq., who dates this and the following portrait somewhat later than I, perhaps 1523, also rejects Hourticq's suggestion and for the Homme au Gant pleads, without any special motivation, for Gianbattista Malatesta, the Mantuan agent in Venice.
Figure (63, 64).

Portrait of a Man. On canvas. Sold to King Charles I of England with the Gonzaga collection in 1627, then to Jabach and to Louis XIV. According to Hourticq a portrait of Pietro Aretino, the one sent to Federigo Gonzaga in 1527 together with that of Girolamo Adorno. As Aretino only came to Venice in that year, the picture in this case could not have been painted before 1527. To the stylistic reasons which contradict this dating must be added the lack of resemblance to the features of Aretino as preserved to us in other portraits.
Figure 59.

PARIS, COMTESSE DE BÉHAGUE

Portrait of Alfonso d'Avalos, Marqués del Vasto. On canvas. First brought to notice by Karl Wilczek in Zeitschrift für Bildende Kunst 1930, pp. 240 seqq. The identification of the subject is based on a miniature in the old Ambras collection in Vienna. Painted at Bologna in 1532/33. L. A. Mayer, Gazette des Beaux-Arts, s. VI, vol. 20, p. 292, suggests the date of 1536.
Figure 122.

⟨PARIS, COMTESSE DE VOGÜE

Portrait of Isabella d'Este. On canvas. Formerly in the Leopold Goldschmid collection, Paris. First brought to notice by Maurice Hamel, Gazette des Beaux-Arts 1903, p. 104. A portrait of Isabella, evidently that after which Rubens made the copy now in the gallery at Vienna, was sold by Vicenzo Gonzaga to Charles I of England in 1627. It is nevertheless doubtful whether this is the same as the Paris version, for owing to the hardness of execution the latter cannot be held to be anything but a copy.
Figure 310.⟩

PIEVE DI CADORE, PARISH CHURCH

Madonna and Child with Saints Andrew and Tiziano di Oderzo. On canvas. Vasari mentions that, when Titian had reached an advanced age, he presented a votive picture to the family chapel of the Vecelli; the acolyte on the left has Titian's features, the St. Andrew according to tradition those of his brother Francesco, who died in 1559. That Titian had a share in the execution, as Crowe and Cavalcaselle asserted, cannot be admitted, and more recent critics have all without exception emphasized the workshop character of the painting.
Figure 285.

⟨*Frescoes in the choir.* In the autumn of 1565 Titian planned to decorate the church of his native place. In the vaulting of the choir the Assumption was represented, on the side-walls the Annunciation and the Nativity, on the ceiling of the arch half-figures of Prophets, and also a Mater Dolorosa and St. John the Evangelist. It is supposed that pupils were entrusted with the execution of these paintings, which were finished in 1567 and by 1813 were completely ruined; several of the pupils, e. g. Valerio Zuccato, Cesare Vecelli and Emanuel of Augsburg appear on October 1st, 1565, as witnesses when Fausto Vecelli was appointed notary. Northcote (Life of Titian II, pp. 301 seqq.) gives a detailed description of these frescos. From this description it is clear that the Adoration of the Child in Pieve conformed with the composition preserved in a woodcut (Figure 322) and in an engraving made from the latter bearing the name of Bertelli. From this composition are derived the pictures of this subject in Palazzo Pitti (Figure 323) and at Christ Church College, Oxford. It is a conception by Titian which must date back to the twenties. See thereon the article by H. Tietze and E. Tietze-Conrat in Jahrbuch der Kunsthistorischen Sammlungen in Wien, N. F. X., pp. 142 seqq.⟩

RICHMOND, COLLECTION OF SIR HERBERT COOK, BART.

Portrait of Ranuccio Farnese. On canvas. Signed: Titianus. Titian painted the youngest son of Pier Luigi Farnese at Venice in 1541/42 (see Gronau in Preussisches Jahrbuch 1906, pp. 3 seqq.). The version in Richmond, which at all events is superior in quality to the copy in Berlin, is held by most writters to be also a copy. Ricketts calls it a workshop picture, mainly by Orazio, but with something of Titian's quality in the draperies. Cook (Cook and Borenius, Catalogue of the Pictures in Doughty House 1913, I) and Suida believe that it is by Titian's own hand.
Figure 144.

⟨*Portrait of a Lady with Moorish slave,* said to be Laura de' Dianti. On canvas. 46¼ x 36 inches. From the collection of the Emperor Rudolf. First brought to notice by Herbert Cook in Burlington Magazine, vol. 7, p. 449. This version was considered the best until Hadeln in Münchner Jahrbuch IV made this claim for the Modena version, which is qualitatively better, but like the Richmond picture probably only a copy from a lost original (Figure 305). In Cook's article other still more inferior versions are mentioned.
Reproduced in Klassiker⁵, p. 55.⟩

ROME, GALLERIA BORGHESE

St. Vincent Ferrer. On canvas. It is assumed that this picture depicts some Dominican monk who—as can be proved in other cases—caused himself to be represented as a saint of his Order (see, for example, L. Lotto's St. Peter Martyr in the Fogg Art Museum, Cambridge, Mass.).
Figure 251.

So-called Sacred and Profane Love. On canvas. First mentioned in a Borghese inventory of 1613, where it is described as 'La beltà ornata e la beltà disornata' (adorned and unadorned beauty). Noted by Van Dyck in his sketch-book. The widely varying iconographic interpretations are collected by Olga von Gerstfeld in Monatshefte für Kunstwissenschaft, October 1910, and by Panofsky in Herkules am Scheideweg, p. 173. W. Friedländer in Art Bulletin 1938, 320, and R. Wischnitzer-Bernstein in Gazette des Beaux-Arts, s. VI, vol. 23, p. 89, rediscussed the subject-matter and stressed the close relationship to Colonna's Hypnerotomachia. The coat-of-arms on the sarcophagus is that of the Grandchancellor Niccolò Aurelio of Venice, who commissioned the painting.
Figures 30 (28, 31, 32).

Allegory, the so-called Education of Cupid. On canvas. Called the Three Graces in the Borghese inventory of 1613. L. Venturi has attempted to interpret the subject on this basis in Arte 1932, p. 484, referring to Giulio Romano's murals in the Palazzo del Tè in Mantua. His interpretation has been repudiated by E. Tietze-Conrat in Art Bulletin 1945, p. 270. Van Dyck made a note of the composition in his sketch-book and on the breast of the foremost woman added the word: *quel admirabil petto.*
Figures 246 (247, 248).

ROME, PINACOTECA CAPITOLINA

Baptism of Christ, with the donor Giovanni Ram. On canvas. This picture was seen by Marcantonio Michiel in 1531 at Ram's house in Venice. Despite these unusually good credentials its authenticity was doubted by Crowe and Cavalcaselle, who suggested Paris Bordone, by Hetzer, Frühe Gemälde, p. 104, and by Dussler in Zeitschrift für Kunstwissenschaft 1934, p. 239.
Figure 24.

ROME, GALLERIA NAZIONALE

Portrait of Cardinal Alessandro Farnese. On wood. Discussed by Gronau in Cicerone 1929, p. 41.
Figure 145.

ROME, GALLERIA DORIA

Salome with the head of John the Baptist. On canvas. Formerly belonged to Principe Salviati,
   Queen Christina of Sweden, and Principe Odescalchi; at the Doria Gallery since 1794. The
   best version of a composition of which several other versions exist; the version in the former
   Benson collection, which many prefer to that in Rome—e. g. Burckhardt, Beiträge, p. 478—
   must be an altered workshop repetition. The picture has been ascribed to Giorgione, Pordenone and Lotto, but is now mostly attributed to Titian in his Giorgionesque period. In the
   head of the Baptist, which reminds others of Ariosto, Hourticq, p. 137—and after him Foscari,
   Iconografia, p. 22—thought to recognize a self-portrait of Titian.
   Figures 15 (16).

ROME, PINACOTECA VATICANA

The Virgin in Glory with six saints. On wood. Signed: Titianus faciebat. Painted as an altar-
   piece for San Niccolò dei Frari at Venice, and brought to Rome in 1770. The top was
   originally semicircular. The statement in Sanuto's diaries that the chapel of St. Nicholas
   in the Ducal Palace was finished in 1523, was erroneously applied by Crowe and Cavalcaselle
   to San Niccolò dei Frari and this picture; this mistake has been corrected by Hadeln in his
   edition of Ridolfi, I, p. 173. A. L. Mayer in Gazette des Beaux-Arts, s. VI, vol. 18, p. 305,
   however, presents stylistic arguments for dating the conception in the early 1520's and the
   execution not after 1535.
   Figures 137 (138).

Portrait of Doge Niccolò Marcello. On canvas. Acquired by Pope Leo XII from the Aldobrandini collection, Bologna. The identification of the subject as this doge, who died (1474/75)
   before Titian's time, is based on medals and a portrait of the doge bearing his name by
   Mazza, at Bologna. Titian must have painted his portrait from a medal. Ricketts and the
   catalogue of the collection date the picture in Titian's early period; Hadeln, who has made
   the most detailed study of the picture (Repertorium XXXIII, pp. 101 seqq.), shows that it
   was more probably created about 1542.
   Figure 131.

⟨ROME, FORMERLY IN THE POSSESSION OF POPE PIUS V

St. Peter Martyr. From a letter of Titian to Cardinal Alessandro Farnese written in March, 1567,
   we learn that he sent the Pope a picture of St. Peter Martyr together with a Mary Magdalen
   and a St. Catherine (Ronchini, Relazioni di Tiziano coi Farnese). The composition of the
   picture has been preserved in an engraving by Bertelli which bears a dedication to the Pope
   (Figure 314). The relationship of this composition to the celebrated large version in Santi
   Giovanni e Paolo has not yet been cleared up; in Belvedere 1931, I, Rothschild remarks that
   in the latter picture the composition has been transformed in accordance with the style of the
   late period.⟩

ROTTERDAM, VAN BEUNINGEN COLLECTION

Child between two large dogs. On canvas. From the Serbelloni collection. The picture, which
   was first brought to notice by L. Venturi, Pitture Italiane in America, Milan 1931, p. 288,
   is a characteristic work of the late period. It presents certain iconographical difficulties,
   the simplest solution of which is the assumption that it is only a fragment of a larger
   composition; this is strengthened by the shape, which leads one to suppose that the picture
   has been cut on the left, above and below. The (later) engraving by Pietro Testa
   (Bartsch XX, 222, 25), which in the foreground has a similar group as subsidiary motive,
   makes it permissible to suppose that the child originally belonged to a mythological composition of similar character. The dog corresponds very exactly to that in the portrait
   of a knight at Kassel (Figure 198), and the child to the youthful satyr, likewise holding
   a dog, on the right of the Marsyas picture at Kremsier (Figure 281).
   Figure 260.

ROTTERDAM, BOYMANS MUSEUM

Faun and Nymph. On canvas. Ascribed to various artists, to Dosso by Schmidt-Degener in
   Burlington Magazine, vol. 28, October, and recently to Titian by Suida in the French
   edition of his Titian monograph and independently by this author in Art Quarterly 1939,
   pp. 207 seqq. Probably from the Barbarigo Collection, Padua, and mentioned in Bevilacqua's
   Catalogue No. 80; previously kept in Titian's studio, where it is mentioned by Ridolfi
   (1, 200): *Siringa rapita da Pane . . . nella casa di Titiano sino al suo morire.*
   Figure 228.

SAN DIEGO, CALIFORNIA, ART MUSEUM

Portrait of Doge Francesco Donato. Canvas. Formerly Rothschild Collection. Published by
   Suida in Gazette des Beaux-Arts, s. VI, vol. 29, p. 139, and by E. Tietze-Conrat in Art

Bulletin, vol. 28, p. 82. Titian's modello for the official portrait. Dated by the years of Donato's reign 1545—53.
Figure 169.

ST. LOUIS, MISSOURI, CITY ART MUSEUM

Ecce Homo. On canvas. First published by A. L. Mayer in Burlington Magazine, vol. 76, 1935, p. 53, as a late work by Titian, about 1565. questioned by L. Serra, L. Dussler and this author. Discussed anew by E. Tietze-Conrat in Art Bulletin, vol. 28, 1946, p. 97, who explained the baffling features by classifying the painting not as unfinished, as Mayer had suggested, but as Titian's preparatory sketch which remained in the studio to serve as model for future replicas, some of which still exist. The painting may be identical with one offered in 1640 to the art collecting bishop Coccapani, in Reggio: *Ecce Homo di Tiziano, parte finito, parte abbozzato, verissimo di sua mano.*
Figure 273.

SANDS POINT, LONG ISLAND, L. M. RABINOWITZ COLLECTION

Portrait of Gerard Mercator. On canvas. 42 x 36 inches. Signed (above the globe): *Titiano* and (at the foot of the table) *Titianus f. anno aetatis XXIV* (later addition). Collection King Charles I of England; Lindenhurst, Philadelphia. Exhibited as portrait of a unknown gentleman in Toledo, Ohio, 1940, No. 66, and dated in the late 1530's or early 1540's, later identified by L. Venturi, The Rabinowitz Collection, New York (1945), p. 51, as the portrait of the famous globe- and map-maker Gerard Mercator. Though the only other portrait of Mercator available for comparison, the engraving by F. Hogenberg, shows him at the age of 62, and thus of course very much changed, the identification seems attractive.

SERRAVALLE, CATHEDRAL

Madonna in Glory with St. Peter and St. Andrew. On canvas. Signed: Titianus. Begun in 1542, finished in 1547. The payments continued until 1553. Mainly an atelier work.
Figure 155.

STOCKHOLM, HERMANN RASCH COLLECTION

Portrait of King Philip II. On canvas. Formerly in the Habig collection, Kassel. See A. L. Mayer, Tizianstudien, in Münchner Jahrbuch 1925, pp. 267 seqq., where the painting is placed a few years before the portrait in Cincinnati, while according to E. Tietze-Conrat in the Art Bulletin 1946, p. 82, it may be instead a finished version after the painting in question which served as Titian's modello. A slightly different copy in a private collection in Göteborg, Sweden, was published by O. Sirén in National Arsbok X, 1928, p. 45.
Figure 214.

TREVISO, CATHEDRAL

Annunciation. On wood. Altar-piece of the chapel endowed in 1519 by Canon Broccardo Malchiostro; the inscription on the frame was paid for in 1523; see L. Coletti, Rassegna d'Arte, 1921, p. 407. Ottinger, in Münchner Jahrbuch, N.F. VII, pp, 319 seqq., attempted to solve the problem of the dating of the picture by suggesting that a typical Annunciation composition was begun by Titian in 1515 as a horizontal picture, and that Paris Bordone in 1525 transformed it into the altar-piece; in this way could be explained the contrast between the Virgin and the Angel, the awkward insertion of the donor, and the spatial depth which is so unusual in Titian. Suida and Coletti (in the Inventory of the Province of Treviso) are not in favour of this theory. It gains probability if one assumes that Bordone made the alterations when he was an assistant in Titian's workshop.
Figure 65.

URBINO, PALAZZO DUCALE

Resurrection of Christ. On canvas. Painted as a processional standard in 1542/44, together with the Last Supper, for the members of the Congregation of Corpus Domini in Urbino; separated from the Last Supper in 1546 and provided with an ornamental frame by Pietro Viti (Repertorium XXV, p. 443). The combination of an older form of composition with elements of the period—the guardian on the left is almost identical with a figure in the Ecce Homo at Vienna (Figure 139)—denotes, together with the arid execution, that it is a workshop production.
Figure 156.

Last Supper. On canvas. Belongs with the Resurrection, see preceding paragraph. Suida has drawn attention to the noteworthy Milanese elements, especially the Bramantesque round building in the background. In addition to this, it should be noted that St. John is not represented with his head on Christ's breast, as is usually the case, and that the composition in other respects differs from those which Titian adopted from Leonardo. The scheme of composition and the single figures became a part of Venetian painting (Tintoretto, Francesco

Bassano, Moroni in the parish church at Romano)—perhaps as a result of a more impressive version (the burnt Last Supper by Titian in Santi Giovanni e Paolo). Figure 154.

VENICE, ACCADEMIA

Presentation of the Virgin in the Temple. On canvas. Painted between 1534 and 1538 for the Scuola della Carità (G. Ludwig, in Jahrbuch der Preussischen Kunstsammlungen XXVI, supplement, pp. 52 seqq., and Cantalamessa, Le Gallerie Nazionali Italiane II, pp. 37 seqq.) and now hung once more in the room for which it was originally painted. Ridolfi identified among the spectators portraits of Andrea Franceschi and Lazaro Grasso. Antonio Lorenzoni, Cadore, Bergamo 1907, p. 30, attempted to identify the mountain in the background with the view of the Marmarole from Roccolo di Sant' Alipio. Figures 108 (109—114).

Pietà. On canvas. The picture was intended for the chapel of the Crucifixion in the Frari, but at the time of Titian's death, perhaps because the monks refused to accept it, it was still unfinished in his atelier; it was completed by Jacopo Palma il Giovane and presented to the church of Sant' Angelo, on the demolition of which it passed to the Accademia. These facts are related in the inscription: Quod Titianus inchoatum reliquit Palma absolvit Deoque dicavit opus. Beneath the statue of the Sibyl is the coat of arms of the Vecelli, and leaning against it a votive tablet showing Titian and his son Orazio praying before the Virgin (on this tablet in relation to other votive pictures in Venice see Fogolari in Dedalo II). Opinions differ as to the share to be attributed to Titian's own hand and to Palma. Figure 280.

John the Baptist. On canvas. From Santa Maria Maggiore. Signed: Ticianus. Hourticq's assumption (Giorgione, p. 88), that the picture is based directly on the engraving by Giulio Campagnola (Kristeller 3) and that a drawing in the Louvre is the connecting link, appears to me erroneous; in the same way the connection with the drawing by Domenico Campagnola in the École des Beaux-Arts, which has been assumed by many writers, seems to me inexistent; A. L. Mayer in Burlington Magazine, vol. 71, p. 178, following a similar trend of ideas, placed the painting around 1530 to 1532. In my opinion Titian drew on an earlier memory in a later painting, as he did in many other instances. Figures 152 (153).

Head of St. Catherine from Palma Vecchio's Santa Conversazione. On canvas. The picture by Palma, acquired in 1901, is reproduced in Rassegna d'Arte I, p. 25. G. Frizzoni, Rassegna d'Arte VI, drew attention to the similarity between the St. Catherine and the St. Agnes in the atelier picture of the Santa Conversazione in the Louvre (reproduced in Suida, Plate LXXXI a). The fact that the style and quality of the head differ notably from the rest of Palma's picture led Hourticq, Revue de l'Art XXXII, pp. 120 seqq., and Suida, Belvedere 1931, p. 137, to suppose that Titian completed a picture which had been left unfinished on Palma's death in 1528. Although Spahn (Palma Vecchio, p. 90) endeavours to explain the extraneous elements in the St. Catherine as due to restoration, it seems to me that there is much to be said for the attribution of the head to Titian. Figure 79.

VENICE, BIBLIOTECA MARCIANA

Wisdom. On canvas. Ridolfi called this picture a representation of 'Historia'. The decoration of the library, built by Sansovino, was executed by Cristoforo Rosa; on September 9th, 1559, Titian was entrusted with the task of valuing his friend's work. It is supposed that in April of the following year Titian took over the middle space, while the other compartments were decorated by younger artists. First mentioned as a work of Titian by Boschini, Minere, p. 67. Although it is generally very favourably judged, and even called by Hetzer, and by Norris in Burlington Magazine 1935, II, p. 128, one of Titian's great masterpieces, it seems to me, on account of the decorative superficiality, to be essentially an atelier work. Figure 232.

VENICE, DUCAL PALACE

Doge Grimani kneeling before Faith (La Fede). On canvas. On March 22nd, 1556, Titian received a partial payment for the votive picture which he had begun by order of Doge Francesco Venier in honour of Doge A. Grimani (1523/29). For unknown reasons, however, he did not finish it, and Vasari saw it still unfinished in his atelier in 1566. Probably it was completed by pupils after Titian's death and placed in the Ducal palace after the fire of 1577. Figures 271 (272).

St. Christopher. Fresco on the staircase by the Sala dei Filosofi. Unanimously supposed to have been painted soon after the election of Doge Andrea Gritti in 1523. On its relation to Ger-

man graphic art see Hetzer, Deutsches Element, p. 112, and E. Tietze-Conrat, in Mitteilungen der Gesellschaft für Vervielfältigende Kunst 1924, No. 4.
Figure 68.

Madonna and Child with little Angels. Fresco, transfered to canvas. 63¹/₄ x 138³/₄ inches. Described by Ridolfi as being 'at the foot of the staircase leading from the court of the Senators to the end of the loggia on the first floor'. In its present state of preservation it is difficult to form an opinion on it, but in view of the very close similarity with the top of the altar-piece now in the Vatican (Figure 137) it can only be an atelier work, after 1530. Its influence on Jacopo Bassano is frequently referred to.
Reproduced in Suida, Plate LXXXV.

⟨VENICE, FORMERLY IN THE DUCAL PALACE, SALA DEL GRAN CONSIGLIO

The Battle of Cadore. In a petition dated March 31st, 1513, Titian offered to paint this battle picture, and this was accepted by the Council of Ten, but Titian, after he received the broker's licence for the Fondaco dei Tedeschi in 1516, does not appear to have proceeded with the execution. Admonitions in 1518 and 1522 had no effect, and it was not until June 23rd, 1537, when the Senate threatened to make him repay the money he had received since twenty years, that he started work on the picture, which he finished in August, 1538. It was destroyed in the fire of December 20th, 1577. We can reconstruct it from a painted copy in the Uffizi, an engraving by Fontana of 1569, an anonymous engraving in the Albertina at Vienna, and a copy of the girl at Bergamo (see above). That the copy in the Uffizi and the anonymous engraving retain the original composition has been proved by E. Tietze-Conrat in Mitteilungen der Gesellschaft für Vervielfältigende Kunst 1925, p. 42. More recently the same author has returned twice to the task of clarifying this painting. In Art Bulletin 1945, pp. 204 seqq., she examined the subject matter and reached the conclusion that the painting, named merely the 'Battle' in the documents and made to replace an early battle scene by the Trecento painter Guariento, was meant to represent the Battle of Spoleto, one of the episodes in the legendary early history of Venice, which offered the favorite subjects for almost all official decorations in the Ducal Palace. The second article, in Gazette des Beaux-Arts, s. 6, v. 34, p. 237, deals with the preparatory sketch of the whole composition, in the Louvre, showing the influence of Leonardo da Vinci's Battle of Anghiari for the general arrangement and many significant differences from the final solution.
Figure 302.⟩

⟨VENICE, FORMERLY IN THE DUCAL PALACE, SALA DEI PREGADI

Votive picture of Doge Andrea Gritti. Painted by Titian in 1531 and described by Vasari as 'cosa maravigliosissima'. Destroyed in the fire of 1574. The composition is reproduced in an anonymous woodcut, in which the head of Gritti is replaced by that of his next successor but one, Francesco Donato, who is also mentioned in the inscription (Figure 303). The composition, however, corresponds exactly with the description in the Diary of Marino Sanuto, Volume LV, under date October 6th, 1531, where the three patron saints of Gritti are mentioned and it is also stated why these three saints were chosen. On the reconstruction of the picture see Hadeln in Jahrbuch der Preussischen Kunstsammlungen XXXIV, p. 234, and Pantheon, 1930, p. 489; Hadeln's theory is corrected by H. Tietze and E. Tietze-Conrat in Jahrbuch der Kunsthistorischen Sammlungen in Wien, N. F. X, p. 191, under drawing No. 22.⟩

VENICE, FONDACO DEI TEDESCHI

Decorative mural paintings. According to the unanimous information of the oldest sources, Titian painted the frescoes on the street side of the Fondaco, while Giorgione, who received the final payment on November 8th, 1508, and was thus evidently in charge of the whole work, painted those on the canal side. The reconstruction of the frescoes, which on the spot are scarcely visible any longer, is aided by two engravings by J. Piccino and the etchings of Zanetti in his work 'Varie Pitture a fresco', Venice 1760. As the oldest attested work of Titian, both Hetzer, Frühe Gemälde, p. 7, and Ottinger, in Belvedere XI, pp. 44 seqq., make them the central point in their analysis of Titian's youthful style. Lately Piero H. de Minerbi in Bollettino d'Arte 1936/37, pp. 170 seqq., has tried to give the literary sources a different interpretation which would involve a new distribution of the murals. His arguments have not convinced me.
Figure 286—291.

VENICE, SANTA CATERINA

Tobias with the Archangel. On wood. 68¹/₄ x 58 inches. Titian mentioned to Vasari that he had painted a picture of this subject at the time of the war between Venice and Maximilian, i. e. 1507/08; Vasari refers this statement to the picture in San Marcuola, which, however, shows a later degree of style. In his edition of Ridolfi, pp. 153 and 158, Hadeln refers the

statement to our picture, which he, and after him Hourticq and Suida, hold to be a youthful picture by Titian, while Öttinger (Magyar Müveszet 1931, No. 4) tried to justify the attribution to Bordone, and Ricketts and Heinemann classified the painting as a copy after a lost original by Titian. Reversing my former opinion, I join those who consider the painting an early work of Titian, perhaps a few years after the above mentioned date. A. L. Mayer's observation that the coat-of-arms on the panel is that of the Bembo family (Gazette des Beaux-Arts, s. VI, vol. 18, p. 304) offers an important additional argument for the attribution to Titian and for the early date. Pietro Bembo was one of Titian's earliest patrons and apparently instrumental for his invitation to the papal court before 1513. The central group of the painting was included in the crowd in the large woodcut of the 'Destruction of Pharaoh's Host'.
Figure 13.

VENICE, SANTA MARIA DEI FRARI

The Madonna of the Pesaro Family. On canvas. Painted between 1519 and 1526 on behalf of Jacopo Pesaro, Bishop of Paphos, and unveiled on December 8th of the last-named year. The arms on the banner are those of the Pesaro and Borgia families; the donors represented are, on the left, Jacopo Pesaro, on the right, according to Gronau, Benedetto, and behind him Vittore, Antonio, Fantino and Giovanni Pesaro. The supposed sketch preserved in the Uffizi and the drawing at the Albertina in Vienna mentioned by the older writers were not made until after the picture had been painted. A. Wolf, who copied the picture in the seventies, discovered (Zeitschrift für Bildende Kunst 1877, pp. 9 seqq.) that the group of figures was originally surrounded by the interior of a church, and that the striking motive of the two pillars in the background was created only during the course of the painting.
Figures 69 (70—73).

Assumption of the Virgin. On canvas. Signed: Ticianus. Commissioned in 1516, the same date being found also on the frame, and shown to the public for the first time on May 20th, 1518. The picture had been in the Accademia since 1817, but after the first world war it was replaced in its original position, in 1919.
Figures 35 (36, 37).

VENICE, GESUITI

Martyrdom of St. Lawrence. On canvas. Signed: Titianus Vecelius Aeques F. The history of the picture has been expounded by Rodolfo Gallo, Rivista di Venezia 1935, pp. 155 seqq. Between 1557 and 1559 it was placed by Elisabetta Querini on the tomb of her husband Lorenzo Massolo, but it was conceived in the previous decade, as we learn from Massolo's will that Titian was already working on it on November 18th, 1548. This is corroborated by the fact that the Spanish Ambassador Garcia states in a letter of 1564, that the picture had been completed many years before. The stylistic elements and the relationship to the later version in the Escorial have been fully discussed by Eugen Rothschild, Tizians Darstellungen der Laurentiusmarter, Belvedere 1931, p. 202. The engraving by Cort of 1571 is closer to the Venice version, without, however, corresponding to it in every detail.
Figures 209 (210).

VENICE, SAN GIOVANNI ELEMOSINARIO

St. John Elemosinarius. On canvas. The usual date of 1533 assigned to this picture is due to hasty reading of the date, 1633, inscribed on the frame, which refers to the construction of the altar. It is, however, partially confirmed by the fact that Vasari and Ridolfi place the picture immediately after Titian's meeting with Charles V in Bologna (1532/33).
Figure 81.

⟨FORMERLY IN VENICE, SANTI GIOVANNI E PAOLO

Death of St. Peter Martyr. Painted in 1528/30, after the Confraternity of St. Peter Martyr had decided in 1525 to replace the older altar-piece by Jacobello del Fiore and Titian had been victorious in the competition against Palma Vecchio and Pordenone. This picture, described by all contemporary writers and by later judges as one of Titian's principal works, was destroyed by fire on the night of August 16st, 1867. The composition has been preserved in several engravings and painted copies; on the spot there is one by Cigoli. Draughtsketches in Lille (Figure 85); on others wrongly held to be sketches by Titian see H. Tietze and E. Tietze-Conrat in Jahrbuch der Kunsthistorischen Sammlungen in Wien, N. F. X, pp. 150 seqq.
Figure 300.⟩

⟨VENICE, FORMERLY IN THE SCUOLA DI SAN GIOVANNI EVANGELISTA

Vision of St. John the Evangelist. According to Ridolfi the decoration of the Albergo della Confraternità di San Giovanni Evangelista was carried out by Titian. After the closing of the school the pictures were removed to the Accademia, where may still be seen nineteen paintings, representing evangelical symbols, angels' heads and masks, all of them unimportant atelier productions. The principal picture was sent in exchange for another to Count Bertalazzone d'Arache, Turin (according to Cadorin, Nota dei Luoghi dove si trovano opere di Tizano. Nozze Morosini-Rombo 1885), and seems after a long disappearance to be in the art market at present. The composition is also preserved in an engraving on copper, and is described as a vision of St. John the Evangelist, without, however, defining to which vision this appearance of God the Father—not that of the Virgin Mary on Patmos—refers. Figure 318⟩.

VENICE, SAN LIO

St. James. On canvas. Nothing is known of the history of this badly preserved work. Previously it was usually dated in the late period, but now most writers assign it to the 1540's. Figure 147.

VENICE, SAN MARCO

St. Marc in ecstasy. Mosaic in the atrium above the principal doorway. Signed : Francesco e Valerio Zuccato 1545. That Titian made sketches for mosaics for the Zuccati is an old tradition, confirmed by statements made by him during the lawsuit against Francesco Zuccato. Stylistic reasons—e. g. the resemblance to the altar-piece in the Vatican Gallery—make it probable that this mosaic is one of those designed by Titian. R. Longhi, however, recently ascribed it to Lotto, in Calepino Veneziano, in Arte Veneta 1947, p. 192. Figure 158.

St. Geminianus. Mosaic in the north atrium. Signed: F. Zuccato 1535. Cf. what has been said above about the St. Mark. Stylistically and also in the colour-treatment agrees with Titian's style in the thirties. Ascribed to L. Lotto by M. A. Muraro in Arte Veneta 1918, p. 100. Figure 296.

VENICE, SAN MARZIALE

Tobias and the Angel. On canvas. On Titian's statement that the picture was painted in 1507/08 and the obvious error caused thereby, see above under Venice, Santa Caterina. Our picture is generally assigned to the thirties or forties (Crowe and Cavalcaselle about 1538, catalogue of the recent exhibition about 1534, Gronau—probably more correct—1540/43, A. Venturi about 1546, A. L. Mayer, Gazette des Beaux-Arts, s. VI, vol. 18, p. 304, between 1532 and 40). Boschini's attribution of the painting in Santa Caterina (see above) to Sante Zago might refer to the one in San Marziale, which L. Fröhlich-Bum (Jahrbuch der Kunsthistorischen Sammlungen in Wien XXXI, p. 198 f.) wished to attribute to Andrea Schiavone. R. Peltzer in the same Jahrbuch, p. 221, assigned it to Lambert Sustris. By a follower of Titian, rather than by the master himself. Figures 140 (141).

VENICE, SAN ROCCO

Christ bearing the Cross, with an executioner. On canvas. The tradition relating to this picture has varied from the beginning. Vasari calls it a Giorgione in his first edition, a Titian in the second. Subsequently most sources call it a Titian, only Van Dyck wrote the word 'Giorgione' after his sketch. Modern opinions also differ widely, and the bad state of preservation makes a decision difficult. On the whole the reasons for assigning it to Titian seem to me to predominate. Figure 284.

VENICE, SANTA MARIA DELLA SALUTE

Cain and Abel. On canvas. Originally painted for the church of Santo Spirito, probably between 1541 and 1544. When the latter church was demolished in 1656, the picture was brought to the Salute. Belongs with the two other ceiling pictures, Figures 149 and 150. L. Fröhlich-Bum, Jahrbuch der Kunsthistorischen Sammlungen in Wien XXXI, p. 204, is inclined to attribute it to Andrea Schiavone on account of the external resemblance to the latter's Samson in Palazzo Pitti; vice versa, A. Venturi, IX/3, p. 310, on account of the same resemblance, would like to assign the Pitti picture to Titian. Figure 151.

The Sacrifice of Abraham. See the preceding paragraph. There is a drawing of the picture in the École des Beaux-Arts in Paris (s. below). Figure 149.

David and Goliath. See above. Figure 150.

Eight medallions with busts of Evangelists and Fathers of the Church. On wood. Diameter
28¹/₄ inches. Originally, and very probably together with the three ceiling paintings (see
above), painted for Santo Spirito and transferred from there in 1656. In the St. Matthew
some have thought to recognize Titian's self-portrait, but this is disputed by Foscari, Iconografia, p. 27; Aretino may have sat as model for the St. Augustine. The participation of
the workshop is considerable.
Figure 148.

St. Mark with Saints Sebastian, Roch, Cosmas and Damian. On wood. Painted for Santo Spirito
and transferred in 1656. According to earlier investigators painted on the occasion of the
plague in 1504, but more probably—as Crowe and Cavalcaselle supposed—after the plague
in 1510.
Figure 14.

Descent of the Holy Ghost. On canvas. In 1541 Titian painted an altar-piece of this subject for
Santo Spirito, which, however, according to Vasari, he had to repaint after a long dispute
with the brethren, because it was spoilt; Titian refers to this quarrel in a letter written to
Cardinal Farnese in 1544. It is not known when he completed the substitute picture; for
stylistic reasons it is generally assigned to the middle of the fifties. It was brought to its
present position in 1656.
Figure 237.

VENICE, SAN SALVATORE

Annunciation. On canvas. Signed: Titianus fecit fecit. The second 'fecit' which has been
interpreted as meaning that Titian wanted to emphasize his own authorship in the face of
doubters or to refute critics of his late style, may perhaps be explained as due to bad
restoration of a date which previously stood there, traces of which may still be discerned
under the letters. A late work, but before 1566, for it is mentioned by Vasari. The picture
suffered badly from earlier restoration; Ridolfi (Hadeln edition I, p. 205) states that even
at that time Philipp Esengren had restored and damaged it.
Figure 256.

Transfiguration. On canvas. This painting still serves as a 'timpano' or covering for the silver
altar of the church, and is shown only during the first days of August and on important
festivals. A late work, probably conceived before 1566. Damaged by bad restoration.
Figure 235.

VENICE, SAN SEBASTIANO

St. Nicholas of Bari. On wood. Signed: Titianus P. Ordered by the Venetian jurist Niccolò
Crasso for his chapel, which bears the date of 1563. Crowe and Cavalcaselle, as well as later
authors, assume a more or less considerable participation of the workshop. A. L. Mayer,
Gazette des Beaux-Arts, s. VI. vol. 18, p. 306, dates the painting long before 1563, perhaps
even before 1540.
Figure 261.

VENICE, SCUOLA DI SAN ROCCO

Annunciation. On canvas. Bequeathed to the Scuola di San Rocco in 1555 by the lawyer Amelio
Cortona. Many writers place it in the forties, but Suida is probably more correct in assigning
it to the early thirties. In any case the workshop seems to have taken a share in the execution.
Figure 115.

Dead Christ. On canvas. 21¹/₂ x 31³/₄ inches. The tradition as to this picture has been uncertain
from the beginning. The serious damage it has sustained through fire and extensive overpainting make it difficult to form an opinion. The iconographical type is the frequently occurring
one of the Gregorian "man of sorrows", cf. Panofsky in Friedländer-Festschrift, p. 263.
Nothing in the execution points to Titian except the general Giorgionesque character.
Reproduced in Suida, Plate CCIC.

⟨VENICE, FORMERLY IN TITIAN'S ESTATE

Flagellation. According to Ridolfi (Hadeln edition I, p. 207) after Titian's death several
'abbozzi', among them a Christ being scourged at the pillar, were acquired by Jacopo
Tintoretto. This composition, of which nothing else is known, is probably that which is
preserved in engravings by B. Franco and by Martino Rota of the year 1568.
Figure 319.⟩

VERONA, CATHEDRAL

Assumption. On canvas. Vasari calls this picture the best modern painting in Verona, but gives
no information about when it was painted. The dating in the modern writers varies between
1523 and 1543. Recently A. L. Mayer, Gazette des Beaux-Arts, s. VI, vol. 18, p. 308,
pleaded strongly for a date before 1530.
Figure 82.

VERONA, MUSEO CIVICO

Portrait of a Gentleman. On canvas. From the Bernasconi collection. Held by Ed. Schaeffer, Jahrbuch der Preussischen Kunstsammlungen XXXI, pp. 136 seqq., to be a portrait of the scientist Girolamo Fracastoro, but this is denied by Giuseppe Gerola and Hadeln, Ridolfi I, p. 192. The subject is now held to be a member of the Castracani family. Originally the picture was assigned to Morone, until it was claimed for Titian by Berenson and, with more ample details, by Gronau in Rassegna d'Arte VII, p. 135. The notable resemblance of the weak hands and pale flesh to the portrait of a gentleman by Lotto in the Brera renders the attribution to Titian very doubtful. Dussler, Zeitschrift für Kunstwissenschaft 1935, p. 237, and A. L. Mayer, Gazette des Beaux-Arts, s. VI, vol. 18, p. 304, also reject the attribution to him, the latter even to the School of Venice altogether.
Figure 179.

VIENNA, AKADEMIE DER BILDENDEN KÜNSTE

Lucretia and Tarquin. On canvas. Purchased in 1907 at the Schroff auction-sale in Vienna. First brought to notice by W. von Bode in Kunstchronik, N. F. XXVII, No. 2. The suggestion of Anny E. Popp, Zeitschrift für Bildende Kunst, N. F. 1921, pp. 9 seqq., that this picture is a reduction, made by cutting on all sides, of the full-figure composition reproduced by C. Cort in his engraving of 1571, has been refuted by Eigenberger in Die Gemäldegalerie der Akademie 1927, I, pp. 408 seqq. For the larger version of the subject, see the picture in the Fitzwilliam Museum, Cambridge, Figure 275. Our picture might be a composition sketch which Titian kept in his atelier.
Figure 276.

VIENNA, GALERIE CZERNIN

Portrait of Doge Andrea Gritti. On canvas. Signed: Titianus E. F. (authenticity doubtful). In his study of Titian's portraits of Doges, Pantheon 1930, Hadeln has stated that this picture could not have been painted before 1533. While it is valued very highly by some writers, e. g. by Dussler in Zeitschrift für Kunstwissenschaft 1935, p. 239, it has been considered doubtful by others. Crowe and Cavalcaselle thought it was certainly by Pordenone, and Norris has recently expressed his doubts in Burlington Magazine 1935, II, p. 127. In A. L. Mayer's opinion (Gazette des Beaux-Arts, s. VI, vol. 18, p. 307) the painting is later than 1545, in view of its technique and its tendency to be colossal; it may even represent a later doge than Gritti and have been painted by Palma Giovine. E. Tietze-Conrat in Art Bulletin 1946, p. 81, on the other hand identified the painting with one in the collection of King Charles' of England and described its type as the portrait of Doge Gritti 'in atto di passeggio'.

VIENNA, KUNSTHISTORISCHES MUSEUM

Ecce Homo. On canvas. Signed: Titianus Eques Ces. F. 1543.—According to Vasari, painted for Giovanni d'Anna (van Haanen), a Flemish merchant residing in Venice, in whose house Henri III of France saw it in 1574 and where it is mentioned by F. Sansovino in 1580. Purchased in 1620 by the Duke of Buckingham and acquired at the auction of the latter's collection in 1648 at Antwerp by Archduke Leopold Wilhelm on behalf of Emperor Ferdinand III; remained in Prague until at least 1718, in Vienna since 1723. According to Ridolfi, the Pilate is a portrait of Pietro Aretino, and the turbaned horseman that of Sultan Soliman the Great; according to the same writer, the horseman in armour is Charles V, the man holding a staff in each hand Titian himself, and the girl dressed in white his daughter Lavinia. All these identifications of portraits, with the exception of that of Aretino, are doubtful. Crowe and Cavalcaselle assumed the participation of pupils in this picture, and Ricketts also criticizes unfavourably its composition.
Figure 139.

Entombment. On canvas. Signed: Titianus. Cut on all four sides. Acquired in the artist's atelier in 1572 by the Signoria as a present for the Spanish Secretary of State Antonio Pérez, and sent to Madrid. Later purchased by the Duke of Buckingham and at the auction of his collection in Antwerp in 1648 probably acquired by Archduke Leopold Wilhelm for Emperor Ferdinand III. Can be traced in Vienna from 1723 on.
Workshop repetition of the lost picture sent to Philip II in 1556, which was small and not in full figure; to replace it Titian delivered in 1559 a new version of the Entombment now in Madrid (Figure 255).
Reproduced in Suida, Plates XX and LXXIII b.

The Gipsy Madonna. On wood.—In the collection of Archduke Leopold Wilhelm in 1659. A youthful picture, in which the influence of Giovanni Bellini and the closeness to Giorgione have always been noted; the latter led A. Venturi and H. Cook to believe that it was by Giorgione, and L. Justi likewise considers this not impossible, while G. M. Richter (Art Bulletin 1934, p. 272) is willing to accept at least an underpainting of the picture by Giorgione. The attribution to Titian has now been confirmed by J. Wilde's 'Röntgenaufnahmen der Drei Philosophen und der Zigeunermadonna', in Jahrbuch der Wiener Kunsthistorischen Sammlungen, N. F. VI, p. 151; in the same article the date first suggested by E. von Rothschild (Belvedere 1932, p. 110), viz. 1510, is upheld, whereas Crowe and Cavalcaselle placed it at the end of the fifteenth century, Morelli six to eight years later, and Fischel about 1502/03. Figure 9.

The Madonna with the Cherries. Transferred from canvas to wood in 1853/58.—In the collection of Archduke Leopold Wilhelm in 1659. The underpainting revealed when the picture was transferred to canvas was preserved in a copy by Erasmus Engert and shows important deviations from the final version; see Graphische Künste III, p. 19, and Belvedere 1932, I (Figure 33). While Crowe and Cavalcaselle date it shortly before 1508 and Hetzer in 1506, Heinemann assigns it to 1511/17, Gronau, Fischel, the 1928 catalogue of the gallery and Rothschild, loc. cit., to 1512/15. In this case the obvious connection with Dürer's Madonna with the goldfinch in Berlin is not, as Glaser, E. Tietze-Conrat and Hetzer assumed, due to a borrowing of Dürer from Titian, but vice versa, as Flechsig states in his book on Dürer, unless—as H. Tietze and E. Tietze-Conrat suggest in Der reife Dürer, No. 326—both pictures are derived from an older Venetian original. Figure 34.

Madonna and Child with Saints Stephen, Jerome and Maurice. On wood. $36^1/2 \times 54^1/2$ inches. Acquired with the collection of Archduke Leopold Wilhelm in 1659; according to Gronau probably the picture which C. Ridolfi mentions as belonging to the heirs of Cardinal Aldobrandini in Rome. Crowe and Cavalcaselle, Klassiker[5], and Ricketts hold it to be the original, while Gronau, A. Venturi, and Phillips consider that it is a repetition of the Louvre version. Heinemann, p. 40, is reminded of Francesco Vecellio, Hetzer attributes both pictures to an unknown Venetian influenced by Titian, about 1530. The Vienna catalogue of 1928 suggests a workshop repetition of a lost original. That pupils also painted such pictures is proved by Ridolfi, I, p. 223, who mentions a 'Vergine col Bambino e tre santi dinanzi' by Nadalino da Murano. Reproduced in Suida, Plate LXXXIVa.

Diana and Callisto. On canvas.—From the collection of Archduke Leopold Wilhelm. An altered repetition of the painting which Titian sent to Philip II in Madrid in 1559 (see under London, Bridgewater House, Figure 226). The preliminary drawing which came to light when the picture was transferred to new canvas in 1912 agrees with this earlier version. The execution is attributed by most writers to the workshop, though Crowe and Cavalcaselle think that a few strokes may be due to Titian's own hand and others assume a rather greater participation of the master himself. The 1928 catalogue of the gallery, supported by the article by A. Stix in Jahrbuch der Kunsthistorischen Sammlungen XXXI, pp. 335 seqq., claims that the repetition is by Titian's own hand. Figure 227.

Nymph and Shepherd, also known as 'Angelica and Medor', perhaps identical with the picture of 'Endymion and Diana' which Titian offered to Emperor Maximilian II in 1568. On canvas. A strip on the left, $6^3/4$ inches wide, which still appears in older reproductions, is now hidden by the frame. Acquired from the collection of Archduke Leopold Wilhelm in 1659. This picture, sometimes held to be a sketch or unfinished, and in any case in a very bad state of preservation, is unanimously assigned to the master's last period of activity, by Gronau about 1565, by Fischel 1566/70, by the 1928 catalogue of the gallery after 1570. The relation to earlier motives has likewise been frequently observed. The resemblance to Giulio Campagnola's engraving of a recumbent nymph (Kristeller 13) has been noticed by Ricketts, Hourticq (Jeunesse, p. 264), Wilde in Jahrbuch der Kunsthistorischen Sammlungen, N. F. IV, and Suida, Gazette des Beaux-Arts 1935, pp. 75 seqq., while Suida also refers to a passage in Michiel, who mentions a miniature by Giulio Campagnola in Casa Bembo at Padua : 'una nuda tratta da Zorzi, stesa e volta'. According to this, Titian must have returned to a motive of Giorgione in this late work. The drawing in the former Oppenheimer collection (Figure 7) confirms this fact. On the other hand the frequently asserted relationship of the goat springing up a tree with a woodcut attributed to Domenico Campagnola has no foundation. Figure 279.

Portrait of the Elector Johann Friedrich of Saxony. On canvas.—First heard of in Vienna in the Stallburg gallery in 1720. It is not certain whether the picture is identical with the portrait which originally belonged to Queen Maria of Hungary and was taken by her to Madrid in 1556. Many investigators have noticed a northern element in this picture and have drawn attention to the resemblance of the conception to that of the Elector's court painter, Lucas Cranach. Wickhoff finds this northern element so pronounced that he describes the picture as a copy by Rubens after Titian (Kunstgeschichtliche Anzeigen 1904, p. 117), and Ricketts suggested a northern portrait model. Nevertheless most writers assume that Titian

painted the portrait at Augsburg in 1548 or 1550/51, at the time when the Elector was a prisoner there. Beneath the left eye the scar of the wound is visible, which the Elector received in the battle of Mühlberg in 1547.
Figure 194.

Portrait of a Man with raised right hand. On canvas. At the bottom a strip 3½ inches wide has been stuck on. The staff and the book, which have led to the subject being described as St. James, are later additions.—From the collection of Archduke Leopold Wilhelm.—A copy in the Kaiser Friedrich Museum in Berlin establishes the fact that the picture originally formed one painting together with the portrait of a boy (Figure 178).
The double portrait was held by Crowe and Cavalcaselle to represent Ranuccio Farnese and his tutor Leoni. According to the 1928 catalogue of the Vienna gallery, L. Burchard identifies it as the portrait of the orator Francesco Filetto and his son mentioned by Vasari, which in 1566 was in the house of M. Matteo Giustiniani at Venice. G. Hartlaub mentions the picture in Repertorium XLVIII, p. 243, as an example of an 'instructional painting' (Teacher and pupil, initiate and adept). The gallery catalogue dates it 1545/48.
Figure 177.

Portrait of a Boy. On canvas. On the left at the top a large portion measuring 18½ x 9¾ inches has been inserted. The arrows, which have led to the subject being described as St. Sebastian, are later additions.—In the collection of Archduke Leopold Wilhelm, 1659.
Originally belonged together with the preceding picture, q. v.
Figure 178.

Portrait of Filippo Strozzi (?). On canvas.—In the collection of Archduke Leopold Wilhelm, 1659. It is not known what the foundation for the naming of the person portrayed is which first occurs in the Mecheln catalogue of the Belvedere gallery, 1783. It is presumably incorrect because Filippo Strozzi, the leader of the anti-Medicean party, died in 1538, and the picture, though dated by Fischel about 1540, was probably created considerably later. On account of the costume alone, A. L. Mayer, in Belvedere V (1924), pp. 184 seqq., gives 1550 as the earliest possible date, while the catalogue of the gallery dates it 1555/60.
Figure 127.

Portrait of Fabrizio Salvaresio. On canvas. Cut below and on the right. Signed: MDLVIII. Fabricius Salvaresius annu agens L. Titiani opus.—In the collection of Archduke Leopold Wilhelm, 1659. Crowe and Cavalcaselle find the negro slave so overpainted that they doubt whether any part of the work as it is at present can be by Titian's own hand.
Figure 238.

Portrait of Benedetto Varchi (?). On canvas. Signed: Tizianus E.—In the collection of Archduke Leopold Wilhelm, 1659. The identification of the subject, which first occurs in the Mecheln catalogue of 1783, is based on the resemblance to a medal of Varchi by Domenico Poggini. This identification, however, is doubted by Crowe and Cavalcaselle and others (Gronau, Suida, Norris), who date the picture about 1550 or later and therefore find that it does not correspond with the age of Varchi, who was born in 1503. The 1928 catalogue of the gallery and that of the 1935 Venice exhibition nevertheless retain the name of Varchi, who as a political refugee and tutor of Filippo Strozzi's children lived in Venice from 1536 to 1543, and date the picture about 1540/43.
Figures 163 (164-5).

Portrait of Jacopo de Strada. On canvas. Slightly cut on the left. Signed: Titianus f. On the letter is the inscription: Al Mag^co Sig^ore il Sig^ore Titian(o) Vecellio... Venezia. In the cartouche, inserted later on the right at the top, is an inscription with the name, titles and dates of the subject.—In the collection of Archduke Leopold Wilhelm, 1659.
According to the investigations of H. Zimmermann in Mitteilungen des Instituts für österreichische Geschichtsforschung, supplementary volume VI, the picture was begun in 1567 and finished in 1568.
Figure 268.

Portrait of Isabella d'Este, Margravine of Mantua. On canvas. Cut on right and left; Jakob Burckhardt (Beiträge 2, p. 236) suggests that this is 'perhaps only the remains of a large, imposing knee-length picture'.—In the collection of Archduke Leopold Wilhelm, 1659. In the 1659 inventory erroneously described as the Queen of Cyprus. The now usual identification is based on the inscription on an engraving by Vorsterman after Rubens's copy of this picture; despite the credibility of this testimony—at the beginning of the 17th century Rubens was court painter at Mantua—the identification as Isabella d'Este was doubted by Suida and in more detail by L. Ozzola (Bollettino d'Arte 1931). It is, however, supported by the fact that from Isabella's correspondence we learn that Titian painted her portrait in 1534/36, using as a model a picture painted by Francesco Francia in 1511/12, which in its turn was not painted from life, but from another portrait. See H. Tietze and E. Tietze-Conrat in Jahrbuch der Kunsthistorischen Sammlungen in Wien, N. F. X, 1936, pp. 139 seqq.
Figure 95.

Girl in a fur. On canvas. Probably cut. First heard of in Vienna in 1705, previously supposed to have been in the collection of Charles I of England, though this is doubted by Ricketts. The same young woman (erroneously described by Moritz Thausing in the Wiener Kunst-briefe as Eleonora Gonzaga) sat as model for 'La Bella' in the Palazzo Pitti and the Venus at the Uffizi. In relationship with these pictures the Vienna painting is unanimously dated about 1535/38.
Figure 96.

Portrait of Titian's daughter Lavinia. On canvas.—In the collection of Archduke Leopold Wilhelm, 1659, where it was ascribed to Tintoretto. The identification rests on the resem-blance to the picture in Dresden bearing Lavinia's name. While Stix in Jahrbuch der Kunst-historischen Sammlungen XXXI, p. 344, and Ozzola, Bollettino d'Arte 1931, maintain that it is a workshop painting, Baldass (Belvedere V, p. 91)—because a participation of the workshop would be probable in a family portrait—and the 1928 catalogue of the gallery attribute it to Titian's own hand. Nevertheless the author of the last-named publication, Dr. Johannes Wilde, after a study of the X-ray photograph, is inclined to hold it for a workshop production.
Reproduced in Suida, Plate CCIV a.

WASHINGTON, THE CORCORAN GALLERY OF ART

Portrait of the Sculptor Martino Pasqualigo. On canvas. 31¹/₄ x 25 inches. Inscribed: *Ticianus* and *Martinus Pasqualigus Statuarius Venetus.* Published simultaneously by W. Suida, Art Quarterly II, p. 326, and H. Tietze, Art in America, 37, p. 181, as the portrait described by Ridolfi (I, 201, and II, 201) in the house of Bortolo Dafino. An origin around 1554 or 1555 seems likely in view of the age of the model.
Figure 213.

WASHINGTON, NATIONAL GALLERY OF ART (MELLON COLLECTION)

Venus with a mirror. On canvas. After Titian's death passed to the Barbarigo family, and from them to the Hermitage. This composition, which exists in several repetitions and numerous derivations has been discussed by Poglayen-Neuwall in Münchner Jahrbuch, N. F. 1929, pp. 16 seqq., and in still greater detail in Art Bulletin 1934, pp. 358 seqq. Accord-ing to these articles, there were two versions due to Titian himself, one of them, now lost, which he painted between 1545 and 1555 for the jurist Niccolò Crasso, and the Washington version, which Poglayen dates about 1555. After a comparison with these two versions, he considers the version formerly in the Nemes collection, Munich, which at one time aroused much interest, to be a workshop repetition. In Art Bulletin 29, 1947, 195, Poglayen defended his theory against the thesis offered by O. Wulff in Jahrbuch der Preussischen Kunst-sammlungen 1941, pp. 191 seqq., that the original contained no Cupids at all as in the version in the Cà d'Oro in Venice.
Figure 218.

WASHINGTON, NATIONAL GALLERY (WIDENER COLLECTION)

Venus and Adonis. On canvas. 42 x 53 inches. Collection Barbarigo, Padua; Lord Bristol; Earl of Spencer, Althorp Park; J. P. Widener, Elkins Park. For paintings representing the same composition on a bigger scale and with numerous differences see London, National Gallery, and Madrid, Prado. The painting in Washington may well be the modello of the second version made later than the bigger one and possibly invented by Titian's son Orazio. A studio replica of this version in the Metropolitan Museum, New York.

WASHINGTON, NATIONAL GALLERY (KRESS COLLECTION)

Young Woman at her toilet. On canvas. 36³/₈ x 31³/₄ inches. Formerly belonged to the Benacose family, Ferrara, then to Count Leopoldo Cicognara and Count Pourtalès-Gorgier, Paris. Dis-cussed in detail by Valentiner, Ein unbekanntes Meisterwerk Tizians, in Belvedere I, pp. 90 seqq., also accepted by A. and L. Venturi and by Suida, and described as a variant of the Louvre picture (Figure 17), painted about 1516. The derivation from the latter is obvious, yet I am inclined to agree with Heinemann, p. 52, and Dussler, Zeitschrift für Kunstwissen-schaft 1935, p. 237, that it is rather to be considered as the work of a follower and not connected with Titian.
Reproduced in Suida, Plate CXXI a.

Portrait of a Young Man. On canvas. 29³/₄ x 24⁷/₈ inches. Collection Henry Doetsch, London; Henry Goldman, New York. Attributed to Licinio, Giorgione, Sebastiano del Piombo or Titian. The last named is favoured by Berenson (who was the first to publish the painting as early as 1897, Gazette des Beaux-Arts II, 273), Cook, L. Venturi, Valentiner and Suida. The catalogue of the collection classifies it as by Titian after Giorgione. An entirely new theory was offered by H. Hahn in 'The Rape of La Belle', 1946, 200, who considers

the painting as the work of a Northern imitator of Giorgione. Nevertheless I am still inclined to accept Titian's authorship, around 1508 to 1510.
Figure 2.

WASHINGTON, NATIONAL GALLERY (MELLON COLLECTION)

Portrait of the Grandchancellor Andrea de' Franceschi. On canvas. $25^1/2 \times 20$ inches. Collection Earl of Wemyss, Gosford House, Scotland; A. Mellon, Washington. Probably Titian's original of which the painting in the E. B. Whitcomb Collection, Detroit, is a replica. For the identification of the model and the relationship of the various portraits some of them separately, and some together with Titian Ch. Holmes, Burlington Magazine 1929, p. 159 seqq., B. Berenson in Festschrift für Friedländer, p. 232, and Poglayen-Neuwall in Münchner Jahrbuch für Bildende Kunst, n. s. IV.
Figure 132.

WASHINGTON, NATIONAL GALLERY (KRESS COLLECTION)

Portrait of Cardinal Pietro Bembo. On canvas. $39^1/2 \times 29^1/2$ inches. Collection Barbarini, Rome; Charles M. Schwab, New York; S. Kress, New York. Titian painted Bembo's portrait repeatedly. The version in Washington may be Titian's study from life which was used for the official portraits. As to Titian's portraits of Bembo in general, see Suida in Burlington Magazine, vol. 68, 1936, p. 281, and E. Wind, Bellini's Feast of the Gods, p. 42.
Figure 133.

DRAWINGS

The most recent and detailed study of Titian's drawings is contained in this author's and E. Tietze-Conrat's book 'The Drawings of the Venetian Painters of the XVth and XVIth Centuries', New York 1944, p. 304 seqq., which supplements and in part corrects earlier critical lists compiled by Detlev Freiherr von Hadeln (Tizians Zeichnungen, Berlin 1924), Lili Fröhlich-Bum in Jahrbuch der Kunsthistorischen Sammlungen in Wien, n. s. II, 163 seqq., and ourselves in the same Jahrbuch, n. s. X, p. 137 seqq. A few more drawings have emerged since the publication of our book. The following list is limited to those drawings which to me seem especially important for the understanding of Titian's paintings.

BAYONNE, MUSÉE BONNAT

Landscape with Satyrs and Nymphs. Pen, 265×410 mm. Our number 1871. Attributed by others to Domenico Campagnola and G. M. Verdizotti, but claimed by us for Titian in the 1530's. To the references to paintings by Titian given in our book another should be added, to Titian's landscape in the background of Bellini's 'Feast of the Gods'.
Figure 88.

Romantic Scene (so-called Roger and Angelica); according to Ridolfi (I, p. 202) Perseus and Andromeda. Pen. 250×395 mm. Our number 1872. The composition is attested by C. Cort's engraving of 1565. Three inferior versions of the drawing in Chatsworth, in the Louvre, and formerly in the Fenwick Collection, Cheltenham, now London, British Museum. We placed the drawing in the 1540's and connected it with the mythological compositions for King Philip II, perhaps Medea and Jason, mentioned in Titian's letter to the King in 1554.
Figure 172.

Landscape with a Castle. Pen. 217×347 mm. Our number 1875 and illustrated pl. LXIII, 1. From the second decade of the sixteenth century. Used in Titian's woodcut 'Landscape with Milkmaid', Pass. VI, p. 242, No. 96.
Figure 26.

BERLIN, KUPFERSTICHKABINETT

Head of a Bearded Man. Black chalk, heightened with white. 312×230 mm. Our number 1878 and illustrated pl. LXVI, 2. Also attributed to Paris Bordone and A. Moretto. We referred for the attribution to Titian in the 1540's to the man on horseback in the 'Ecce Homo' in Vienna.

Study for the St. Sebastian in the Brescia altar-piece. Pen. 162×136 mm. Our number 1880. 1520 or a little earlier.
Figure 53.

CAMBRIDGE (ENGLAND), FITZWILLIAM MUSEUM

Jupiter and Io. Black chalk, on blue. 225×265 mm. Our number 1886. A copy in the Louvre.
Figure 229.

FLORENCE, UFFIZI

Man on Horseback. Black chalk, on blue. 524 x 395 mm. Study for the horseman in the left background of the 'Battle'. Our number 1908.—On the back: *Head of a Moor*. A similar head may be found on the left edge of the Pesaro Madonna.
Figures 78, 77.

Study for St. Bernardino in the Votive Painting of Doge Andrea Gritti. Black chalk, heightened with white, on blue. 380 x 264 mm. Our number 1904. Corresponds exactly to the woodcut made from the composition.—On the back two studies for the cloak of the kneeling doge. This drawing shows that in the original picture the doge was represented kneeling in sharp profile, as in the woodcut.
Figure 100.

Preliminary Drawing for the portrait of Duke Francesco Maria of Urbino. Pen. 240 x 142 mm. Our number 1911. On squared paper with a view to transfer to canvas. The picture must, as Hadeln has also stated, have first been painted in full figure and subsequently adapted to the format of the portrait of the Duchess.
Figure 101.

Study for the Executioner in the Martyrdom of St. Lawrence in the church of the Gesuiti at Venice. Charcoal, heightened with white. 403 x 253 mm. Our number 1906. On the back of the sheet are some small details, part of them not by Titian's own hand.
Figure 208.

Angel of an Annunciation. Black chalk, heightened with white. 420 x 280 mm. Our number 1905. On the back of the sheet study of a draped standing figure, illustrated in Gazette des Beaux-Arts 1937, II, 305, and in our book pl. LXIX, 2.
Figure 255.

FRANKFURT ON THE MAIN, STAEDELSCHES KUNSTINSTITUT

Studies for the St. Sebastian in Brescia. Pen. 183 x 115 mm. On the back various sketches. Our number 1915.
Figure 51.

LILLE, MUSÉE WICAR

Sketches for the Martyrdom of St. Peter in S. S. Giovanni e Paolo, destroyed by fire in 1867. Pen. 141 x 188 mm. Our number 1923.
Figures 297—299.

Faun. Pen. 128 x 130 mm. Our number 1926. Formerly called Titian, ascribed by Morelli to Sebastiano del Piombo, an attribution which we tried to refute in favour of the traditional name. Other critics, as for instance R. Pallucchini, Sebastian Viniziano, 1944, p. 80, still claim the drawing for Sebastiano, L. Fröhlich-Bum, Art Bulletin 1938, even for Annibale Carracci. To our arguments in favour of Titian offered in our 'Titianstudien', p. 174, we added a few more in 'Graphische Künste', n. s. III, p. 53.
Figure 40.

LONDON, BRITISH MUSEUM

Study for St. Peter in the 'Assunta', Frari. Chalk, 157 x 134 mm. Our number 1929. Dated by the painting.
Figure 38.

Two Shepherds in Landscape. Pen. 193 x 290 mm. Our number 1932. In an article on Domenico Campagnola's woodcuts, in Print Collectors Quarterly 1939, 457, we emphasized the close resemblance to Domenico Campagnola, but insisted on the difficulty of separating the drawing from the sketch for the Jealous Husband, in Paris, see there.

MUNICH, GRAPHISCHE SAMMLUNG

Horseman Leaping over a Fallen Man. Charcoal on blue. 346 x 252 mm. Our number 1941. Formerly related to the 'Battle' so-called of Cadore, but by E. Tietze-Conrat, Old Master Drawings 1936, April, to the battle picture by Orazio Vecelli, in the Ducal Palace (around 1562—64). The authenticity was questioned by Hetzer, in Thieme-Becker, 34.
Figure 264.

NEW YORK, METROPOLITAN MUSEUM

Group of Trees. Pen. 218 x 320 mm. Our number 1943. Used by Titian in two different places in his woodcut of the Sacrifice of Abraham, around 1516.
Figure 47.

NEW YORK, E. & A. SILBERMAN

Two Satyrs in Landscape. Pen. 213 x 152 mm. Formerly Wiltonhouse and Henry Oppenheimer Collection. Our number 1948. First ascribed to Titian in our 'Tizianstudien', p. 169,

ascribed to Sebastiano del Piombo by R. Pallucchini in L'Arte, n. s. VIII, 32, and called by A. L. Mayer, Gazette des Beaux-Arts, s. VI, 20, p. 305, 'at best copy from a Titian drawing'.
Figure 7.

OXFORD, ASHMOLEAN MUSEUM

Rider on a Falling Horse. Black chalk, on blue. 274 x 262 mm. Our number 1949. Stylistically related to the Horseman in Munich and like the latter belonging to Titian's late period.
Figure 263.

PARIS, ÉCOLE DES BEAUX-ARTS

Jealous Husband killing his Wife. Supposed sketch for the mural in the Scuola del Santo, 1511. Pen. 188 x 177 mm. Our number 1961. In agreement with the almost universal opinion of critics we accepted the attribution to Titian, but stressed the confusing divergences from the mural and the stylistic closeness to Domenico Campagnola.
Figure 10.

The Sacrifice of Abraham. Black chalk, heightened with white. 232 x 258 mm. Our number 1962. Design for the ceiling now in the Sacristy of Santa Maria della Salute, which originally had been commissioned of Giorgio Vasari in 1543. This fact may explain the striking approach to Central Italian Art in the ceilings and correspondingly in the drawing.

PARIS, LOUVRE

Group of Apostles. Pen. 231 x 302 mm. Our number 1952. Probably about 1516/18.
Figure 39.

Madonna and Child. Pen. 131 x 196 mm. Our number A 1951. I included the drawing in the first edition, but now believe that the doubts expressed by L. Serra in Bollettino d'Arte 1935, 549, were well justified and that the drawing is by a later artist under the influence of Titian.

Sketch for the 'Battle' so-called of Cadore. Black chalk on blue. Square. Discovered and circumstancially discussed as Titian's general sketch for the 'Battle', showing an early stage of the conception, by E. Tietze-Conrat in Gazette des Beaux-Arts, s. 6, v. 34, p. 237. The drawing is unique in Titian's oeuvre as a design for a complete composition.
Figure 105.

SEATTLE COLLECTION L. BACKUS

Mother and Child. Black chalk, heightened with white. 324 x 240 mm. Published by Hans Tietze, Art in America 1945, pp. 148 seqq., and in European Masterdrawings in the United States, New York 1947, No. 27.

STOCKHOLM, NATIONAL MUSEUM

Dog. Oil sketch on brown paper. 222 x 293 mm. Ascribed to Domenico Campagnola. Discussed as by Titian by this author in Gazette des Beaux-Arts 1949, p. 182.
Figure 104.

STOCKHOLM, PRIVATE COLLECTION

St. Christopher. Pen. 330 x 200 mm. Closely related to Titian's drawings of the 'Two Shepherds' in the British Museum and the 'Jealous Husband' in the École des Beaux-Arts in Paris and likewise close to Domenico Campagnola. First published in Gazette des Beaux-Arts 1949, p. 178.
Figure 67.

VIENNA, ALBERTINA

Two kneeling Boys in Landscape. Pen. 236 x 213 mm. Our number 1970. Constable in Burlington Magazine, April 1923, and Hadeln assumed that the landscape was by another hand than the figures, but this hypothesis had been rightly rejected by A. Stix and Fröhlich-Bum in the Catalogue of the Venetian Drawings in the Albertina, p. 29, No. 38.
Figure 6.

WOODCUTS

The woodcuts previously treated by Bartsch and, with additions, by Passavant and later on by Wilhelm Korn, Tizian's Holzschnitte, Breslau 1897, have been re-examined by this author and E. Tietze-Conrat in two articles: Tizian-Graphik in Graphische Künste, n. s. III, pp. 8 seqq. and 52 seqq., and Titian's Woodcuts in the Print Collectors Quarterly, vol. 25, pp. 333 seqq. and pp. 465 seqq., to which we refer for further information. Still more recently appeared Fabio Mauroner, Le incisioni di Tiziano, Padua 1943. In the following list only those woodcuts are included which are discussed or mentioned in my text.

The Triumph of Faith. Printed from five plates which have a total length of 148 inches. That the drawing is the work of Titian is stated by Vasari (VII, p. 431); the name of the woodcutter of the first edition has not been handed down. On the suppositions regarding this woodcut and the various editions of it see the facsimile edition by Paul Kristeller, Publication of the 'Graphische Gesellschaft in Berlin' 1906. Around 1511. Dated 1508 by Vasari, but evidently a few years later.
Folting Plate.

The Sacrifice of Abraham. Printed from four plates, 31 x 41¹/₂ inches. A later state bears the inscription: *Sagrificio del Patriarca Abramo del celebre Tiziano.* The first state, which is inscribed: *In Venezia per Ugo da Carpi...* is discussed by Lippmann, in Jahrbuch der Preussischen Kunstsammlungen I, p. 275. Around 1516. A drawing by Titian used in the woodcut is preserved in the Metropolitan Museum, New York (Figure 47). For a detailed discussion of the woodcut see also our Tizianstudien in Jahrbuch der Kunsthistorischen Sammlungen, n. s. X, pp. 163 seqq.
Figure 320.

Destruction of Pharaoh's Host. Printed from twelve plates. 47³/₄ x 86⁹/₁₆ inches. According to a long inscription designed by Titian, cut by Domenico delle Grecche. Detailed discussion in our Tizianstudien, l. c., pp. 162 seqq.
Figure 321.

Samson and Delilah. 12¹/₂ x 20 inches. Not signed, but certified by Lampsonius in his letter of March 13, 1567. The conception is from the early 1540's, the execution probably by Boldrini.
Figure 326.

Nativity. 15¹/₂ x 19³/₈ inches. Certified by Vasari and Lampsonius and through the inscription on an engraved copy made by Luca Bertelli while Titian was still living. The woodcut reproduces in reverse the composition of a picture which is preserved also in two painted versions, see Florence, Palazzo Pitti. The woodcutter who signs with the monogramme B was formerly erroneously identified as Boldrini. See about him Wilhelm Korn, l. c., pp. 60 seqq.
Figure 322.

Six Saints. 15¹/₄ x 21 inches. Certified by Vasari, who reports that the altar-piece with six saints (now in Rome, Vatican Gallery, see there) was drawn on wood by Titian himself and then cut and printed by others. The second edition repeats the picture, though with essential alterations, in reverse, and is attributed to Boldrini.

Saint Francis receiving the Stigmata. 11⁵/₈ x 17¹/₄ inches. Certified by Ridolfi, the execution probably by Boldrini. From the 1540's.
Figure 325.

St. Jerome in Forest Landscape. 15³/₈ x 21 inches. Certified by Vasari and Ridolfi, cut by Boldrini. From the 1530's. A drawing used for the big tree at the left in the woodcut exists in a private collection in France; see our Drawings of the Venetian Painters, number 1912, pl. LXII, 1.
Figure 324.

St. Roch. 15¹³/₁₆ x 8³/₄ inches. Not signed. Ascribed to Titian by stylistic considerations and dated around 1523. Illustrated in Graphische Künste, l. c., p. 65, and in Print Collectors Quarterly, l. c., p. 468.

Doge Francesco Donato adoring the Virgin. 17¹/₄ x 20⅛ inches. Hadeln, Jahrbuch der Preussischen Kunstsammlungen 1913, p. 34, recognised the composition as a reproduction of Titian's votive painting of Doge Andrea Gritti, painted for the Ducal Palace, the figure of the Doge having been replaced by that of his next successor but one, Francesco Donato. This alteration permits us to date the woodcut during the years of Donato's rule, 1545—53. No explanation has yet been offered as to why the portrait of the doge should have been substituted, although Gritti's patron saints have been retained.

Caricature of the Laocoön Group. 11 x 16¹/₂ inches. Boldrini is usually held to have been, the woodcutter of the drawing, which Ridolfi attests as being by Titian. O. Fischel in Amtliche Berichte der Berliner Museen 1917, pp. 60 seqq., discussed the woodcut in connection with the attitude of Titian, and of Venice in general, to the classicistic trends of the period. In a recent study in Art Bulletin 1946, p. 49, H. W. Janson denied Titian's alleged intention of satirising Bandinelli or classic art in general, and explained the woodcut as connected with the Vesalian-Galenist controversy which raged in 1543 and in which Titian may have become interested through his acquaintance with Vesalius.
Figure 327.

CHRONOLOGICAL TABLE

Between 1480 and 1490, probably between 1487 and 1490, Tiziano Vecellio is born at Pieve di Cadore; his father, whose name was Gregorio, was the son of Conte Vecelli, his mother was called Lucia.

Probably between 1496 and 1499 Titian comes to Venice, where he studies at first under Sebastiano Zuccato, and then under Gentile and Giovanni Bellini.

1507/8. The Emperor Maximilian makes war on Venice.

1508. Titian collaborates with Giorgione in the painting of the Fondaco dei Tedeschi.

1510. Death of Giorgione.

1511, December 2nd. The Fraternity of St. Anthony in Padua pays Titian four ducats as last instalment of his fee for the three frescoes in the Scuola del Santo.

1513, March 31st. Titian petitions the Council of Ten to grant him the order for painting a battle picture in the Sala del Grande Consiglio, and obtains the commission together with the reversionary right to a broker's licence at the Fondaco dei Tedeschi.

1516. Titian finally obtains the broker's licence which he has been striving for against repeated opposition since 1513.

1516. Titian comes into contact with Alfonso d'Este of Ferrara.

1516-18. Assumption for Santa Maria dei Frari, unveiled on March 20th, 1518.

1520. Altar-piece for the church of San Francesco in Ancona.

1520-22. Altar-piece for Santi Nazaro e Celso in Brescia, of which the St. Sebastian panel was finished in 1520.

1523. Titian comes into contact with the Margrave Federigo d'Este of Mantua.

1523-38. Doge Andrea Gritti.

1519-26. Madonna of the Pesaro family.

1525. Titian marries.

1527. Sack of Rome.

1528-30. Martyrdom of St. Peter Martyr in Santi Giovanni e Paolo in Venice.

1530, February 25th. Coronation of Emperor Charles V at Bologna.

1530, August 5th. Death of Titian's wife Cecilia.

1531, September. Titian moves to the house in Birri Grande, which he inhabited until his death.

1531, October. Unveiling of the votive picture of Doge Andrea Gritti in the Ducal Palace.

1532. Beginning of Titian's relationship with Francesco Maria della Rovere, Duke of Urbino.

1533, May 10th. Titian appointed court painter to Charles V and promoted to Count Palatine.

1534-49. Papacy of Paul III.

1537, April. Titian sends Federigo Gonzaga the first picture of the series of twelve Caesars.

1538. Completion of the Battle of Cadore in the great hall of the Ducal Palace.

1539-45. Doge Francesco Donato.

1542. Portrait of Clarissa Strozzi (Berlin).

1543. Ecce Homo (Vienna).

1543. Portrait of Paul III (Naples).

1545-53. Doge Marcantonio Trevisan.

1545, October. Titian's journey to Rome.

1546, March 19th. Titian granted the citizenship of Rome.

1547, April 24th. Battle of Mühlberg.

1547/48. Titian's first sojourn in Augsburg.

1549. Woodcut of the Destruction of Pharaoh's host.

1550/51. Second sojourn in Augsburg.

1552, October 29th. Titian restored to the office of broker at the Fondaco dei Tedeschi.

1553, September 21st. Titian makes his offer to paint a large picture for the Scuola di San Rocco in Venice.

1553. First deliveries of pictures to Philip II.

1554. Philip II becomes consort of Queen Mary of England.

1554. 'Gloria' for Emperor Charles V.

1554. Altar-piece for the parish church at Medole.

1555, October. Abdication of Charles V.

1555. Titian's daughter Lavinia marries Cornelio Sarcinelli at Serravalle.

1558, September 21st. Death of Charles V.

1561. Portrait of the so-called Palma (Dresden).

1566. Vasari visits Titian.

1566, February 4th. Titian receives from the Signoria a privilege for the publication of engravings.

1568. Portrait of Jacopo Strada (Vienna).

1569. At Titian's request his broker's licence is transferred to his son Orazio.

1571, October 7th. Battle of Lepanto.

1576, August 27th. Death of Titian; August 28th, his burial in the Frari.

LIST OF ILLUSTRATIONS
ACCORDING TO SUBJECTS

(For notes on the pictures see the Catalogue arranged in alphabetical order of places.)

1. RELIGIOUS WORKS.

a) Old Testament.

b) New Testament.

2. MYTHOLOGICAL, ALLEGORICAL AND HISTORICAL SUBJECTS.

3. ANIMALS, LANDSCAPES AND KINDRED SUBJECTS.

4. PORTRAITS.
a) Known Persons (Men):

b) Known Persons (Women):

c) Unknown Persons (Men):

d) Unknown Persons (Women):